Philosophy and Action of RSS for the Hind Swaraj

Philosophy and Action of RSS for the Hind Swaraj

Father Anthony Elenjimittam

Published by
PRABHAT PRAKASHAN PVT. LTD.
4/19 Asaf Ali Road,
New Delhi-110 002 (INDIA)
e-mail: prabhatbooks@gmail.com

ISBN 978-93-5562-580-9
Philosophy and Action of RSS for the Hind Swaraj
by Father Anthony Elenjimittamji

Edition
2025

Paperback Price
₹ 500.00 (Rupees Five Hundred only)

Printed at
R-Tech Offset Printers, Delhi

Dedication

Ye anti-communal, anti-secular, caste-creed-sex-free, steel-nerved, iron-willed, all-renouncing patriots of New Bharat,

Ye countless sages, seers, bards, prophets, rishis, missionaries and apostles of Hindu-Buddhist Dharma who built up Greater India in Asian continent,

Ye intrepid, chivalrous, indomitable soldiers who will defend the inviolable Unity, Freedom, Humanity, Catholicity, Culture, Civilisation of Aryavarta,

Ye youth of Bharatvarsha, boys and girls, men and women of the New World Order, New Dispensation, whose lofty ideals, purity and strength of character will make India impregnable,

Ye artisans and architects of India's all-sided nation-building, peasants and labourers who struggle and strain to wipe out exploitation of labour by capital, destroy money-mammon-power that kills values and ethics, to emancipate Indian womenfolk, eradicate illiteracy, ignorance, poverty, unemployment from India,

Ye members, friends and sympathisers of the RASHTRIYA SWAYAMSEVAK SANGH, the vanguard battalion for national Unity and Solidarity, the auto-charging dynamo of Bower and Light, the well-knit, solid, disciplined, National Army in renascent and reflorescent Vedantic India;

Ye who repudiate the liability of birth-religion-labels and will consecrate, immolate, crucify, annihilate your individual interests for the good of your bigger whole, your family, sacrifice your family for Society, give up society for the welfare of Mankind, and renounce Mankind, universe and all for attaining Truth, God, Over-Soul, Reality Supreme, Paramatman, according to the Vedic dictum:

त्यजेदेकं कुलस्यार्थे ग्रामस्यार्थे कुलं त्यजेत्।
ग्रामं जनपदस्यार्थे ह्मात्मार्थे पृथ्वीं त्यजेत्॥

To you, to you, to you
Are the following pages dutifully,
conscientiously and lovingly dedicated.

—Anthony Elenjimittam

R.L. Trust Research Institute,
55, Girgaum Road, Bombay-4

30th October, 1951
Depavah Day

Foreword

At last somebody with courage of conviction and clarity of vision has come forward to say some kind words about the Rashtriya Swayamsevak Sangh (RSS), which has been held to ridicule, condemnation and obloquy, quite dishonestly and unfairly, by Pandit Nehru and his crowd.

Shri Anthony Elenjimittam, author of this book, is a highly educated and widely travelled young man who had unique opportunities of studying social and religious problems at close quarters in many countries of the world. He studied Philosophy, Social Sciences, Comparative Religion and Literature in Rome and Oxford, graduating himself with distinction in Divinity, and spent well over a decade in Europe, engaged in social, cultural and journalistic activities. He has studied and thought deeply on the ethical, social and spiritual problems of this ancient country with an unerring and deep insight. He does not believe in mere superficial shibboleths; he goes to the very root of the matter and takes out the kernel from the chaff.

He has traced the history of the RSS movement from the date it was started by the late lamented Dr. Hedgewar, more than a quarter of a century ago at Nagpur and has taken us through all its subsequent stages of development, organisational and functional expansion, in its manifold cultural and patriotic and youth activities throughout the country to this day. He has proved to the great confusion of the detractors of the movement that it is nothing like the communal organisation—that it is alleged to be—nor is the RSS against any particular religious creed or community, or has any political, economic and social gospel of parochial character, or racial animosity, or contemplates any violent revolutionary overthrow of the present order in India.

Shri Anthony has conclusively shown in this book, to which I have the great pleasure to write this foreword, that the RSS has a very broad vision and catholic outlook on life. It does not stand for sectional interests, as many a communal organisation in India does, for example, the Anglo-Indian Association, the Muslim League and the Sikh League. And he is right. True, the RSS stands for the rejuvenation of the national culture of the Hindus. That in itself does not mean that it is anti-non-Hindu, because the Hindutva of the Sangh is tantamount to *Bharatityata,* or Indianisation, on p. 48, the author makes this point lucidly clear when he writes:

"If only we had known what we are by our birthright as Indians, we should have then known that these communal strifes between Hindus, Moslems, Christians or Parsees are mere quarrels about straw. We are all primarily and essentially Indians, not Hindus, Moslems or Christians. We are children of the soil of Mother India and it is on this basic fact of our national life that the new resurrection of the Indian nationals has to take place. The only enemy of nationalism is communalism, which consecrates birth-privileges and birth-religions, saps humanistic solidarity and undermines national strength."

Earlier on p. 18, he had shown that the social distinctions of the ancient Indians into the intellectuals, warriors, businessmen and artisans were not based on birth, but on inherent qualities and ways of professional and vocational life. Under some guise or other, such professional and vocational division is bound to exist and is good for all times, but should never be based on accidents of birth. This idea the author stresses anew on p. 146 and elsewhere in the book.

The leaders of the RSS are also strongly against any caste or communal divisions amongst the Hindus themselves. A man belonging to the bluest blood of ancient nobility or princely order must sit cheek by jowl with the humblest and the lowly within the Sangh. All arc equal there. Nobody is high or low and everybody is expected to render unselfish and silent service. The super-discipline of the Sangh is but the indispensable means to achieve this supreme end. The obedience of the army of the RSS is to an ideal not to a cult or to an individual. The members of the RSS have an unshakable faith in the indivisible unity of our Motherland and an abiding faith in the greatness of the cultural heritage of India in many walks of life. They certainly wish to revitalise and strengthen all that is best and of lasting value in Indian civilisation, which is necessary for the health, self-respect and independence of the Indian nation, although this is distorted as 'revivalism' by the advocates and hirelings of pseudo-secularism. The present leaders and conductors of the Sangh have declared the aims and objectives, the ideals and policy of the movement in its very constitution, which is there for anybody who cares to know the truth.

Shri M.S. Golwalkar wants Hindi to be the national language of India, not so much merely on the statute book as in the actual life of the people. He does not believe in any kind of provincialism and the Sangh proclaims that the demand for linguistic provinces is a reactionary claim. Service is the motto of the RSS. Silent sacrificial offering at the altar of the Motherland is their method, on p. 149, the author says:

"In this burning crucible of self-sacrificing service will melt away the remnants of communalism, pauperism, injustice, indiscipline, indifference, hypocrisy and such other weak points that have kept us divided and disorganised, and have made India a laughing stock to foreigners. The embryo, the nucleus that is there in the form of the RSS for the national resurrection still needs tending, watching, ordering and organising, until India is built up anew on the foundations of Vedantic humanism and socio-economic justice restored to the common man. Culture is no culture that cannot provide bread and butter to the shrivelled bellies and walking skeletons."

It is this strictly nationalistic and patriotic, self-sacrificing and nation-building RSS that is being denounced by Pandit Nehru and his stooges as a fascist organisation. Its leader and members by the thousand were imprisoned by the Congress Government out of sheer spite and political animosity. Their only crime was their spotless idealism and their sturdy refusal to bow their heads to the arrogant hate of the Pandit. All these vital points Shri Anthony brings out again and again in the pages of this book in a language of unexampled polish, vigour, profundity and grace. He has studied the movement with sympathetic insight, but without any preconceived bias and it will be an eye-opener to many ignorant and sceptical folk in this country who will realise for the first time how cruelly they misunderstood the RSS movement and strengthened the hands of the Nehru Government for crushing it—vainly though, as sequel proved it. The author deserves congratulation for his intrepid and thought-provoking work.

Not unfrequently, it so happens that two minds, thinking and working independently, often come to the same conclusion. This is illustrated by the essential principles of the RSS being independently embodied in the Manifesto of the Indian National Youth Movement, about which we heard a good deal during the Nasik session of the Congress—this could be verified by reference to the Appendix.

The presentation of the whole case of the RSS in this book is sometimes marked with adjectival flavour. In one case the author is, in my opinion, incorrect when he describes the Hindu Mahasabha as a communal body. The unrivalled richness of the author's appreciation of the RSS movement samples him out as a gentleman who does not allow his judgement to be warped by mopped psychology or political partisanship.

I congratulate Shri Anthony Elenjimittam for presenting to the thinking public the gospel of the RSS in a nutshell. With the publication of this book, there is no excuse for anyone to remain ignorant about the Sangh.

Jamnadas Mehta

—Jamnadas Mehta

Pandit Bhagavanlal Indraji Road,
Malabar Hill, Bombay-6

9th October, 1951
Vijaya Dashami Day, Sneha Smriti

Foreword

Among the many definitions of the Rashtriya Swayamsevak Sangh (RSS), the one offered by Shri Dadarao Parmarth stands out for its clarity and content: "RSS is an evolution of the life mission of the Hindu Nation." This insight was not a mere abstraction but the result of his deep internalisation of Sangh values, shaped through his close association with Dr. Hedgewar, the founder of the RSS. When asked to define the Sangh, Parmarth responded spontaneously in English, articulating its essence in a manner that combined its core principles into a profoundly poetic mantra. His words captured the spirit, history and aspirations of the nation, reflecting the sacred connection between the Sangh and Bharat. They underscored that the RSS is not a conventional organisation but a vital organ of the Hindu Rashtra, an organic evolution in its national journey.

Over the years, numerous critics, scholars and adversaries have attempted to define the Sangh, often driven by prejudice or a desire to misrepresent it. Yet, one of the earliest and most sincere studies came from an unexpected quarter—a Catholic priest named Father Anthony Elenjimittam. His work remains one of the most overlooked and under-appreciated explorations of the RSS and deserves greater attention in the contemporary discourse.

What makes this book significant is not merely its attempt to present the Sangh in its true spirit, but the genuine sincerity of the author, who approached the subject as a seeker rather than a sceptic. Apart from a few works intended for internal circulation, 'Philosophy and Action of RSS for the Hind Swaraj' may well be the first comprehensive book on the Sangh to be published. As noted in the foreword of the original 1951 edition, it should be read as a sympathetic and honest effort to understand the Sangh from an outsider's perspective.

Father Anthony Elenjimittam is also credited with the coinage of an oft-quoted term in Indian politics, i.e., pseudo-secularism. And he was a vehement critic of Jawaharlal Nehru, who is now widely held as the father of pseudo-secularism. Even in this work, Father Elenjimittam used the term pseudo-secularism not less than five times. Notably, he never raised the 'minority question' or an iota of doubt about the all-inclusive approach of the Sangh towards religions.

He has also sought answers to many questions and doubts about the RSS, most of which arose from the widespread propaganda against the Sangh promoted by the then Nehru government. One of these was the 'bogey of fascism'. Father Elenjimittam responded to such propaganda in highly polemical language:

""But then are not the RSS youths fascists?" ask the pseudo-secularists. This bogey of fascism and communism are quarrels about straw and the might-fever caused by seeing a ghost at a distance which, from near, however, is nothing but a scarecrow. If discipline, organised centralisation and organic collective consciousness mean fascism, then the RSS is not ashamed to be called fascist. All hallucinations and sophistication are about name and form—Namaroop. This silly idea that fascism and totalitarianism are evils and parliamentarianism and Anglo-American type of democracy are holy, should get rid of from our minds if we want to approach problems realistically and bring in solutions for them. Did they not condemn Subhas Bose as a fascist? And yet it was Netaji who was the most realistic politician among the Congress trinity of Gandhiji, Nehru and Subhas," he writes.

Some of his observations may appear to be in support of fascism as an ideology, possibly influenced by his admiration for Netaji, who was also labelled a fascist by the Nehruvian faction within the Congress. Father Elenjimittam believed that the accusations of fascism against the RSS should be viewed in the context of similar allegations made against Netaji. As mentioned earlier, the sympathetic view of a Catholic cleric should be seen as a sincere attempt to understand the Sangh from a nationalistic perspective, not as an autobiographical account of the Sangh.

From the Sangh's perspective, there are several points in the book that would merit a dissenting note. However, I have refrained from doing so, as it is already well known that the book should be read and interpreted from the author's viewpoint. Since a brief overview of the book's contents is already included in a study featured in this volume, I am refraining from commenting further.

The re-publication of this remarkable work, originally written around the time of the Sangh's 25th birth anniversary, coincides with the centenary of the RSS. Most importantly, the first edition was published in the aftermath of the Gandhi assassination. This book also highlights the importance of understanding the prevailing narratives and discourses of that era. The political propaganda by the Congress-Islamist-Communist conglomerate linking the RSS to Gandhi's assassination gained momentum during the post-Emergency period and was used as a political tool to hinder the organisation's growth. Although, the Sangh was banned following the assassination, the move was rightly perceived as a politically motivated act by Nehru to suppress the RSS. It is also worth noting that the author himself was an admirer and follower of Mahatma Gandhi and countered the propaganda against the Sangh in this book.

Cutting through many such adverse circumstances, the Sangh has grown into a powerful organisation contributing to national rejuvenation. The RSS now attracts global scholars who seek to understand its extraordinary growth. While books like *The Saffron Swastika* by Koenraad Elst and *The Brotherhood in Saffron* by Walter K. Andersen and Shridhar Damle have documented the organisation's expansion, this book may be the first to capture the nascent stage of the budding Sangh in all its vigour and beauty. Revisiting it on the occasion of the organisation's 100th anniversary offers a special treat for those interested in its journey and legacy.

As the Sangh completes a hundred years of its long march along the path shown by Swami Vivekananda and other great sages who contributed towards the reconstruction of this nation, we witness Sangh-inspired organisations flourishing across various fields, including education, employment, science, economy and more. Today, over 35 such organisations operate with ideological clarity. Even after a century, the Sangh continues to explore new horizons. The RSS is steadily progressing toward fulfilling its life mission, an evolved Hindu Rashtra shaped by the will of the nation.

Even though, the true philosophy and action of the Sangh can only be fully understood through the Shakhas. For those who are sceptical of Hindutva, and the philosophy of the RSS, this book serves as an introduction. In this context, what Gurudev Rabindranath Thakur writes in his seminal work Swadeshi Samaj holds great relevance and should be read alongside the observations of Father Elenjimittam.

Gurudev says, "To feel unity in diversity, to establish unity amongst variety. That is why without sacrifice or destruction, she wants to accommodate everybody within one great system. That is why she accepts all ways and sees the greatness of each in its own sphere... Because of this virtue in Bharat, we shall not be frightened considering any society as our opponent. Each fresh conflict will enable us to expand ourselves. The Hindu, the Buddhist, the Muslim and the Christian will find a meeting point. That meeting point will not be non-Hindu, but very specifically Hindu. However, foreign may be her body parts, her life and spirit will be Bharat...".

As we can see, Father Elenjimittom also shares the exactly same definition and views of the RSS and its Hindutva philosophy, which is holistic in its philosophy, integral in its approach and all-inclusive in its action. He was truly a pioneer in fostering religious and cultural harmony in independent Bharat. Through his works in comparative religion and his efforts to infuse nationalism and Bharatiyata into Christian theology, he made significant contributions to interfaith understanding. His sincere attempt to engage with the history and philosophy of this Hindu nation, and his deep appreciation for its cultural heritage, were remarkable. He was among the few Christian theologians who grasped the profound essence of Swami Vivekananda's Chicago address, where Swamiji described Hindu Dharma as a faith that has taught the world both tolerance and universal acceptance.

In an age where interfaith dialogue and religious harmony are more crucial than ever, we must not allow the legacy of such a noble soul, who dedicated his life to social cohesion, to fade into obscurity. In his honour, why not commemorate his birth anniversary as National Interfaith Harmony Day? Such a gesture would be a fitting tribute to his enduring spirit. Let us hope that both Bharatiya Christian community and Hindutva organisations will uphold his legacy and continue the meaningful dialogue which he hopefully initiated.

On a special note, I would like to extend my sincere gratitude to Prof. Neerja Gupta, the Vice-Chancellor of Gujarat University, for helping us recover some of the missing pages of this edition in our possession.

Republishing this magnificent book, originally written on the occasion of the Sangh's 25th birth anniversary, in 2025 holds special relevance as the Sangh completes its 100-year journey this year. We are grateful to Prabhat Prakashan for taking up this mission and bringing this valuable work back to readers after a gap of seven decades. We hope this unparalleled work, which has had no match even after 75 years, will be received by readers and embraced in both letter and spirit.

—J. Nandakumar
National Convenor, Prajna Pravah

Foreword—The Catholic Priest Who Authored The First Popular Book About RSS

Over more than seven decades of its legacy, *Organiser* has served as a national platform for numerous eminent scholars, intellectuals and writers from India and abroad transcending political and religious boundaries, to voice their thoughts. Adopting the slogan: 'Voice of the Nation', the weekly featured articles that are characterised by the true spirit of cultural nationalism that transcended politics and religion. Among these luminaries who contributed to the weekly in the 1950s, is a Catholic priest who wrote a series of thought-provoking essays that drew national attention. His name is Father Anthony Elenjimittam.

Born on June 22, 1915, in a Christian family in Kochi, Anthony Elenjimittam later emerged as a philosopher, theologian, writer and political commentator. Well-versed in Hindu and Buddhist philosophies, he authored over fifty books. His works spanned interfaith studies, political critique and included translations and interpretations of major Hindu-Buddhist texts.

He also made significant contributions to India's political thought. The phrase "pseudo-secularism," which gained wide traction in Indian politics through senior BJP leader L.K. Advani, was in fact first coined and repeatedly used by Father Elenjimittam in his political writings. Through his essays in *Organiser* and his books, he introduced this term as a critique of the hollow secularism of Nehru and the Congress. It is quite likely that Advani, who served as an editor of *Organiser* during that time, was influenced by Elenjimittam's writings and later popularised the term during the Ram Janmabhoomi movement to expose Congress's political duplicity.

A Decade-Long Association with *Organiser Weekly*

A staunch anti-Nehruvian Father Elenjimittam began contributing to *Organiser* in 1949-50 and continued for over a decade. A passionate nationalist, an RSS sympathiser, and a staunch opponent of Islamism, pseudo-secularism and communism, his razor-sharp articles stood as testaments to his uncompromising ideological positions.

In the early 1950s, when the Rashtriya Swayamsevak Sangh completed 25 years of its service, Father Elenjimittam authored his book *Philosophy and Action of RSS for the Hind Swaraj*. The book was published on Vijayadashami Day, 1951, by Lakshmi Publishers in Mumbai. Spanning over 200 pages, it was arguably the first comprehensive and positive study of the RSS.

Interestingly, the term 'pseudo-secularism' also made its appearance in this book, in which he criticised Congress leaders for their superficial commitment to secularism. A review of the book, published in *Organiser* on December 3, 1951, describes it as "a sympathetic attempt to understand the ideology and working of the RSS, despite the natural limitations of an outsider's perspective."

"The book is welcome as a sympathetic attempt to understand the ideology and working of RSS despite its all shortcomings and natural incompleteness of an outsider's insights into the Sangh," the review reads. At the same time, it also shares an apprehension that the preface of Jamnadas Mehta and the introductory chapters of the author lend an anti-Nehru anti-Congress tinge to the book.

The review also acknowledges the book's anti-Nehru and anti-Congress undertones while praising Elenjimittam's understanding of the Sangh's perspective, noting that "Hindu" was presented not as a narrowly religious concept but as a territorial and cultural identity. "The quintessence of the Sangh's standpoint is that Hindu is not a narrowly religious but a catholically territorial-cum-cultural concept, and the author of this book is to be congratulated upon for being one of those very few outsiders who have grasped it, though he expressed his understanding a bit clumsily," it added.

While his early writings for *Organiser* focused on critiquing Jawaharlal Nehru and the Congress party's pseudo-secular agenda, his later work reflected a deeper interest in spirituality and comparative religion. One such article, *Buddhism: The Daughter of Hinduism*, published on May 21, 1956, explored his growing engagement with Hindu spiritual traditions, the Ramakrishna-Vivekananda movement, and Buddhist philosophies.

His Views on RSS as described in the Book

The book is divided into two parts: the first part elaborates on the RSS's philosophy and ideals, while the second delves into its organisational structure, discipline, the concept of economic self-reliance and the challenges posed by communism.

In his long and marvellous dedication to the book that reflects his patriotic fervour and pride of nation, he wrote:

"To the vanguard battalion for national unity and solidarity, the auto-charging dynamo of power and light, the well-knit, solid, disciplined National Army in renascent and reflorescent Vedantic India—the members, friends and sympathisers of the Rashtriya Swayamsevak Sangh."

He dedicates his book to the following category of people:

- *Anti-communal, anti-secular, caste-creed-sex-free, steel-nerved iron-willed, all-renouncing patriots of the New Bharat.*
- *Countless sages, seers, bards, prophets, rishis, missionaries and apostles of Hindu-Buddhist Dharma who built up a greater India in the Asian Continent.*
- *Intrepid, chivalrous, indomitable soldiers who will defend the inviolable unity, freedom, humanity, catholicity, culture, civilisation of Aryavarta.*
- *Youth of Bharatvarsha, boys and girls, men and women of the New World Order, new dispensation, whose lofty ideals, punty and strength of character will make India impregnable.*

- *Artisans and architects of India's all-sided nation-building, peasants and labourers who struggle and strain to wipe out exploitation of labour by capital, destroy money-mammon-power that kills values and ethics, to emancipate Indian womenfolk, eradicate illiteracy, ignorance, poverty and unemployment from India.*
- *Members, friends and sympathisers of the RASHTRIYA SWAYAMSEVAK SANGH, the vanguard battalion for national unity and solidarity, the auto-charging dynamo of power and light, the well-knit, solid, disciplined, National Army in renascent and reflorescent Vedantic India.*
- *Who repudiate the liability of birth-religion-labels and will consecrate, immolate, crucify, annihilate your individual interests for the good of your bigger whole, your family, sacrifice your family for society, give up society for the welfare of mankind and renounce mankind, universe and all for attaining truth, God, Over-Soul, Reality Supreme, Paramatman, according to the Vedic dictum:*

"Tyajet ekam Kulasyarthe,
Gramasyarthe Kulam tyajet,
Gramam Janapadasyarthe,
Atmarthe prithivim tyajet."

To you, to you to you...Are the following pages dutifully, conscientiously and lovingly dedicated Anthony Elinjimittam

About the mission of the Sangh, he writes: "The historic mission of the RSS, as a successor to the Indian National Congress, will be to work for and achieve the national unity at all cost. As Sri Aurobindo said, "India is free, but she has not achieved unity, only a fissured and broken freedom. But, by whatever means, the division must and will go." (SRI AUROBINDO'S MESSAGE ON 15TH AUGUST 1947) This unity means that all nationalist Indians, whether they are labelled as Hindus, Muslims or Christians, have always believed that they are all children of the soil and that they have not acquiesced in any way to the artificial vivisection that has been brought about as a passing political expediency."

In his views, the RSS translates the patriotic heritage of the Congress into action.

He writes: "In an independent India, the RSS is destined to combine the nationalistic and patriotic heritage of the Congress with the most dynamic urge for action, as embodied in the lives of men like Bal Gangadhar Tilak and Netaji Subhas Chandra Bose, the great hero of Hindustan, whose sacrifice became the life-blood and inspiration to the new patriotic soldiers of the INA in free India."

Countering the propaganda against the RSS that it distributed sweets when Gandhiji was assassinated, Father Elinjimittam writes: "The RSS owes much to Gandhiji's inspiration and guidance. Only there is not going to be any exclusive hero-worship to the detriment of the integrative and complementary mission of the rivals to Gandhiji in Indian politics. In fact, it was not the RSS that distributed sweets at Gandhiji's martyrdom, but it was the black-marketers and many Congresswalas who felt secretly happy because the old saintly man, Bapu, would no longer preach to them about brahmacharya, asteya and abaya."

"We have now to choose which ideology is to be presented to our youth so that they may arise from slough and despondency and work for the much-needed socio-economic and cultural revolution in the country. It is at this juncture that the RSS offers the youth of India an ideology, a dream which is not the undiluted materialism of orthodox Marxian Communists, but the saving leaven of centralised discipline and highest self-sacrifice based on the idealistic patrimony of Indian culture. Because the RSS base their stand on the philosophy of the Upanishads, the Ethics of the Sermon on the Mount, the psychology of Buddhism, the metaphysics of Vedanta, the so-called secularists say, "These are Hindu revivalists, let's put them down." These secularists have no philosophy, no ideals to build up Indian youth, nor their own sweet selves," he adds.

Father Elinjimittam goes on to add: "we shall take pride in being called Hindus, if by the term 'Hindu' we mean to be true to the cultural heritage and national spirit of the Indian soil. If the Muslims, Christians, Parsiees should still be called Muslims, Christians and Parsiees, even within the confines of their sectarian religions, why should a Hindu be ashamed to be called a

Hindu if Indian culture remains to this day the Universal Mother of Religions, the broadest possible Catholicity and the most philosophical and enlightened humanism of history?"

In the book, he extensively quoted Dr. Keshav Baliram Hedgewar, Doctorji to narrative the mission and growth of the Sangh.

Father Elinjimittam writes: "The life of Dr. Hedgewar was itself a lesson of service, sacrifice, purity embodied. He did not wear the gerua colour nor he put ashes and sack clothes around him, but he was a sanyasi without these external paraphernalia, which more often are being utilised by the sycophants to deceive the ignorant and serve their own selfish ends. Similarly, today Shri Golwalkar is at heart and spirit a sanyasi who teaches a practical vedantin, and yet there is no show and glamour about him, for his eyes and heart are firmly fixed on the rock of Indian culture. "Culture, which", he says, "includes also food."

"Young Keshav Baliram Hedgewar will ever remain in Indian history as a supreme pattern of patriotism, political realism and social justice and one of the boldest soldiers who fought the battle of righteousness and fell to consolidate the defences and inner resources of young India. His short life (1890-1940) is the argument and proof of a dedicated soul who lived but for one sole purpose—the resurrection of Mother India. Because he sought and fought to revive Bharatiya culture, there is no justification whatsoever to charge him of the sin of communalism. For the fundamental thesis all sane nationalists hold is that India is their Motherland and the culture and spirit of the soil, prior to the Muslim or Christian domination, is the spirit and culture of every true Bharatiya."

When he brought out his book, the RSS had just survived the ban imposed following Mahatma Gandhi's assassination. In such a sensitive situation, if a prominent Catholic priest chose to publicly support the RSS and write a full-length book in its favour, it shows the author's nationalistic spirit and his faith which he reposited on the Sangh. This historical context amplifies the book's importance alongside its content.

His Social and Spiritual Life

Father Elenjimittam's academic journey began in Kerala, before he joined the Dominican Order in 1935 and moved to Italy. During his ordination, Bishop Monsignor Benedetto Cialiò remarked:

"... you are the first Indian Dominican appointed priest in this modern era, after centuries of decadence since the Dominicans left India [...] Your country has a rich and vast spiritual culture that you have inherited in your veins. You have a mission to fulfill in India, and is to find a meeting point between Tomistic philosophy and our theology with the immense and valid spiritual traditions of your country. I know how much you love St. Thomas Aquinas, who was a pioneer in the attempt to integrate the Catholicism of the Middle Ages with Greek philosophy, especially Aristotle."

—*Cosmic Ecumenism*

However, his progressive views and intense nationalism invited suspicion from British intelligence agencies and discomfort within the Catholic hierarchy. From 1936 to 1941, he studied philosophy in Rome. During his return journey to India in 1942, he came into contact with Subhas Chandra Bose in Lisbon—an interaction that made British agencies wary of him.

Intercepted letters to Mahatma Gandhi and various handwritten documents in his luggage led British authorities to block his entry into India at the Liverpool port, stating:

"You are an Indian nationalist and a potent patriot, so we cannot allow you to return to India, we have to examine all your notebooks, notes, diaries and manuscripts contained in your trunks and suitcases, to make sure that you are not a spy sent to England for the Italian Government...".

—*Cosmic Ecumenism*

While detained in England, he enrolled as a research scholar at Cambridge University. He returned to India in 1945 and became chief editor of *The Indian Messenger*, an English weekly inspired by the Brahmo Samaj. After his return, he also visited Mahatma Gandhi at Santiniketan and later wrote:

"...because I saw in him the authentic copy of Jesus Christ,

Socrates and Abraham Lincoln, the three fused in him surrounded by the halo of a Saint Francis of Assisi."

—*Cosmic Ecumenism*

His nationalist leanings and sympathy for Hindu-Buddhist ideals earned him resentment from conservative factions within the Church. Possibly, it was one of the reasons behind his strained relationship with the Archbishop of Mumbai, eventually leading to his exile. In 1975, Father Elenjimittam returned to Italy, choosing to dedicate the rest of his life to causes beyond the confines of institutional religion, in spaces that offered greater freedom for his ideals.

He passed away in Italy on October 5, 2011, as he had once quoted Bhagavad Gita and written: "The body is but a garment: once worn, it must be cast off..."

Father Anthony Elenjimittam lived a life that stands as a luminous example. A visionary who grasped the potential of the RSS in shaping modern India from its very inception, he remained a steadfast patriot and nationalist even as he served as a devoted man of God. Advocating interfaith harmony, he collaborated closely with Hindutva and nationalist movements, perhaps becoming the first Christian cleric to recognise and act upon the need for national Christian-RSS cooperation. He will be remembered for his lasting contributions towards interfaith harmony, inculcating Bharatiya values in Christian theology and recognising Hindutva in its true sense.

—Ganesh Radhakrishnan

Contents

Part-I
PHILOSOPHY AND IDEALS OF THE RSS

Chapter-1

Laws of Individual and National Survival

Indian National Congress, which was once the leavening force, the clarion call and the representative mouthpiece of the country, once the mighty force in the struggle for national emancipation, is today a decrepit grandmother with its face turned towards the funeral[1] pyre. The stalwart men and women whose sacrifice, patriotism and service built up the Congress are either gone or are today old marionettes with no creative imagination, adventurous spirit and risky living The few Congressmen who count something in the life of the nation are engripped within power-madness, office-hunting and money-grabbing with the result that the Congress, to all intents and purposes, has ceased to be a living soul in the life of the nation, hardly three years after the enthusiasm and jubilation of Independence that resounded the land of the Ganges and Himalayas.

That the Congress got diseased beyond the hope of cure, that the Mother of Indian Freedom is today gasping for breath lying on her death-bed, that the great minds that built up the Congress, specially Mahatma Gandhi, Netaji Subhas and Sardar Patel, have gone from our midst, is no reason for us to weep or pine away. This is the law of life—birth, childhood, adolescence, youth, maturity, decrepitude and death. This is the law that creates and re-creates life. It is futile to resist this inevitable course of life. It is this unceasing death of individuals and groups that preserves life in its higher and better forms, if and when the succeeding generations are wise and intelligent enough to learn the lessons of their historical past.

In the history of the rise and fall of various civilisations, we learn the unmistakable laws of survival of nations and peoples, of culture and spirit of a given individual or group. Life being a continuous movement and change, every form of staticity and stagnancy spells death. Peoples and nations survive through vital transformation, through such changes that make life-currents adjust themselves to the ever-changing circumstances and environment. Refusal to move with the moving wheels of history, to change with the changing times, is to court premature and unnatural death. From this foremost law of survival it could be gathered that the Congress today is in the agony of death, because it lost its hold on the fountain-head of life, because it refused to change with the changing times, because it betrayed the trust that was given to it by the people.

Congress is today decrepit, incapable of enthusing and energising the people of India not only because it refused to change with the changing times and survive through vital inner transformation, but also because it forfeited the mandate given to it by the people. The office-holders within the Congress still continue to cash and tax the people with the post-dated cheques of their past sufferings and sacrifices. To cash people's loyalty and confidence, their money and life, merely repeating the name of Mahatma Gandhi and of the past trials in prisons and sacrifices is to expose one's own hollowness. Many who were returned to Government services on the Congress tickets have today lost that seal and imprint of character and self-sacrifice which once gave birth to the Congress, nurtured it and built it into a mighty movement under Gandhiji for our national liberation.

Congress was pledged to win "a united, democratic and independent India," as Shri Nehru puts it. But today we have neither a united nor democratic nor independent India in the sense one understands these words from any dictionary meaning or from common people's concept. Vivisection of the country alone is the crime which the common people of India are not easily going to forgive or forget. "Pakistan is a sin," insisted Gandhiji. But this sin was committed, this major operation was resorted to, by the then Gandhi-Nehru-dominated Congress High Command with the hope of saving the rest of the body politic from (a) the British domination, (b) Muslim communal fanaticism and (c) from the domestic forces of socio-economic anachronism. British domination is partially got over but the apron strings that tie us to the Commonwealth is the very denial of the spirit of the resolution of Complete Independence which Congress voted for and we continued to celebrate on every 26th January. After the withdrawal of the British political power, tremendous responsibilities have been shouldered by the less experienced and more servile Indian Congressmen, whereas the economic advantages for India after partition and Independence have definitely diminished and deteriorated. Muslim communalism cannot be cured by merely creating Pakistan; on the contrary, the communal cleavage between Muslims and Hindus has become more real, accentuated and intransigent. Pakistan has become a springboard for the communal Muslims to reach out to their wider scheme of re-constructing their old Mogul Empire in India and making it the centre of the entire pan-Islamic confederation. The basic and fundamental idea that we are all children of this soil of Mother India, of Mother Nature, is killed, destroyed by communal fanaticism of the anti-national religionists. Partition has proved that the real answer to communalism was nationalism and not vivisection of the country.

While East and West Pakistan have become the mutilated limbs of the Motherland, the heart and mind of the rest of the Muslims in India do not lie in Delhi, but in Karachi. What else could be expected of the illiterate, ignorant, poverty-stricken, communalism-infected sections of the Muslims than to look to their holy land, the new Jerusalem which was carved out of the bleeding limbs of this indivisible, historical and cultural unit, India, Bharat, Aryavarta, which Nature has marked out to be an indivisible 'geographical and spiritual unit'?

Our domestic socio-economic anachronism has not been solved. The Interim Government came into being in 1946 and Independent Government in 1947. Three or four years in this Atomic Age mean much to the peoples and nations who are engripped in a battle of life and death. The growing deterioration in the economic and social life of the people is to be stemmed forthwith if the revolutionary violent forces of Hunger, Disease, Social Insecurity, Unemployment and Famine were not to turn the country upside down. Communism is not culture; it is the easiest and cheapest answer to end exploitation of Labour by Capital, to save the hungry, jobless and poverty-stricken destitutes of Asia. Mere Security Bills and Nehru-Liaquat Ali Pacts and Preventive Detention decrees cannot stem the tide of frustration and languor that rage wild in the country today. Bayonets cannot kill ideas; mere paper schemes do not fill empty bellies and soothe the pangs of walking skeletons and shrivelled bellies.

It is when the bankruptcy of our Government is becoming obvious on all fronts and in every way that we see the symptoms of new forces surging forth throughout the country to replace the present weak, suicidal, decrepit Congress Government. Since Nehru is a well-read man, tolerably good in leading an opposition to any government, foreign or national, indeed, a great Indian with noble qualities, but he is not the man of destiny to face and solve the socio-economic problems in the country, the statesman with iron will, self-discipline and one-pointedness of mind and heart, destined to preserve India's national heritage; the hero who with single-minded devotion and unflinching character could lead the country and people to the promised land of socio-economic freedom, without which political freedom from the British Crown means little, a mockery to the nationally-minded children of the Motherland. Gandhiji's guidance is no longer there, Netaji's iron will and sacrificial powers are gone, Sardar's steely realism also gone. Now Pandit Nehru has hardly any check and his continued hold on the present weak Government will spell disaster to the country. Nothing is too late; even resignation from exalted posts, if by that way rejuvenated and revitalised nationalist forces could find expression and service for the resurrection of the moribund Motherland, for the creation of men and women with muscles of iron and nerves of steel to fulfil their duties in the great uphill work of nation-building that await us today, which is the paramount duty of all national-minded children of India.

Socialists and Communists, jointly with other Leftist parties and co-operating with the progressive undercurrents of the Congress, could have displaced and replaced the present weak Nehru Government had they not displayed their extra-territorial loyalties. Besides, the Leftist parties and organisations in India today merely parrot-wise repeat some sayings of Marx and look to Moscow as their Mecca without exploring the unfathomable depths of their own country, their nation, their national culture and the spirit and aspirations of the Indian people. The narrow outlook of imprisoning life within the Socialist and Communist platitudes is the very denial of the spirit of India, the soul of our culture, the essence of India's philosophy and outlook which seeks integration of Man *qua* Man and not merely exclusively as an economic entity. The Leftists may rally mass meetings, but they have no tap-roots as long as they forget, neglect or positively eschew the message of our ancient *rishis*, the *Vedas*, *Gita*, Epics, *Darsanas* and such other imponderable values and spiritual traditions that form the bed-rock of our national life; the life-blood of every citizen of India who is conscious of his national identity and humanity.

Why is it that Lokamanya Tilak, Mahatma Gandhi, Rabindranath Tagore, Vivekananda, Netaji Subhas and such spiritual giants captivated the imagination of the people? Were they not modern enough to discriminate gold from dross and wheat from chaff? All the greatest men of Indian history, even the most radical revolutionaries like Buddha, Charvakas, Sankara and, in our own age, reformers like Ram Mohun Roy, Keshub Chunder Sen, Ramakrishna and others took their stand on the imperishable treasures and priceless riches of India's specific humanity, her culture, her philosophy, India's outlook, her spirit, her life, her blood and her soul. They were modern, they were radicals, they were revolutionaries, but their tap-root went solidly deep down the Mother Earth of their land of birth and love. The unsophisticated and instinctive intuition of the common people could discern easily that such revolutionary reformers were the true heirs to their Aryan *rishis* and sages and that they kept continuity with the vital traditions and healthy heritage of the country as a race as a whole, people as a whole. But in many Leftist leaders of India today, the people, the masses cannot discern the heirs of ancient wisdom and there is no guarantee that the people's trust will ever be safe in their hands. Indian soul is incurably Vedic and idealistic.

If the present Congress and the Leftist parties cannot deliver us goods, then, is our condition so precarious and hopeless, as political ideologies are sharply divided between the Right and the Left? To leave the destiny of the country in the hands of the present Congress leadership, as we experience it today, or in the hands of mutually exclusive Socialists and Communists, is definitely detrimental to the national interests and can mean perpetual bondage to our posterity. But the situation is not so desperate if we look again to the forces of nationalism that now continue to surge forth as a result of the failure of the Congress on the one side and the risky uncertainties of the Leftists on the other. If the Congress quit office today, the Leftists are not united and disciplined enough to take hold of the reins of the Government. The Indian National Front is the main strength and new hope.

What then is this new nationalistic resurrection which, if properly organised and canalised, can save the country from the very real dangers of pan-Islamism on the one side and roboted destruction of human values on the other? This new force is not Hindu Mahasabha, which was the rival communal organisation to the Muslim League, with this difference that the Muslim League achieved its first target, viz. of creating Pakistan as a springboard for further conquests, whereas the Hindu Mahasabha has practically failed in its main objective which was to neutralise and frustrate the machinations of the League. This new force is not the old reform movements like the Brahmo Samaj, Arya Samaj, Ramakrishna-Vivekananda Mission, Theosophical Society, Deva Samaj, etc., for they all came to meet certain needs of the hour and today they are out of date, out of place. But their influence and mission and message are not to be kept in cold storage, museums and libraries, but their purpose and mission must continue to leaven and influence the people of the entire sub-continent. Does this new nationalistic power spring from such religions like Islam, Christianity, Parsiism, Judaism and other community groups that live in India? No, for they remain as exotic plants insofar as their communal character is stressed, accentuated and buttressed. Where then is the new national force to leaven the country, to redress the past and face the present socio-economic problems realistically and guarantee India's future? That new force is the Rashtriya Swayamsevak Sangh in its ideal character. The emergence of this new force in the spiritual, cultural and political horizon of India is itself the proof that the law of individual and national survival is working and we are going to survive the present partitioned independence crisis also. The instinct for survival becomes conscious in those individuals who have set a purpose in life, who are conscious of their duties and responsibilities as human beings and citizens of a particular country, society and nation. Society is necessary, but State is a concession to the weakness, limitations and ignorance of the common masses who form the herd on whom the State officials rule and overlord. But State must exist as long as men are animals, but with gradual education and spread of illuministic ideals and humanistic philosophy that Government will become the best which rules the least. In the ideal plane of perfected human beings, of groups and peoples who have risen from their animality to their potential humanity and divinity, there will be no more need of the State as we understand it today. The State will wither away when higher human beings are evolved, when there can be only free co-operation of equals in various differing vocational spheres without that humiliating subjection of the unthinking many, the herd and the thoughtless many, to the dictates and laws of the ruling few, the exploiting clique.

But whether it is through voluntary co-operation, through State-dictated, centralised control or through the minimum possible government, the one thing essential to be achieved is that Indians, as individuals and as a people, as a nation and society must survive, keeping vital and organic continuity with their historical past, with the essential philosophy of life and aspirations and character of the people. Here the question whether nation is to be improved after all the individuals are made perfect or whether it is through the change of society and nation that the individuals are perfected and bettered is as irrelevant as the cross-purpose whether the hen comes first or the egg. The obvious fact is that the work of individual perfection and national re-discovery and revitalisation must go hand in hand, although it is true that only a few individuals turn the wheels of history and that human beings are largely the product and victim of the socio-economic environment of the society in which they are born and grow.

Today India is confronted with the vital question of survival, to be or not to be is the question. If we continue to sleep and close our eyes to the stark realities and problems that our country is confronted with, the question of survival of the Indian nation will be answered negatively. The feasibility of Pakistan was once laughed at and ridiculed by such leaders like Shri Nehru and Mahatma Gandhi and yet both of them had to put their signatures to the partition of the country. There is nothing that is impossible underneath the sun. Nothing that is great is ever easy. Eternal vigilance, they say, is the price of freedom. It is this vigilance and alertness, this seriousness and business-mindedness, in safeguarding vital national and cultural interests of India that are so miserably lacking in India today. When that seriousness and business-mindedness dawn, then the path towards survival of India as a nation, as a distinct cultural entity, and as a people, will become clear.

Gibbons, Spengler, Lecky and Cantii, eminent authorities in the history of rise and fall of civilisations, have clearly stated that peoples and nations rise when they become conscious of their potential powers as substantiated with the deeds and facts of their past. It is this lack of national awareness and consciousness that stand in the way of national resurrection in India. The sleeping are to be awakened, the ignorant are to be educated and the potential perfection inborn in man, in an Indian, to be developed.

उत्तिष्ठत जाग्रत प्राप्य वरान् निबोधत।
क्षुरस्य धारा निशिता दुरत्यया दुर्गं पथस्तत् कवयोवदन्ति॥

—*Kathopanishad I 111 14*

"Arise, awake, by talking to the wise get yourself illumined, the sages say that life is as risky as walking on a razor's edge," say the *Upanishads*.

The second law that is at work behind the survival of individuals and nations is discipline. Man left to himself is like a ship tossed to and fro without a rudder or compass. It is for this reason that man has to discipline himself to find out a purpose in life, a vocation, mission which alone make the potential powers of man to grow and develop to the maximum pitch of efficiency and power. When the majority of people or nation are disciplined, the nation becomes disciplined and out of national discipline is derived the mightiest impetus for the growth of the people.

The rise of Sparta, of the Chinese Empire and of modern Japan, Germany, Italy, Soviet Union and Great Britain are all the results of strong national discipline. Is this discipline to be self-imposed, born out of conviction, or dictated from the top? The obvious answer is that discipline should be possibly borne out of conviction, but imposed from the top authorities if necessary, when it concerns the question of national survival. Discipline, as we could learn from the lessons of history and from our own personal experience, is vital for the survival of both individuals and nations. Discipline, more discipline, iron discipline is what is so needed for India today if we mean business and are determined to survive the crises that are in the air everywhere.

The third law of human survival that holds good for both an individual and nation, is the eternal law of *yagna* or self-sacrifice. We have to give first if we have to receive. We have to die to ourselves if we are to live for others. The seed does not germinate unless it falls to the ground and dies there. Then a new plant sprouts out, blossoms and fructifies. The blood of martyrs has always been the seed of the Church. It is only from sufferings, struggles, toils and sweat that the greatest achievements are made, that we are enabled to know the secrets of life, that we could unveil the mysteries and unlock the Ali Baba's cave, which is the inner chamber of life. "Self-sacrifice, not self-assertion, is the law of the highest universe," says Vivekananda. The essence of *Gita* is what we get when we repeat it six times, for, the word '*gita*' becomes *gi-tygi-tygi*—'*tyagi*' and ends in '*tyag*', which means self-sacrifice. The sign of Christianity is Cross which is again symbolic of sacrifice. Self-indulgence contracts life, whereas self-sacrifice, love, service expand the heart of man. Every expansion is life, every contraction is death. Brahmo Samaj, Arya Samaj, Indian National Congress, all were built on the solid rock of self-sacrifice. When that rock was removed, the entire superstructure also collapsed. India's national ideal is again self-sacrifice, but not sacrifice as an end in itself, but as an indispensable means for creation, growth, expansion, service and dynamic apostolate.

The fourth law of individual and national survival is the axiom, 'To thine own self be true'. This means rational and emotional attachment to our tap-root, to the very spiritual and imponderable values that sustain us in life. Man does not live by bread alone. Every child of India, merely by being born in this land, becomes heir to the *Vedas, Upanishads, Gita, Darsanas*, epics and all those monuments of human civilisation. Then only we survive when we analyse them rationalistically and critically and cling to the best of them with even some emotional and nostalgic romance. Social anachronism such as caste, sub-caste and untouchability, outdated laws regarding marriage, enslavement of the womenfolk. etc. are to be ruthlessly swept aside. But let us be on our guard not to empty out the baby with the hot water from the bath. Indian Philosophy, *Gita, Upanishads*, Yoga, Indian Art, Music, Dance, Literature, etc. are monuments of human civilisation. It is only by rooting ourselves deep into the soul of such civilisation that we become truly Indians and truly humans. Charity begins at home; they say internationalism without healthy nationalism is nonsense. World citizenship without dutiful citizenship of one's own Fatherland mean vagueness, defeatism and indolence.

We need to cling to that culture, that philosophy and religion that has sustained our lives for centuries, the past that has proved to be the Himalayan rock whence were hewn out Buddhas and Asokas, Chandraguptas and Akbars, Sankaras and Kabirs, Tagores and Gandhis. The glamour and glitter of machine civilisation may come in; but that should not be allowed to destroy and displace the Light of the East, the philosophy and Culture that is by birth in our blood. The nemesis of denationalisation is too bitter to contemplate. We need return to our own soul, get anchored on our own soil, to grow on our own national tap-roots, on that very spirit, civilisation and culture which make us Indians and humans, which is the pride and glory of our land, the perennial philosophy and Sanatan Dharma of our people, the indestructible and invincible rock of Truth and raft of salvation that persists through ages, that gives us power and poise, that pledges our national resurrection and is the lighthouse and pointer to our ideal, 'United, Democratic, Free Indian Republic'.

□

Chapter-2

The Birth and Growth of The RSS

यदा-यदा हि धर्मस्य ग्लानिर्भवति भारत।
अभ्युत्थानमधर्मस्य तदात्मानं सृजाम्यहम्॥
परित्राणाय साधूनां विनाशाय च दुष्कृताम्।
धर्मसंस्थापनार्थाय सम्भवामि युगे-युगे॥

'O Descendant of Bharatiya race, when, whenever Dharma declines and Adharma gains the upper hand, then, then I body myself forth.

For the protection of the Righteous, destruction of the wicked,
To restore Dharma back to its pedestal,
I come on earth from age to age.'

—*Bhagavad Gita, IV 6*

To meet the challenge of undiluted materialism, for upholding human values, for the glorification of the economic and military man there stands aloft the unshaken might of the Himalayas, the flowing streams of the Ganges in the land of Bharat, in this Aryavarta, in this Hind, this Hindustan. To the challenge of communalism of either the Muslim League, Christian Church or the Hindu Mahasabha there stands the eternal philosophy of Vedanta, the psychology of Buddha and Buddhism, the metaphysics of non-dualistic idealism of Sankara, the integrated ethics and psychological religion of the *Bhagavad Gita*, to the communal-minded religious fanatics who want separate Pakistan, Sikhistan, Christianistan or Hindustan, the dormant spirit of the ancient seers of Bharatvarsha, the philosophy of the Vedanta, the redemptive message of the *Bhagavad Gita* and the *Vedas* proclaim—एकं सत विप्रा बहुधा वदन्ति। Truth is one, the wise called it by different names.

The communal, caste and separatist divisions among the children of the soil of India are merely names and forms, *namarupa*. The quarrels between various communities, castes and sub-castes of India are merely fights for bones, quarrels about straw and nothing more. Yet this quarrel is so real and powerful today that the British diplomacy could exploit both the communalism of the League and the weakness of our Congress leaders and manage to vivisect the indivisible Mother India. The caste, sub-caste and under-caste divisions among the Hindus have again kept the children of the soil, born of the grace and love of Mother India, into separate camps, warring one against the other, barring healthy social living, national solidarity and cementing friendship and love among the various communities of the country. Such internal divisions have in the past enabled the Greeks, Turks, Moguls and the European nations to conquer our people without much difficulty or resistance and enslave us for centuries. Now political slavery is the worst form of slavery for any self-respecting and nationally-conscious people with a long, glorious and rich history behind, with a luminous philosophy of Light, Love and Life. Today we have forgotten our own national soul and bewitched by the dazzling glitter of the machine civilisation, we have forgotten to see, understand and appreciate the inborn qualities, inherent traits and birthrights of the philosophy of India. We have imitated, copied and aped Western life without that vital assimilation and absorption, without which exotic plants can only produce indigestion, constipation, ill-health, poisoning of the bloodstreams of our national and cultural life.

It is nationalism alone that is the remedy to the cancer of communalism, not partition of the country, acquiescing to the cry of communalists. It is patriotic love alone that heals the wounds of mutilation of the country, not the assumption of partition as *fait accompli* that has come to stay forever and ever. *Error corrigitur ubi apprehenditur*—There and then is corrected the error where and when it is detected, says a Latin proverb. But true to the spirit of India this united, nationalistic and patriotic India is still to be built up slowly, patiently through education, spread of illuministic ideas, healthy nationalistic propaganda, through high ideals made flesh and blood in the lives of those who cherish the dream of a united republican India, and through press and platform turned into educative vehicles and creative universities. Pen is power and tongue is fire, if only we know how to use the written and spoken words, which must spring from intense *sadhana,* self-discipline and lofty unsullied character. All the possible avenues are to be exploited to check the present rolling-down-the-hill of India's national life, to embark upon the positive ideals of the up-hill job of nation-building.

The emergence of the RSS as a strong nationalistic force, after the collapse and fall of the once mighty Indian National Congress, is itself the proof that the laws of national survival are working. Now it is up to the children of Mother India, to the loyal sons and daughters of this country, to know what it means to be born in India, what is the purpose of life which Mother India points out to her children, what is her gnosis, *jnana,* her culture, her philosophy, her methods of human development, her ideal social structure, her answer to the economic and political problems that confront the children of India and the world at large. The spirit of India is not a closed fist of an esoteric teacher, nor the walled protection of the dogmatic religions. Indian spirit is essentially receptive, open, all-sided asymmetrical, creative, enterprising and power-engendering philosophy of life.

The term 'Hindu', in its technically religious and communal connotation, does not go back beyond the last three or four centuries. The term 'Hindu' today stands for the essential Indian spirit—as we speak of the Hellenic spirit, Roman or American spirit. The word 'Hindu' stands for anyone who is born in the land of Ganges, who is conscious of his cultural heritage, specially of the Vedanta, Yoga, *Gita*, Buddha, Sankara, Indian art and literature, who struggles to realise those vital truths in his life, whose purpose of life is self-realisation or God-consciousness for himself and the subsequent dynamic service of his fellow-beings, in leading his people, his society, country, mankind to a better social, economic and political pattern. Birth is of little significance, quality life means everything. The social distinctions of the ancient Indians into the intellectuals, warriors, businessmen and artisans is based not on birth but on inherent qualities and ways of life. "*चातुर्वर्ण्यं मया सृष्टं गुण कर्मविभागश: ।*"—The four castes were created by me according to inherent qualities and professional fields of work," says the *Gita*.

Today there is again darkening of the sun of righteousness and the triumph of unrighteousness all around. The purpose for which Independence has been achieved is today miserably defeated. The common man has not enough food, clothing and decent shelter to live in. He has no social security, no guarantee of job, no environment, inspiration and encouragement to grow. Tragically enough, our various religious communities continue to fight one against the other through propaganda, backbiting, public and private calumny. All are apparently immersed in their own petty personal, group, party or community squabbles and a few there are who have the vision, conviction, heart and realisation to look to the country as a whole, to the nation, to Mother India as a whole and say, "I am the child of Mother India, of her love and truth. I am born to realise my highest Self and serve my fellow-humans in India and the world."

What sort of democracy we are witnessing today? Mushroom parties and factions spring up here and there, one fighting against the other and weakening the country in every way. To sink smaller differences in view of major issues, to understand the rules of citizenship, to fulfil the purpose of human existence and to draw out our fellow pilgrims from the mud, we are so few left today. Those who do feel for their country, who mean business, who feel proud of the country's cultural heritage, who are receptive and assimilative enough of the light and life from abroad, are isolated, stranded and, not infrequently, frustrated. If they organise and do some useful work, embark upon the nation-building-task, then the black-marketeers, profiteers, nepotists and power-seekers, who are favoured by the present weak government, will raise alarm and the easy-going, over-democratic government will not hesitate to take action against them. Of such a hard trial the foremost and most convincing example was the action taken by the Government against the RSS since Gandhiji's martyrdom. It must be so; for all the great redemptive movements must spring from the streams of sufferings, persecution and agony. The blood of martyrs is indeed the seed of the Church, the crucifixion of the *homo sapiens* is the prelude to the resurrection that awaits him, even as winter hailstorms precede the advent of the spring. Suffering and sacrifice are the royal roads to the victory of spiritual truths, of human values and Eternal Freedom of the Great.

Out of the agony of the national crisis was born the RASHTRIYA SWAYAMSEVAK SANGH with most humble beginnings in the year 1925 under the inspiration and guidance, patriotic and nationalistic romance of Dr. Keshav Baliram Hedgewar of Nagpur, a man whose breath was nationalism, patriotism, service, sacrifice. Being instinctively an heir to the brave revolutionary spirit of RSS, such defenders of Indian culture, like Rana Pratap, Sivaji and Tilak, Dr. Hedgewar could not for long co-operate with the Gandhian wing of the Congress. From his student days at Poona and Calcutta, the passion for delivering the country from the clutches of foreign imperialists and domestic socio-economic tyrants was burning in his breast. Like Socrates of old became a 'midwife' to help others to bring forth strong, sturdy, intelligent youth for Athens, Dr. Hedgewar transmuted his medical profession to heal the spiritual maladies of his people. In intuitive moments of prophetic vision, Dr. Hedgewar could have visualised that he was being utilised by a Force bigger than himself to found an organisation, which in decades would grow to several millions of brave sons and daughters, disciplined soldiers and brave warriors, to resurrect the ethical, moral and spiritual forces of their country, to plant the tree of Indian wisdom in every corner, village and home of India, to make her strong, invincible, impregnable from every front, to unite her, strengthen her, lead her to the highest peaks of development, organisation and power. The little *Sangh*, that was formed after the non-cooperation days of Gandhiji, after the Nagpur communal riots, after the triumph of Gandhian Congress against the naked realism of Tilakism, consisted of ten boys. But today under the banner of the RSS are millions. The Christian Church began with one Jesus and twelve fishermen, but soon it conquered even the mighty Roman Empire and Greek Philosophy and gave a wonderful synthesis to the West—the synthesis, the strongest and the mightiest organisation in history, the Church, born of the love and sacrifice of one Jesus, the greatest Asian, supreme yogi, who spanned East and West through the Cross—the banner of his sacrifice that is Cross but supreme pattern of sacrifice. The root of religion is sacrifice, bursting of the bubble of selfishness and becoming one with the Ocean of Life, Reality, the Absolute, the Oversoul.

ईशावास्यमिदं सर्वं यत्किञ्च जगत्यां जगत्।
तेन त्यक्तेन भुञ्जीथा: मा गृध: कस्यस्विद्धनम्॥

All this universe is paraded by the Spirit-Consciousness
Enjoy Him by renouncing desire, not the yearning of another.

—*Isa Upanishad I*

Renunciation, sacrifice is the root of strength, power and invincibility. Only this pure love borne of sacrifice can make us serve our fellow-humans, the living gods in the form of walking skeletons, shrivelled bellies and exploited and dispossessed many everywhere.

The birth of the Sangh in the twentieth century may be compared to the vast spiritual and humanistic movement of nationalistic and rationalistic character in the history of Buddhist India. Where there is *Buddha,* there should be both *Dhamma* and *Sangh*. India in centuries past has said and taught other nations:

बुद्धं शरणं गच्छामि धम्मं शरणं गच्छामि संघं शरणं गच्छामि।

"I take refuge in Buddha (enlightenment), I take refuge in Dharma (moral law), I take refuge in Sangh (organisation)."

The new Sangh that is born is the crowning and fulfilment of all that is best in Hindu and Buddhist traditions with its hands outstretched to receive with critical acumen all that which is great and bright in other civilisations also. India has never been a closed book; she is the most open, naturalistic, humanistic and rational country among the civilised nations of the world. That is her history, that is her tradition, her soul and it is on this spirit of India the new Sangh arose "for the protection of the good, for the destruction of wickedness—परित्राणाय साधूनां विनाशाय च दुष्कृताम्।" as the *Gita* puts it.

One of the basic characteristics of the Rashtriya Swayamsevak Sangh is its insistence on organisation, discipline, efficiency, canalisation and utilisation of the youthful forces in the country for the constructive side of nation-building. India has lost much in her social structure through her individualistic philosophy. Today we are confronted with dangers and perils from outside the geographical frontiers of India, from within the country that the time has come for the nation to stand up as a solid rock like the mighty Himalayas, with living faith and unsullied purity of character like the white snow on the Everest and Kanchenjunga peaks. Organisation and social *sadhana* are now to be stressed, for it is only when Mother India as a whole, her culture and civilisation as a whole, survives that individuals, citizens can survive. Neither orthodox individualism of the stereotyped, uncritical, caste-ridden type vested interests nor the parliamentarian debates nor paper schemes could help the resurrection of the country. What is needed is unity, discipline, character and the ideal that nation before national, society before individual, community before private and group interests should prevail.

It is with this creative urge for collective *sadhana* that the RSS was born, has grown and will continue to grow and fulfil its mission in India. While the individualists, like Mr. Bombay and Mrs. Calcutta, Mr. Promode and Mrs. Fatima continue to indulge in self-seeking and self-aggrandisement, the brave boys and girls of the RSS continue to immolate themselves on the altar of the Motherland, in that creative and dynamic service that is born of the purest self-sacrifice and nationalist zeal. They will remain the watchdogs and guardians of India's national soul. These national guardians are the members of the ideal RSS, not in any communal, sectarian stereotyped or orthodox sense, but as spiritual dynamites to uphold the fundamental ethical values in life, for the preservation of the Aryan culture in the world, for giving and setting patterns of healthy tolerance and wide catholicity, to give enthusiasm and inspiration, purpose to life and meaning to the human pilgrimage, to vindicate the ontological and metaphysical truths in life, for the protection and defence of the righteous and the noble, not in India alone, but in this planet which itself is *vasudaiva kutumbakam*—the household of Vasudev, the Absolute, the temple of God.

Keshavraoji Hedgewar, like his predecessor in nationalist politics and religious revivalism, Bal Gangadhar Tilak, clung to the ideal of action, *karmayoga,* as the path for individual and national liberation. The ancestral Telugu family of Dr. Hedgewar from Hyderabad had transmitted to him the sense of organised action, political realism and cultural illuminism, which found expression when he moulded his first disciples, including Guruji Madhav Sadashivrao Golwalkar, who succeeded him as the second RSS chief, after the demise of its founder in 1940. As a school boy in Poona, as an undergraduate in the Medical College, Calcutta, and in mature years of his nationalistic apostolate, Dr. Hedgewar stuck to his gun, viz. to emancipate his country from ever-degrading forms of political, economic and social slavery. This could come about only through infusing the power-generating philosophy of Vedanta and the psychological militant energism of the *Gita*. No wonder that his nationalistic realism and political clear-mindedness clashed with the broad, but inefficient and inoperative liberalism, good-for-nothing moderatism and security-seeking caution of the phantom politics of the then arm-chair liberal and capitalist Congress.

While the classical Liberals of Indian Renaissance, like Pherozeshah Mehta and the Nehru family looked to foreign countries for the mainspring of their inspiration, the stalwart realists among the Indian nationalists looked to their own history, their own traditions, their own psychology and ethics, to the land and soil that gave them birth, for their main resourcefulness and action. Mazzini and Bismarck, Emerson and Gladstone are all great men and we will learn wisdom from them. But to the children of the soil of India they will remain as outside strength and corroboration of the treasures that are already in our soil, the external bulwarks of the inner castle that is there in the land of Aryavarta. This cult of the soil of India is not narrow nationalism, for it aims at the self-disciplining and self-sacrifice of the thoughtful nationals in safeguarding their own spiritual and political freedom, economic and social self-respect as against the evil eyes of communalists and imperialists who have for long subdued and destroyed many best national monuments and treasures of the land of Bharat.

The very air and breeze of India is dear to us—the flowing *sarees* and pyjamas we prefer to the imported frocks and suits, the epics of *Ramayana* and *Mahabharata* and the broad scriptural lore are all sacred to those born on the land of the Ganges. But they call this reactionary spirit as obscurantism. They say that we should be ashamed of being called Hindus. Ashamed? No, we shall take pride in being called Hindus, if by the term 'Hindu' we mean to be true to the cultural heritage and national spirit of the Indian soil. If the Muslims, Christians, Parsis should still be called Muslims, Christians and Parsis, even within the confines of their sectarian religions, why should a Hindu be ashamed to be called a Hindu if Indian culture remains to this day the Universal Mother of Religions, the broadest possible catholicity and the most philosophical and enlightened humanism of history? We do not speak of caste and sub-caste divisions and other factors that have degraded Indians and have divided Indians against Indians, but we mean the broad cultural and spiritual heritage of India to which every child born of the Indian soil is an heir.

All those who are gravitated towards the lap of their Motherland are Hindus. It is this conscious realisation of the spirit alone that counts, not the old anathema of being born of Brahmin or Chandala parents. Life, ideals, realisation, character alone count in the new setup of new India, not birth and parentage.

The genesis, then, of the RSS is to be sought in that historical necessity wherein are fulfilled the laws of individual and national survival. Until the year 1942, the dream of Dr. Hedgewar remained like a seed fallen in fertile soil, but during the last one decade, the seed has germinated and has become a pretty big tree that is today becoming the shade and protection to all the loyal children of the soil of India, those who are the born-heirs or adopted children of the Humanism, Rationalism and Philosophy, Metaphysics and Sociology of India. After the August Movement was crushed by the British in 1942, the Congress leaders gaoled and the nationalist forces banned and burnt by the high-handedness of the foreign ruler, Providence entrusted the task of safeguarding the national soul to the young RSS. The second phase of the history of the RSS then, began with the failure of the August Movement under Gandhiji's leadership, after the greatest realistic politician, statesman and loyal child of Bharatmata, Netaji Subhas Chandra Bose was humiliated and defeated by the vested interests and pacifist group of the Congress, during and after the Tripuri Session.

The most sensitive nationalists, whether within the RSS or outside, feel that their own individual deaths are far better and nobler than to see their country, their people, their culture enslaved any further. Shri Guruji Golwalkar, the pilot of the RSS, its captain and head said, "What is the use of being alive after Bharatmata is dead? It is better that Bharat should go under sea rather than become a carbon copy of others. Today people talk so much of the love of nation, but where is that love? Is it patriotism to go on simply copying others? No, it is rather an insult to the Mother. We are determined to keep Bharat as Bharat."

The new emphasis, the mainspring of inspiration, the *raison d'etre,* the very breath of the RSS then, is the identification of individual interests with the social and national interests. This runs diametrically opposed to the weak tradition in India and the separatist philosophy of the individualists who preach, "Let individual leave even if the society and the nation were to go to dogs, get enslaved." The new force to bring the collective *sadhana* and social living in the life of new India is the RSS. Here again says Shri Golwalkar:

"The RSS saw the light of the day at a time when the Hindu community was like a house divided against itself. It was as it is even today, ridden by invidious distinctions of caste and creed. These were further accentuated by the foreigners and those who could not tolerate the sight of a united and well-knit Hindu community. The result was there for all to see. The people had lost all character; they had been estranged from even the most basic concepts and ethical standards. Corruption, nepotism and other ills were rampant and in the medley of confusion engendered by the race for wealth and power, the individual had forgotten that he was an integral part of the Hindu society. He no longer considered his and the community's interests as identical. This was sure to mean the country's fall and it did. A people divorced from discipline, character and spirit of service and sacrifice could not but come to grief.

"It was the mission of the RSS to bring home to the individual the realisation that he was not merely an individual, but an integral part and important member of the entire community, a limb of the body social."

—Shri Golwalkar's speech on 25th anniversary of the RSS

The increasing sense of personal and collective discipline imparted to the members of the RSS volunteers is meant to cement this sense of nation-consciousness and collective *sadhana*. Even from a merely tactical point of view, out of mere self-preservation and self-interest, the Hindus and all those who consider India as their Motherland must hug the sense of unity, discipline and solidarity, without which the nation will not be able to withstand the religious fanaticism and political aggressiveness of the Pakistanis and pan-Islamists, foreign imperialists and vandals from across India's borders. And political bondage is the worst, for, with it goes down self-respect, self-culture, self-confidence and all that are really great and lofty in the accomplishments of any civilised nation. The supreme need of the hour in Indian history today is strong organisation and steely discipline—whatever name be that strong disciplined decentralised centralisation may be called—so that India may live as a free country, united and economically self-sufficient and socially emancipated and politically progressive.

We should sound a note of warning that if in the name of nationalism and patriotism we uncritically cling to anything and everything that is in the social, religious and economic life of India today, we may be sure that the final doom of Indian civilisation is not far off. Today there is only Pakistan and the threat of materialistic communism. But if patriotic and nationalistic Indians abandon the goddess of Reason, Humanity and Justice and adore mere custom, meaningless traditions and priest-craft, religion-sanctioned caste and sub-caste system, untouchability, unenlightened idol worship, totemism and unhealthy taboos, then we may know that India will lose her national heritage and thus when the dreams of pan-Islamisation and materialistic hedonism become a *fait accompli,* then streams of tears will be too late, repentance will be without remission, and the very purpose for which the nationalistic forces once fought for Independence, will be defeated.

In this critical, rational and humanistic resurrection of Indian nationalism, the vanguard is to be the ideal RSS and the Rashtriya Swayamsevaks remain untouched by the blemish of cheap and easy emotional religion, skin-deep nationalism and journalistic applause, which the uncritical nationalists and emotional communalists champion and fight for. It is when mankind goes astray from the right ethical path, from the psychological path of self-knowledge and self-realisation that great prophets and movements appear in history to set the derailed humanity back to the ethical foundation-stone on which the entire universe subsists. Law, both physical and moral, is the very foundation of life, existence. Derailments from the right path are many, but the right path itself is just one, although the wise may call it by different names. Thus without self-knowledge and self-purification it is impossible to reach the rock of deeper Humanity and potential Divinity inborn in man. Among these ethical giants, among these humanistic and rationalistic revivalists stand such eminent prophets like Manu, Vyas, Yajnavalkya, Buddha, Asoka, Sankara, Kabir, Tulsi and such other saints who went deep into the source of Strength and Power, Ethical Law and Divine Humanity inborn in the heart of man and taught the way of peace and progress to the weary world.

Of the new mission that awaits the new National Army of the RSS in partitioned, economically bankrupt and internally disorganised India, the first and foremost will be to unite, cement into one solid national block the various waning communities, creeds and castes on the rock of Indianism, which is the highest form of Hinduism, says Shri Golwalkar.

"The RSS was founded and has been working with a view to revive all that is best in Hindu, i.e. Bharatiya culture and on that sound basis to knit together in bonds of abiding brotherhood the people imbued with the culture of our land. It tries to destroy the fissiparous tendencies in the Hindu society by inculcating the truth of our having a common heritage and making all individuals realise that all apparent vanity is but the expression of a common underlying unity, by creating mutual trust, love and regard for one another and by instilling intense love for the Motherland—Bharat as a whole—in the hearts of the people."

Here also Shri Golwalkar, repeating the message of the latest prophets of modern India, the voice of seers like Ramakrishna, Vivekananda, Dayanand and Tilak, sounded the same note of national unity, solidarity built up and cemented on the rock of Indian cultural heritage, her national humanity with eyes and minds open to any new thought that may be thrown from any part of the world, with arms outstretched for learning science, industry, politics, economics from the greatest thinkers and seers of the West as well as of the East, so that India may rise anew as the Mother of Philosophy and Dharma, the Mother of human understanding, sympathy and tolerance, Mother of universal brotherhood and universal peace. Her message is that of:

सत्यं ज्ञानमनन्तं ब्रह्म। यो वेद निहितं गुहायां परमे व्योमन्।
सोऽश्नुते सर्वान् कामान् सह ब्रह्मणा बपिचतेति ।

—Taittiriya Upanishad II 1

These words could be paraphrased as follows:

"Truth, Knowledge, Bliss is Brahman

That man who discovers this Brahman hidden within his heart

He attains the objects of all his desires in that omniscient, omnipotent God."

These words, *सत्यं ज्ञानमनन्तं ब्रह्म: ।* are the highest wisdom

India can teach her children and the world at large. In the entire theological and philosophical literature of the whole world there is not another word that could compete with or surpass the term India has given '*sat-chit-ananda*', to Reality as TRUTH-CONSCIOUSNESS-BLISS. This is the highest metaphysics, highest psychology, lofty philosophy, sublime theology and religion the history of civilisation ever knows. Those who have the courage to realise these truths in their own lives will have thereby acquired immortality, invincibility, fearlessness and emancipation which is the gospel which India holds out for her children and to the world at large.

From the nationalistic passion and political business-mindedness and cultural life of the RSS let none imagine that it is merely a fanatical 'fascist organisation'. Against the glorification of brute force the RSS will take its stand on soul-force, again the pomp and glamour of Western militarism will be replaced by the RSS through an intense educational and missionary propaganda, against the complicated State apparatus and mechanised war machines will stand out the simplicity, self-discipline, orderliness, humanity and creativity of the new Sangh, which, instead of being an isolated movement in India, will be the main stream of the best revolutionary economic struggles, social, political and spiritual movements, incorporating the best from such forces like the Brahmo Samaj, Arya Samaj, Ramakrishna Mission and such other organisations that once gave life and still the original word in this particular text might have been '*anandam*' which means bliss, and not '*anantham*' which means infinite. Paul Deussen and other critics hold this view continue to point out the way for national unity, social reforms, human solidarity, based on Reason, Humanity and Faith.

This latest and newly-born child of Mother India, the extant, chivalrous, rationalistic, humanistic, disciplined, iron-willed, centralised Rashtriya Swayamsevak Sangh will be both the Brahmin-Kshatriya-Vaisya-Sudra, the brain-soldier-trader-peasant-labourer hierarchy plus the torch-bearer of the twentieth-century wisdom of India to the entire mankind. The betrayal of the country, the selling of India's humanity by the present Congress clique, the denationalisation advocated by the extreme Marxian Communists, the religious poison injected into the body politic by both the Muslim League, Hindu orthodoxy, Christian League and all such communal and separatist groups will all find their meeting ground, their redeeming feature, corrective and strength, expiation and remedy in the new ideal RSS, which must be the synthesis of the *nova et vetera,* New and Old, East and West, Idea and Matter.

The march of the RSS is now inexorably fixed. Persecutions and calumnies, slandering and back-biting can only strengthen the RSS all the more to cling to the vital source of then Indian humanity, their unsullied nationalist philosophy, their disciplined and purified army of brave sons and daughters of new India to face the terrible economic, social, educational, cultural and political problems of their Motherland. For achieving this dream, their stand is on the perennial philosophy of life, taught by Mother India through her sages and *rishis,* her reformers and thinkers, her representative men and women. India has taught for ages that all fields of human life, political, military, psychic, psychological or philosophical, yogic or spiritual activities wax all of the divine origin. Self-realisation is impossible without strength. "*न अयं आत्मा बल्हिनेन लभ्यः*—that *atman* is not realised by a weakling" warn the *Upanishads.*

It is this dynamic character of neo-Vedantism that needs stressing. If our ancient *rishis* conceived self-realisation, the union or yoga of the *jivatma* with *paramita,* of the Soul with the Over-Soul, of the Shadow with the Substance of the universe, of the relative consciousness with the Pure Act, the Absolute, as dewdrops melting and falling into the shining sea, the modern neo-Vedantists conceive Self-realisation as the awakening of the 'Lion of Divinity asleep in man' as Vivekananda puts it. It is the potential infinite powers that are latent in man that are to be awakened, aroused, developed, mobilised, canalised and utilised for the constructive nation-building purposes. Man is potentially both the personal God and the impersonal Absolute. This is the keynote of Vedanta. But this neo-Vedanta is in no way an abstruse, unpractical metaphysics, unrelated to practical details of our economic and political life. On the contrary, Vedanta furnishes the rock-bottom to the social, educational and economic superstructure that is to be built in the land of the Ganges and the Himalayas, the impregnable eternal Rock of Man, the Universal, Eternal, Powerful and Divine.

The practical details of Vedanta must enter every field of our national life, even the luxury chambers of cinema stars and business-merchants and professional men. For, in the new resurrected and self-respecting, strong and powerful India, even movies, radio, industry, scientific and technical advancement will all be made instrumental to the building-up of the nation, of the people, to instill hope and truth, build up character and power in every son and daughter of Mother India. The present hoarding of black money through exploitation of film stars and pornographic art will be ruthlessly removed from the path of India's nation-building. If we mean business, no anti-national, fissiparous and anti-social forces will have any more a free hand to strike at the root of India's national unity, solidarity, creative urge and her unsullied character.

□

Chapter-3

The Philosophical Basis of The RSS

नित्योऽनित्यानां चेतनश्चेतनानाम्-
एको बहुनां यो विदधाति कामान्।
तमात्मस्थं येऽनुपशान्ति धीरा-
स्तेषाम शांतिः शाश्वती नेतारेषाम्॥

Eternal amidst the transient things,
Consciousness pure amidst the unconscious beings,
The Supreme One whose dispensed life is breath to all,
Him who realises in his own heart, his is peace, not of others.

—Katho Upanishad, V 13

"BRHAMAN is the Absolute, universe is relative, the soul of man is one with the Over-Soul."

—Sankara

"The central dogma of all true religions is the possible perfection of man, his inherent divinity, the indivisible solidarity of all beings with each other in the life of God."

—S. Radhakrishnan (Kalki, p. 68)

The real strength and credentials of the RSS is its stand on the bedrock of Indian philosophy, which is *philosophia perennis* par excellence. That psychological philosophy that is embodied in the *Upanishads* is for all peoples, for all times, for everywhere. Herein is fulfilled the veritable conditions of catholicity of doctrine, being *quod semper, quod ad ominbus, quod ubique*—for always, for all, for everywhere. This is the Himalayan basis of Indian thought. Most modern scientific discoveries of the West have done nothing more but to confirm the eternal verities proclaimed by the sages of the Himalayas, the philosophical speculations and life-wisdom contained in the *Upanishads*, *Vedas*, Vedanta and the *Gita* of the Indian lore.

'OM' is the traditional symbol of that positive, optimistic philosophy that takes its stand on the Absolute, conceived and realised as the *summum bonum* of human life. Relativity of the universe postulates the Absolute *maya* or cosmic illusion, the power that creates, preserves and dissolves the relative universe, postulates *satya* or Reality. Supreme Reality is Truth, Truth of all truths—*satyasya satyam satya* and *maya* are, as it were, intertwined and mixed in the created universe, everything partaking of the shadow and substance of Existence (*Sat*), Consciousness -Thought (*chit*) and Bliss-Happiness-Good (*ananda*), being derived from the Supreme Reality and the negative side like evil, grossness, misery, etc. being caused by *mahamaya*. Relativity, which, if ontologically analysed, vanishes into mere nothingness. Hence creation is not mere transformation of something into something; it is the emergence of something out of sheer nothing, *production rei ex nihilo sui et subjecti*. Nothing on the one side postulates everything on the other side. Hence it is in the supreme stages of metaphysical realisation of the relative with the Absolute, of reducing the many into the One, of creation into the power of the Creator, of the universe into the realm of Substance, that thinkers, philosophers, seers of the perennial philosophy have arrived at the concept of *ekam evadvitiyam*—of the One without a second. This monistic idealism is the peak of all philosophic speculations not only in India, but also in ancient Greece, Rome, China and everywhere where monuments to the Temple of Man, the Universal and True, have ever been raised. In Plato's idea of Good, Aristotle's idea of Pure Act, Spinoza's idea of *Substantia* and Kant's idea of *Ding an sich* (the Thing in itself), and in all other philosophical systems where systematically and persistently an inquiry has been made into the nature of the Absolute, thinkers have always arrived at the same concept as in the *Upanishads*, in the Vedanta, in that terse well-proved axiomatic truth: *ब्रह्म सत्यं जगन् मिथ्या। जीवो ब्रह्मैव नापर: ॥* —"Brahman, the Absolute, is Truth, universe is transient flux, Relativity, the living soul is one with the Over-Soul, man is potentially the Infinite, from which he is not distinct, not different." The philosophy of the 'one without a second' is the philosophy of India. On this *Advaita Vedanta,* this non-dualistic metaphysics, on this translucent and powerful ontology of 'Being and Becoming, of the Absolute and the relative, of the One and the many,' will be built up the Hind Swaraj that awaits to be born after the cure of the political vivisection and economic bankruptcy caused by the present easy-going, hedonistic and pseudo-democratic leadership in India.

Man is veritably a microcosm. Man, through his consciousness, is the reflection of the Absolute. The embodied speck of consciousness, which we call *jivatma,* is the mirror of the Supreme Soul of the universe, the Over-Soul. The perfect man is indeed the pattern of the Most High, the God of religions, the Absolute of the philosophers, the Unknown of the agnostics, the Over-Soul of the psychologists, the One without a second of the ontologists. The ideal of perfected intelligence and will-power is indeed the incarnate God, the tangible God, as opposed to the vague gaseous vertebrate which the ignorant and the superstitious believe to be presiding over the destinies of the world somewhere up in the heavens. This human, rational and psychological aspect of personal God is seen in the definition which Patanjali gives when he says:

ईश्वरप्रणिधानाद्वा।

ल्केश कर्मविपाकाशवैरपरामृष्ट: पुरुषविशेष ईश्वर: ॥

'Concentration of mind can be attained either through devotion to God. Now God is a particular soul untouched by afflictions, deserts of consuming desires, devoid of burning flames and all-consuming passions.'

—*Yoga Sutras I 24*

The Universal Self—the great I AM WHO AM of the mosaic revelation, the Over-soul of the universe, is residing in every creature, more specially in the mind and consciousness of man. This potential divinity of the *Homo sapiens* is what is the life-giving force in every religion. It is to this omnipotent, all-pervading consciousness-force the Vedic *rishis* sang, before whose majesty and immensity they acknowledged their limitations and whom they strived to realise in their own souls. They said:

यो देवीऽग्नौ यीऽप्सु यी विश्वं भुवनमाविवेश।
यो औवत्रौत्रु यो बनस्पतिषु तस्मै देवाय नमोनमः ॥

"That consciousness-force-God that is in the burning fire, in the rippling water, who is all-pervading force in the universe, who is in the herb as well as in the biggest forest tree—that God we bow down to."

—*Swetaswatara Upanishad II 17*

Little knowledge is always a dangerous thing, we need to drink deep or else better touch not the Pierian spring, where shallow draughts intoxicate the brain, whence drinking deeper, the brains are sobered again. True science, whose devotees are men like Sir Isaac Newton and Galileo, Kepler and Albert Einstein, is always humble. But it is the semi-cranks who become self-conceited with their shallow intellectual attainments and mental gymnastics. The pride of positivistic hedonism separated physics from metaphysics, religion from psychology, economics from ethics and mysticism from pornographic romance with the result that man lost his equilibrium, wholeness and integration, his inner poise and power to face the problems of life with grit, coolness and character. Man is not an isolated entity; he is helplessly part and parcel of the universe, of the Whole; this Stupendous Whole, whose body is Nature and God the Soul. Laws of Nature which cause determinism in the physical world continue to work in the invisible world of ethics, human values, imponderable elements of human growth and development to perfect humanity, divine personality in human beings.

At a time when our shallow political leaders, in the name of secularism and opportunist politics, are deliberately shelving aside the eternal and immortal treasures of Indian philosophy and religion, it will be the task of the new nationalist forces, notably the RSS, to vindicate these human values in their own exemplary lives and, then, through a nation-wide campaign to resurrect the dynamite of Indian metaphysics with a view to giving infinite vision and horizon to the youth of the country, to appreciate the best and eschew the dross, to accept the gram and throw away the chaff, from what is transmitted to us as the sum total of Indian culture and civilisation. It is not mere nationalist passion or emotional politics that is going to save India against the fury of communalists, Muslim, Hindu, Christian or of any other religious group, but it is the knowledge, gnosis, of Truth, love of justice and passion for Humanity that should be the *terra firma* for us to stand. India, at her best, is Humanity, and here is the highest Religion of Man, *Manava Dharma,* that has been developed. It is this Eternal Humanism that is going to stand the test of times, the crisis of human civilisation in a world given to the orgy of violence, hatred, lies, in a mechanised, atomic and roboted society. India has taken her stand on the knowledge, *jnana*—gnosis, of mere, "Knowledge is power. Knowledge is invincibility. Knowledge is Humanity. Knowledge is emancipation. Knowledge is God. Knowledge is beatific vision and immortality," says Thomas Aquinas.

Today the thoughtful children of the Indian soil look to the Vedanta and the *Upanishads*, the *Gita* and to Buddha, not any longer for the attainment of isolated individual emancipation and *vairagya,* a sort of stoic imperturbability. We look back to those monuments of human thought, pinnacles of Indian civilisation, to get the needed inspiration, to find the guide, an ideal pattern, and not to remain drowned in the dead past, but to find a springboard to face the living present with courage and determination to launch into the unborn future, into the blossoming of a hope that is bound to be materialised, given the sound and cool brains for Indians to think and an indomitable will-power to forge ahead, move onward. It is this dynamisation, action, social service and collective *sadhana* that characterise the neo-Vedantic revival started by the Brahmo and Arya Samajis, in the fiery zeal and apostolate of such men like Vivekananda and Netaji Subhas Chandra. The power that is born of purity of heart and self-sacrifice, which is born of the realisation of "*Tatvamasi*", of the "I and my Father are one", is now to be utilised to solve the economic, social and political problems of the country. This is the new urge, the new call of Indian renaissance and the RSS is built upon this neo-Vedantic renewal of action, service, collective *sadhana* and intensified passion for social and political justice. We cannot put the clock back. We are moving forward.

The cardinal tenets of this new revival of Indian philosophy with its most practical bearing on social and economic, political and international life, then, could be stated as follows:

(1) Man is not merely an animal, matter without values and rules. His perfection lies in the development of Humanity to the highest possible peaks. Man is potentially perfectible *ad infinitum,* because the embodied soul is potentially one with the Over-soul, *jivatma* is one with the *paramatma*. All are one, all are parts of a stupendous Whole, whose body is Nature, whose life is Brahman, the Real. The inherent divinity and potential perfectibility of human nature *ad infinitum,* then, is the first principle of the perennial philosophy which Mother India has taught her children in ages past and is now being re-discovered in the changed historical conditions of India today.

(2) But there is no triumph of Human Values, Ethics, Philosophy and Culture save when we have tackled the social and economic problems, have restored justice to the victims of exploitation and have changed the socio-economic structure of the people of India in such a way as to suit the laws of survival, and enable our society to keep pace with the changing tunes, in a world ever-growingly becoming smaller and more united towards the ideal of world citizenship based on world culture and world unity. Hence economics first and then culture. Says Sri Ramakrishna, "Religion is not for empty bellies." Culture becomes mockery when its songs are played or sung into the ears of walking skeletons, shrivelled stomachs and dried-up limbs. That is why Raja Ram Mohun Roy, Surendranath Banerjee,

Kamakshi Natarajan, Gandhiji and others insisted on social reforms and economic justice. If we dismiss these social reformers and champions of the downtrodden, of the victims of exploitation, the scum of the earth, then we lose our hold on Humanity. Then mere nationalism becomes betrayed of Humanity, which refuses to restore socio-economic justice to the downtrodden millions and which becomes mere emotionalism that will not endure in times of trial and peril. If all the universe is *vasudaiva kutumbakam*, God's family, then all humans are brothers. It is this human solidarity that should be deeper than nationalism. In fact, the justification of patriotism and nationalism springs from this wider and deeper passion for Humanity and Justice." "Blessed are they who hunger and thirst after Righteousness", says Jesus.

(3) All traces of communalism including the Hindu and Muslim, is to be fought against, because ontologically all humans have the same source, the Supreme Reality, 'OM', Brahma, Allah, Elohim, Jehovah, Theos or by whatever name the Supreme Reality might be called. The only way to justify and strengthen the culture of the soil is by opposing all communal organisations, whether Muslim, Hindu or Christian, and by strengthening the more intensified, purified and enlightened forms of patriotism, nationalism. It is by being rooted in the national soil that we begin to learn and discover the power of regeneration through national culture. The *swadharma* is not decided by birth, but through the conscious realisation of the culture of the land and discriminating dross from gold. It is in this sense that *paradharma,* or cultures from other lands and other peoples, is to be received and assimilated into the main nationalistic streams of Indian life.

यो देवीऽग्नौ यीऽप्सु यी विश्वं भुवनमाविवेश।

यो औवत्रौत्रु यो बनस्पतिषु तस्मै देवाय नमोनमः ॥

"Better one's own dharma (duty) well-done than another's

dharma well-done,

Better death in one's own dharma, another's dharma is fraught with fear."

—Gita III 35

Here the word *swadharma*, however, means more the duty acquired through conscious and vital assimilation of Truth than any religious label based on the accidents of birth, the glories of our blood and state are shadows, not substantial things. It is the conscious realisation of the basic Human Values in life that gives character, that makes one a Brahmin or an Arya, not pedigree, not accidents of birth.

From what has been stated above it is clear that the pure springs of nationalism are not to be poisoned with any form of communalism. In fact, the acceptance of the letter and spirit of Vedanta and the factual exigencies of our social and political life in India today demand that only unalloyed nationalism, crystal-clear gems of humanism and rationalism, form the true basis of that united, invincible and strong India we envisage, which the ideal nationalistic Rashtriya Swayamsevaks are pledged to work for and achieve. These national springs, however, are not that amorphous and colourless secularism of our British-trained leaders; this nationalism is basically and essentially Indian, which, when conjoined to the cultural moorings, we may broadly call 'Hindu', if only *Hindutva* connotes the tap-root of Indian philosophy, religion and culture, our *Bharatiyata.*

"This is the nationalism, caste-free, creed-free Hindu nationalism which the RSS advocates," says Shri Golwalkar. "Instead of keeping this Hindu patriotism and love of Motherland alive—Hindu nationalism has a long and ceaseless line of heroes from King Dahir of Sind to Rana and Guru Nanak and Guru Govind Singh to Shivaji and Madanlal Dhingra and countless patriots—they (the British and the British-trained denationalised Indians) have done their worst in stabbing Hindu nationalism. Greatness of leaders does not lie in the following they command but in their independence and their strength of character with roots deep in national tradition and drawing inspiration from national heroes.

"The present leaders, lacking true patriotism and national tradition, could not be expected to do better than what they have done. Without patriotism and without love for Bharatmata, no real good of the country or nation is possible.

"But this love of Bharatmata, to be endurable, acceptable and powerful, must be backed up with the philosophic and cultural traditions of the soil of India. Hence, the resurgence of neo-Vedanta to revitalise and reinterpret the soul and spirit of Indian civilisation to the modern world. In this *Kali Yuga,* Iron Age, after the lapse of the *Satya, Treta* and *Dvapar* ages of the Indian sages, what other ground we have to stand up with heads erect and well-founded hopes for our resurrection, save on the rock of Indian culture which is in the marrow of our bones, in our blood, sinews, in our very breath, in our whole being, so deeply implanted, so deeply engraved, so sacredly enshrined within our hearts." But *Kali Yuga,* the age of iron and atom bombs, of strife and war, is not the last word. Indian *rishis* foretold the advent of a fifth *yuga* which is *Krita yuga,* the age in which nations of the world will rise again and restored back to *Satya Yuga,* the Age of Truth. Hinduism, Buddhism, Christianity and Islam agree in this apocalypticism.

With the revival of pure, anti-communal, anti-caste, anti-idolatrous nationalism is vitally linked the question of our national language, customs, traditions, character, mental outlook and all those which make us Indians first and everything else afterwards. Language, religion, race, customs of the land must first be purified, filtered and only the best in them should be preserved and by preserving these national traits, we survive as Indian nationals. Our culture, philosophy, religion and literature are preserved in Sanskrit, Pali and the languages derived from Sanskrit. As for the betaking ourselves to English education, without having solid roots in Sanskrit and Indian vernaculars, has made us slaves, subservient to foreign interests, foreign ideologies and foreign in everything save the colour of the skin, so in the new all-India national revival, which the ideal RSS envisages, Sanskrit language will again be enshrined on her due throne, the venerable mother of Indian languages, the root of our culture, the mainspring of our inspiration and action.

Why should we look to a Max Muller, Schopenhauer, Monier Williams and Estlin Carpenter to learn Indian philosophy or Indian philology? Is it not a disgrace? Does it not reflect an abject slave mentality? Of course those great orientalists have done us a great service by studying and interpreting our ancient culture in a language and in a way understandable to the modern mind in the West. India certainly will remain grateful for their scholarship, erudition, labour, patience and character that enabled them to persist in unearthing pearls of Indian wisdom and presenting them to the world outside in a rational, dignified and purified form. While acknowledging our debts, it will be up to the children of the soil of India to explore still further the unexplored regions of Indian lore, to revive them, revitalise them with new interpretation, giving them new significance so that what is lasting, true, eternal in Indian culture and philosophy may be preserved, defended, propagated and made a living reality in the lives, mental habits of our people and in every sphere of Indian life.

When the present denationalising fad of commercial secularism is got over and the truly national, patriotic and humanistic forces have taken control of the Government, revolutionary steps are to be introduced in the educational life of nationalist India. Education must be made free, compulsory and nationalistic for all. Sanskrit, the mother-language of Indian civilisation, will have to be made compulsory. For, no Indian, truly wishing to be a citizen of India, can afford to ignore the very fountain-head of his civilisation which is conveyed through language, philosophy and religion. To read and write Sanskrit should be the minimum qualification for an Indian student to begin college and university studies. It is ignorance, ignorance of Indian language, her traditions, her culture and philosophy that has made us slaves of foreigners, that has made us ape and imitate without holding on to the soul that is ours, losing our national identity, character, strength, conviction, inner poise and power. Now it is this demon of ignorance which we have to fight against through knowledge, *vidya*. *Vedas* means *vidya,* knowledge. Ignorance has caused our downfall; knowledge shall resurrect us to our pristine position, restore us back to our coveted thrones. No, ignorance does not pay; ignorance is curse; knowledge alone is bliss and freedom.

If only we had known what we are by our birthright as Indians, we would have then known that these communal strifes between Hindus, Muslims, Christians or Parsis are mere quarrels about straw. We are all primarily and essentially Indians, not Hindus, Muslims or Christians. We are children of the soil of India and it is on this basic fact of our national life, the new resurrection of Indian nationals has to take place. The only enemy of nationalism is communalism, which consecrates birth-privileges and birth-religions, saps humanistic solidarity and undermines national strength. The old distinctions and divisions, which our British masters taught by dividing up our country into innumerable castes, communities, factions, still continue. These factions weakened us and our strength will come in forming a united national front with strong, unmistakable national character. "National character and national unity before everything," is the motto that Guruji of the RSS has placed before the nation.

The national philosophy of India, in its universal and catholic significance, the Vedanta of all times, the neo-Vedanta of modern Indians, as expounded by men like Vivekananda, Dayanand, Ram Mohun, S. Radhakrishnan and a few other intellectuals, acknowledges an infinite vauet of approach towards Reality, infinite paths according to the individuals concerned to reach out to the Real from the transient flux of this phenomenal and ephemeral world. "Awakening of religious consciousness and philosophic wisdom are in fact after-growths of man when he has outgrown his animality. Outgrowth of our animality is the entrance to the second birth, *dwijahood,* of Indian traditions. Philosophically cultural, historically and nationally we have to insist more upon personal character and upon the soil of our birth to decide upon the who's who of Indian citizens and not the sham shows of birth, wealth or social status. If there is one fundamental doctrine that has been insisted upon so clearly and unmistakably in our philosophical literature, it is the psychology of second birth, the analysis of human consciousness and the equality and unity of Man and Mankind. All caste and sub-caste divisions and all fissiparous tendencies are aberrations from the lofty ideal of unity and solidarity that is the keynote of Indian philosophical speculation and mystical experience. Thus the Himalayas of the Perennial Philosophy of Man the Universal, the Divine, the Catholic will always be in India. From the Orient the rising sun of Vedanta will again be the torchlight to strengthen and energise not only Indian citizens but also the peoples of the world," says Swami Vivekananda.

"The debt which the world owes to our motherland is immense. Taking country with country, there is not one race on this earth to which the world owes so much as to the patient Hindu, the mild Hindu. I do not see into the future, nor do I care to see. But one vision I see clear as life before me—that the ancient Mother has awakened once more, sitting on her throne rejuvenated, more glorious than ever. Proclaim her to all the world with the voice of peace and benediction."

Thus spoke, thus dreamt Vivekananda, the most dynamic neo-Vedantic philosopher of our century. But now the 'mild and patient Hindu' is not going to let his country and culture to be swept away by any outside intruder. Here again, the weapon of India's fight will not be rifles, canons, atom bombs and mortars, but Truth, Humanity, Love, Understanding. Untruth will be fought in Truth, injustice conquered in Justice, weakness in Strength and Power borne of God. For, our culture teaches all her children this sublime truth, heirs of *Mahabharata*.

अक्रोधेन जयेत् क्रांधम् असाधुं माधुना जयेत्।
जयेत् कदर्थ्य दानेन जयेत् सत्येन चानृतम्॥

Which means "Conquer anger by Forgiveness, wickedness by Goodness, enmity by Service and untruth by Truth."

—Udyoga Parva (Mahabharata), 38, 73, 39, 73

It will be the soul-force of Indian philosophy that will now be aroused, unified, canalised and mobilised to wage the war of spiritual, economic and social freedom of Mother India. This battle will be planned, fought and won by the children of Mother

India. Mere birth privileges will count for nothing, but character, national identity and realisation of the essential spirit of Indian culture alone will count in our struggle. This second birth, *dwijahood,* based on personal character and intrinsic merit of the person is what is contained in our scriptures, repeatedly taught by the greatest and noblest prophetic minds of India. Says Buddha:

"A man is not a Brahmin by reason of his matted hair or his lineage or his caste; he in whom are to be found Truth and Law, he is pure (v.1. Happy), he is a Brahmin."

—Dhammapada, 393

Not amassing of riches, not pot-bellied indulgence, not the boast of heraldry, nothing counts in the new setup which neo-Vedantins of India envisage. Nothing but pure character, the unsullied national character, willpower, discipline, purity, integrity and inner power matters; only these count in the new thought of new India, which keeps vital continuity with the past in all that are of permanent value in the cultural heritage of India. There, there was the eternal cry of Indian sages who upheld that not through wealth, not through progeny, but by self-sacrifice and service alone immortality is to be attained.

न धनेन न प्रजया
त्यगिनैव अमृतत्वामनुभव॥

"Not through wealth, not through progeny, but by self-sacrifice alone is immortality to be attained."

In fact it is only the nationalistic revival that is the effective answer, rational refutation and humanistic remedy to the vices of communalism, sectarianism and provincialism and parochialism. The conscious realisation of the spirit of the Vedanta, the psychology of yoga and the practical religion of *Bhagavad Gita* will heal the present narrow, caste-arrogant, stereotyped orthodoxy of the idle, indulgent, pot-bellied high castes who still support the criminality of untouchability, caste and sub-caste ostracism and so many types of narrow restrictions and divisions that stand in the way of what Shri Golwalkar preaches as "national unity and national character".

The metaphysics of Vedanta, the ontology of idealistic monism, the psychology of yogic discipline and Buddhistic ethics, the social and aesthetic spirit of the *Mahabharata*, the integrated religion of the *Bhagavad Gita*, these, these alone stand out as the Mount Everest of Indian cultural genesis. These lofty truths and highest humanistic principles are today to be understood, propagated in every corner and village of Bharatvarsha, for, on this self-knowledge of India by Indians will arise the new promised land, the new celestial city, *Dharmarajya,* the real Swaraj of our dreams. In this pioneering work of national awakening are needed not only the Ramaknshna-Vivekananda Mission, but also a hundred other new disciplined orders, congregations for both men and women and schools of thought, which, after having felt the sublimity of their vocational mission and missionary vocation, will light the torch of Indian culture in their own hearts and minds, in their everyday life and through an ideal exemplary life and character, irradiate the light of Indian culture, the hidden treasures of Indian lore to the four corners of their motherland, to entire human family at large. In this sense, the Rastnya Swayamsevaks shall be the vanguard of this new missionary awakening and dynamic zeal to defend, buttress and strengthen the permanent bases and imponderable values in the cultural heritage of India.

The present state of despondency, country-wide frustration-complex and misery are not, as our secularists patronise, due to the religious and philosophical bend of the Indian people. On the contrary, the downfall of India, her millennial political slavery—with all the hellish consequences of that political slavery—was due to ignoring the message and mission of the prophets of Indian civilisation—the *rishis* who have taught us the path towards self-realisation and the God-realised dynamics in life. Says again Vivekananda:

"The truths of the *Upanishads* are before you. Take them up, live up to them and the salvation of India will be at hand."

To those who incriminate religion and try to identify religious philosophy with dogmas, creeds, caste, idol worship, etc., the same dynamic apostle of neo-Vedantic religion, says again:

"Each soul is potentially divine. The goal is to manifest this divinity within by controlling nature, external and internal. Do this either by work or worship, or psychic control or philosophy, by one or more or all of these and be free. This is the whole of religion. Doctrines or dogmas or rituals or books or temples or forms are but secondary details."

—Swami Vivekananda

Indian renaissance, to be truly and deeply Indian, its tap-root must be Vedanta which is the most catholic, integrating and accommodating system. In fact, not only India, but all those countries which have been influenced by Indian philosophy, whether the Mahayana or Himayana Buddhists, the Sufi Islam or Greek transcendental monists, all had the core of Vedanta adjusted and re-interpreted to suit the various schemes and times of the development of human civilisation. Similarly that part of intellectual Europe, which was influenced by Indian thought, look to Vedanta as the masterpiece of Indian wisdom. This is no matter for self-complacency or national pride; it is a matter for greater humility and self-searching so that, being heirs to such universal, humanistic and rationalistic philosophy as Vedanta, we may be worthy heirs to the *rishis* of old, to the sages of yore, to the saints whose vision, wisdom and self-sacrifice laid the foundation-stone of cultural India.

Why should the nationalistic revival, as advocated and instilled by the Rashtriya Swayamsevaks, look back to philosophy and culture when the majority of Indians have to solve their problems of food, clothing, shelter, job and a decent material living? The advocates of materialistic secularism further say, "Religion has proved to be the opiate. It divides and vivisects the country and peoples into so many compartments. India has fallen because of overdoses of Vedanta and culture and religion. Now let there be only electricity, science, glamour and gross materialism through which the Western nations have subjugated economically-backward and industrially-underdeveloped countries of Asia. No more culture, philosophy and religion, but more of industry, science and Western life."

To these senile marionettes of Western education everything eastern is dark. Because electricity comes from the West, they think that this Vedantic light is darkness. Now we mean business and we will meet the rationalists on the plane of reason, humanists on the plane of humanism and logicians on the plane of logic. We do not run away, we do not retreat, we do not retrace from the stand we have taken on the rock of Indian philosophy. We do not apologise, we do not advertise, we do not seek approbation from the Westernised *sahebs*; we stand on the strength of our intrinsic merit, on the strength of conviction and rationalistic logic. The present secularistic and materialistic politics is largely responsible for the crucifixion of the true Indian nationals who look upon Vedanta, not as a static metaphysics to be enshrined in museums, but as a treasure-house of powerful ideas which should galvanise, dynamise and urge humans to creative action, potent ideas that have power to transmute animality to humanity and humanity to divinity. The philosopher's stone is not to be thrown overboard because the pseudo-scientific maniacs revel and rage against both the philosopher, his philosophy and his magic stone that can create a Sivaji, Lakshmibai of Jhansi, a Vivekananda out of a sceptic, rationalistic and university-trained Narendra, that can create a Buddha out of Gautama, an Asoka, a Christ, a Sankara, a *mahatma* out of M.K. Gandhi, all those big names that still stand out as the signposts and lighthouses for the benighted mankind to look to and march with purpose and conviction to the destined goal of human pilgrimage of ours on earth.

The re-awakening of Vedanta is necessary to infuse new ideas, for the growth of humanity and all-sided catholic receptivity within us. The resurrection of Vedanta is necessary to instil and transfuse life-giving ideas and ideals to our disorganised, despondent and dejected youth of India. Vedanta is necessary to cement national solidarity and human comradeship on thought basis—and not on the shifty sands of emotionalism, slogan-mongering—to weld Indian national solidarity between warring communities and divided castes and creeds of this sub-continent, whose inspiration should be their country, the soil of their birth and love. In this new dispensation, in the new Indian Republic of our dreams, there shall no more be divisions based on caste, creed or race, but only pure Indian nationality shall remain, those "who are loyal and true to their cultural heritage, no matter what the colour of their skin or privileges of birth or religious labels are.

To those who think that the RSS is merely a revivalist organisation for exclusive 'Hindu interests' with no philosophy and practical programme except 'fascist' and dictatorial methods, we say that the RSS absorbs the best in the Indian cultural renaissance, all that are best in the Brahmo and Arya Samaj movements, in the Ramakrishna-Vivekananda movement, in Theosophy and the best in the cultural heritage of not only geographical India, but also of the entire world. But now philosophy is not going to remain merely a matter for speculation and mental gymnastics, but a practical and systematic thinking, a new power-generating category of ideas, a new outlook on life and inspiration so that the motive force and moving wheels of the RSS may not be merely shifty sands of political expediency or passing waves of emotional patriotism, but the solid rock of a philosophy that is as old as the Himalayas, as pure as the snows of Mount Dhaulagiri, as strong as the rock of Nanda Devi, as fresh and green as the pasture around Mount Kailash and Manasarovar lakes. The RSS has a philosophy which is the philosophy of India, the Vedanta, neo-Vedanta, as transmitted to us by the best of our seers, as interpreted and re-interpreted by the prophets and sages of modern India.

This new philosophy will descend from its celestial heights of *advaita* to the most practical details of national discipline, to the basic problems of hunger, nakedness and starvation of human beings, of the underdogs that today are the victims of economic exploitation, priest-craft and religious communalism. For the strengthening of that true democracy, secularism and humanism, we look to Indian culture as our guide, our rock, our hope and inspiration.

In the words of Dr. Hedgewar, "It is clear that every child of this sacred Bharatvarsha is a potential Vivekananda and Tilak." It is this potential power and locked-up force that the RSS intends to release, develop and unfold in every son and daughter of India. This is an uphill job, a revolutionary idea and a lofty ideal.

Again as the RSS leader said, "After the first greedy taste of materialism, vulgarity and emptiness of modern life, men find in the ideology and objectiveness of the Sangh strangefulness and a long-sought satisfaction."

As the successor to the decrepit Congress, the Rashtriya Swayamsevaks are now called upon to hold the trust of the people in their hands and through self-sacrifice and discipline show the path of national unity, solidarity and character to the people of this land.

□

Chapter-4

Mission and Message of The RSS

धर्मा एव हतो हन्ति धर्मो रक्षति रक्षितः।
सस्मात् धर्मो न हन्तव्यी मा नो धर्मो हतो वर्धात्॥

"Righteousness destroys the man who destroys Righteousness and saves the man who saves Righteousness. Hence destroy not Righteousness. May Righteousness never be destroyed."

—Manu Samhtta, VIII 15

"Thou canst walk on a path unless you become the path thyself."

—Dr. Hedgewar

"Personal salvation was to be forsaken and the cause of the nation upheld."

—Shri M.S. Golwalkar

"With all my love for India and with all my patriotism and veneration for the ancients, I cannot but think that we have to learn many things from other nations. We cannot do without the world outside India. It was our foolishness that we have thought we could, and we have paid the penalty by about a thousand years of slavery. That we did not go out to compare things with other nations, did not make the workings that have been around us, has been the one great cause of this degradation of the Indian mind. We have paid the penalty; let us do it no more."

—Swami Vivekananda

The historic mission of any movement is to be seen, gauged and upheld from the justice of its cause, from the historical circumstances which give birth to the new idea, new leader, new movement, new organisation. The new force that is thus generated is there to see the problems realistically and solve them satisfactorily. The mission of such a movement is unique, because no other movement could at that particular historic moment deliver goods to the people, could have the vision, creative drive and dynamism to face the crisis, to launch into the open sea of struggle and achieve the impossible.

Organisation is not movement, although organisation may follow a movement. In fact, it is the movement that becomes the driving force when the organisation usually gets self-imprisoned within its own constitution, rusts inside stereotyped protective walls of their vested interests. When the creative drive of the movement stops, the organisation becomes outdated and, however the members of such an organisation may strive to preserve it, it fades out, having outlived its utility and completed its *raison d'etre.* The genesis of any movement, it can be seen clearly from the history and critical study, begins with a new idea, or an old idea interpreted and lived in a new way, under a new light. This idea incarnates—as it were—in the life of an individual, or a group of indviduals, who become the centre and circumference of such a movement. This general law that governs the birth, development and decay could be studied in modern India if we cast a glance at the history of the Brahmo Samaj movement, Arya Samaj, Indian National Congress and other forces. The need for social and economic reforms in the life of India took shape in the mind of one Ram Mohun Roy, which later on vitalised the dormant forces of a few individuals, like Vidyasagar, Keshub Chunder Sen, Debendranath Tagore, Rabindranath, Surendranath Banerjee, Kamakshi Natarajan, Chandravarkar, Gama, Ranade and others who became the pillars of the Brahmo Samaj movement. But no movement moves without creating its corresponding organisation. The organisations may come and go, but the creative power of the movement remains. Thus the Sadharan, Navavidan, Adi and Prarthana Brahmo Samajas are today decrepit and may finally collapse, but (native time behind the Brahmo Samaj) the movement remains and it survives in the form of the Indian National Congress, in the Arya Samaj and such other progressive, nationalistic forces that came after it.

The physical law of preservation of energy is truer in the realm of ethics, morality and spiritual dynamics than in physics. One wave of the sea never falls without giving rise to another wave. One generation comes and goes giving birth to one new generation. So movements rise and fall, giving birth to newer and fresher movements. The RSS in the historic setting up of the country, has its mission to be the cultural, spiritual, social and political heir to the various progressive and nationalistic forces that have preceded it and have bequeathed to it their best with this trust and command to move forward, to preserve the eternal verities and indestructible treasures and permanent values in the history of Indian civilisation.

In an independent India, the RSS is destined to combine the nationalistic and patriotic heritage of the Congress with the most dynamic urge for action, as embodied in the lives of men like Bal Gangadhar Tilak and Netaji Subhas Chandra, the great hero of Hindustan, whose sacrifice became the life-blood and inspiration to the new patriotic soldiers of the INA in Free India. Pakistan is made a reality. "Pakistan is a sin," was the litany recited by Gandhiji and this sin was perpetrated, resorted to in order to placate the cry of communal Muslims for the vivisection of Mother India. This calamity would have never overtaken us if we were conscious of our nationality, if both Hindus, Muslims, Christians, all had recognised that they were first and foremost children of the same soil. It is strange that some of our leaders and those foreign vested interests still continue to sanctify and canonise the sin of partition of the country on communal basis, and take it as a *fait accompli* to be perpetuated. But they forget that if communalism is to be acquiesced to, it will end not only in the present partition of the country, but it will also tend to final restoration of the medieval Mogul Empire, with Delhi as the eventual centre of pan-Islamism. "We ruled India for a thousand years. Why cannot we rule over her again?" writes *Dawn* in Karachi. This is the history of the Islamic conquests. If Charles Martel had not stopped the Muslims at Tours in 732, today the entire Europe would have been under the banner of the Star and the Crescent. But even among the fanatical and communal Muslims arise such a great leader as Mustafa Kemal Pasha to arrest, check and remedy the communalism and mechanical expansionist fanaticism of the Koran-bound Muslims and lead them to the deeper core of Humanity, which the great Muhammed realised in his life and preached to the world as the means for human solidarity and ideal social democracy. It is the enlightenment of Sufis through Vedanta, of the revolutionary reformers and leaders of feminist emancipation like Attaturk and Dr. M. Mussadiq in our century that Muslim fanaticism and show them the new path they should take to build their faith on human and rational grounds, and not on the doctrine of sword and *jehad*, on pillage, plunder and forced conversion. In India we have the outstanding examples of men like Maulana Azad and the Khan Brothers, the Nationalist Muslims, the *Khudai Khidmatgars,* whose stand is on national culture.

The wounds of the partition of Mother India are still bleeding. The economic-social problems are on the increase, whereas the answers to these ever-increasing problems are becoming fewer. The present government is composed of too old, out-of-date, secular-minded, foreign-trained ex-patriots. With the few exceptions of such men, like the late Sardar Patel, Pandit Nehru, Dr. B.C. Roy and a few others, the whole government is run by inefficient, weak, old, comfort-seeking, money-grabbing career-seekers. The day-to-day administration is being run with the same machinery left by the foreign masters. We have inherited their government machinery, but not their qualities like character, self-discipline, efficiency and sense of fairness. Under foreign rule, the Indians could live cheaper. Today the cost of living goes higher every day, even postage and railway fares are soaring higher beyond the reach of the common man. Of the wealth of the country the lion share, the ninety per cent, go to the ten per cent of Indian capitalists, and the ten per cent to the rest of the ninety per cent. Tatas and Birlas control both the Government machinery and the government officials, but the cry of the poor, downtrodden and the exploited is today a voice in the wilderness. The problems of these shrivelled bellies and walking skeletons are not solved through additional Security Bills and Preventive Detention Acts. The answer to hunger is food, answer to ignorance is education, to grinding poverty the answer is raising the standard of the people. The population tide should not be allowed to swell beyond the actual economic resources of the country. The law of self-control is the best answer to the population flood and not the patent medicines for contraception and means of birth-control, which are invading our country to wreck her people morally. Nobody flunks or acts in terms of the ancient well-tried truths of self-knowledge, self-control and self-purification, a legacy of Indian culture from the times of Vedic *rishis* to the days of Mahatma Gandhi, Ramana Maharshi, Netaji, Dr. Hedgewar and Golwalkar.

True, the Indian constitution is democratic. But Constitution is paper and ink and nothing more. Democratic freedom, as in the great democratic countries like France, Switzerland, England and the United States, is found in a small measure in India under the benign and constitutional government of Pandit Nehru. It is undoubtedly more difficult to preserve the broad democratic traditions and yet maintain the helm and structure of the Government than to impose totalitarian dictatorship and give social security to the have-nots, to the hungry, semi-starved, poverty-gods, *daridryanarayans.* But in another sense it is better to raise the subhuman level of the living conditions of the vast majority of Indian citizens, make them healthy, educated and strong than to glorify in freedom, which only the rich and the powerful enjoy and monopolise in the good old parliamentarian way. Even culture and philosophy are merely after-growths of right economic and social order. It is this economic-social revolution, regeneration, that should be the first prerequisite for the effective establishment and working of such social democracies as we find them in Switzerland, England or in Scandinavia. It is this economic basis that should first be laid if we mean business and build up the India of our dreams. Culture and philosophy and religion can wait, but not the problems of hunger, ill-health, illiteracy and degradation that are eating into the vitals of the Indian nationals, of the overwhelming majority of the Indian citizens today. Says Swami Vivekananda:

"First of all, our young men must be strong. Religion will come afterwards. Be strong, my young friends; that is my advice to you. You will be nearer to Heaven through football than through the study of Gita. These are bold words, but I have to say them, for I love you, I know where the shoe pinches. I have gained a little experience. You will understand the Gita better with your biceps, your muscles a little stronger. You will understand the mighty genius and the mighty strength of Krishna better with a little of strong blood in you. You will understand the Upanishads better and the glory of Atman, when your body stands upon your feet and you feel yourselves as men."

—Swami Vivekananda's Speeches

It is for doing that the leaders of the RSS begin to work for the strengthening and disciplining of the volunteers who come to serve the cause of the country. A healthy mind works only in a healthy body. It is the bodily fitness that makes one receptive to the higher truths of Vedanta and the *Upanishads.* Only when the *jivatma* is properly fed and nurtured, it can enter the sanctuary of the *Paramatma.* In fact, economics is the basis of culture and civilisation. A Sanskrit proverb says, *"Shariramadyam khuladharma sadhanam"*—the well-being of the body is the foundation of practice of Dharma.

So, then, the sense of Justice, Fairness and Righteousness that a movement upholds will be the real strength and power of that movement. The RSS, then, while rooting itself on the rock-bottom of Indian culture and her civilisation, is receptive and open to any light that may come from any side. The warning of Swami Vivekananda is significant, for it is the narrow isolation of our country from the rest of the world, for the sin of not comparing and contrasting our country with other countries of the West, that we paid the heavy penalty of political bondage for over a thousand years and now the partition of the country, with all the potential dangers of external aggression and internal disruption. Time has come for India to end this isolation and launch out into the wider world.

The historic mission of the RSS, as a successor to the Indian National Congress, will be to work for and achieve the national unity at all cost. As Sri Aurobindo said:

"India is free, but she has not achieved unity; only a fissured and broken freedom. But, by whatever means, the division must and will go."

—Sri Aurobindo's message on 15th August, 1947

This unity means that all nationalist Indians, whether they are labelled as Hindus, Muslims or Christians, have always believed that they are all children of the soil and that they have not acquiesced in any way to the artificial vivisection that has been brought about as a passing political expediency. This unity is to be achieved through education, propaganda and all peaceful means. Violence solves no problems and violence only brings more problems. But Truth is invincible and it need not feel afraid of anything or anybody, for Truth is God, Reality. The Muslim League might have resorted to Direct Action to achieve their partition, but the soul of India should not retaliate nor pay them back in the same coin. We have taken our stand on Nationalism, Humanism and Rationality and this trinity is powerful enough to undo the wrong of vivisection and bring again a "united, democratic and Republican India," which Pandit Nehru once proclaimed as the supreme objective of the Congress struggle.

Besides political unity, all measures are to be taken to achieve internal unity by cementing the solidarity of the Indian nationals from within. We are one people, one nation, one culture, one language, and not, as the "perfidious Albion" taught us, a "country of many peoples, races and cultures." The country is still to be united through one common language, which now is recognised to be Hindi-Hindustani for all-India purposes. Besides the provincial and regional languages, there should be a uniting lingua franca, which today is admittedly Hindi. No provincialism, no sectarianism should stand in the way of our accepting one language as the common link of the people inhabiting the subcontinent of Bharatvarsha," says the RSS leader:

"The country to us being one homogenous whole, all the

indigenous languages enjoy in our hearts equal regard and love. A common language for bringing about a close unity is natural and necessary and from among these languages, Hindi, originating from the great Mother of Bharatiya languages—Sanskrit—is the most suited to fulfil this need, being simple to master, having for a long period been in actual use as a lingua franca of our country and having immense possibilities of becoming into a first-grade language of the world."

"Looking at the related question of script, country's name etc., the RSS feels that no storm could be raised over these issues for, with Hindi the Nagari script, one of the most perfect (scripts in the world), is naturally associated. And so far as the country is concerned, the name Bharat with historical and cultural significance and its indirect acceptance in everyday use in such expressions as Bharatiya Kala, Bharatiya Natya, suggests itself as one to be revived. This name helps in arousing memories of-the great past and inspires one to strive for a still greater future."

—Shri M.S. Golwalkar

The language, script, racial features, common cultural traditions, the country, atmosphere, history, physical features of the land and of her people, these form the solid basis for national unity and solidarity. Then the old decrepit and anti-social and unhealthy traditions of priest-craft, caste-distinctions, untouchability, obscurantism, etc., will go and will, in that way, create such conditions that will justify the non-Hindus to recognise their national identity and common heritage and pave way for a strong, united, nationalistic India that can cope with any danger that may come from outside or from within to wreck the national unity and solidarity of the Indian people. But conditions should be created so that equality of opportunities and justice for all may prevail. Not diplomacy, but truth alone wins, wins, wins.

Historians are right when they say that Bengal became a majority Muslim province because the caste Hindus reduced the Muslims to the state of helotage, to the level of mere drawers of water and hewers of wood. It is the bane of untouchability and caste-arrogance that have been largely responsible for the internal divisions of the country, which later on reflected in the outward vivisection of India by conceding and creating Pakistan. It is the social disabilities of the lower castes and non-Hindus that made them adamant in separating themselves from Hindus and make the Indian nation not one national State, but what they call—a multinational State. Now it is time to remove all social evils with our own hands, to expiate for our own sins, not through arrogance of a numerical majority, but through Truth and Rightouesness of healthy nationalism and Humanism which can still undo the wrongs of the past and pave way for a bright future.

To those diehard, equally sectarian, exclusive rationalists and compartmental scientists, we should say that anti-religionism, anti-philosophy and anti-spiritualism are today things of the past. Even in Russia and China, religion does not live. In Europe, the more thoughtful leaders are favouring the return of mankind back to the perennial fountain-heads of philosophic wisdom. Mr. Aldous Huxley, C.S. Lewis, Gerald Heard, Nicholas Berdyaev, Albert Einstein, Jacques Maritain and such leaders of modern thought, after getting disillusioned with the soulless materialism and utilitarian pragmatism of the modern industrialised life, have taught the world that mankind needs something like religious background, philosophical speculation, metaphysics and ontology to sustain them in the pursuit of Truth, Happiness and Peace on this earth. If the RSS is dubbed as reactionary in so far as it aims at revitalising what is lasting and permanent in the Indian traditions, then, it is better to be called 'reactionaries and revivalists' than to swing back to immoral, unscrupulous and anti-ethical slogans of materialist pragmatism and opportunist political wire-pullings. Here the RSS stands on a surer basis than their opponents. The RSS does not propose to revitalise everything that is traditionally transmitted to us as Indian culture, but only those which are of permanent value in our traditional culture. Here again, says Shri Golwalkar:

"Revitalisation of a culture is sometimes mistaken as a reaction, and as such, a work, to use that oft-repeated word, is dubbed reactionary. I think revitalising the past is not reactionary, if it is found that it has got an abiding value. Only such things that drag the society into worse condition can be called reactionary. Our worse condition can be called reactionary. Our work is the reviving and revitalising of that which is of some permanent value, i.e., Hindu culture."

This mission of preserving what is best in Indian culture is not confined to the RSS. It was the sincere desire of all the reform and renaissance movements of the past, beginning with Buddha's greatest reform movement of Indian history which gave birth to Buddhism. The fight against caste, sub-caste, priest-craft, superstition etc., did not begin yesterday. It is as old as the history of human thought. As long as human reason works within the categories of logic, as long as the core of Humanity remains the self-same, these perennial truths are to be diligently studied, assiduously propagated and diffused for strengthening human solidarity and for man's happiness and peace on this planet.

The new mission, however, that definitely is of the RSS, is the one resulting from the historic circumstances arising from political independence of mutilated India, where there are still so many internal divisions and communal factions, varied forms of social degeneration and all-sided economic bankruptcy. The neo-nationalistic gospel of the RSS is not an end in itself, but the necessary mainspring for the machinery to work, for the people to get the needed encouragement, inspiration and enthusiasm to move forward. If this nationalism, they say, is a myth, then we are ready to accept this myth of the twentieth century more readily and reasonably than the racial myth of Rosenberg, as it was proposed to the youth of national socialist Germany. This nationalism is not narrow, not aggressive, but it is merely the solid rock, the *terra firma,* for us to stand erect and move onward, forge ahead into the Yonder Shore of Existence, to the Unseen Beyond of future Indian history.

Similarly, the special accent and the new mission of the revived 'Hindu' culture can be justified only as long as there is an Islamic or Christian or Parsi culture threatening to absorb or defeat the "Hindu" culture. If this communal antagonism is removed, if the threat of Pakistanisation of the whole Indian sub-continent is not there, the idea of reviving "Hindu culture" also vanishes. For then what remains is the culture of India, the soul and spirit of Indian philosophy, literature, art, poetry and mysticism, which will remain, fructify and vivify every child of the soil as long as India remains India. But once India becomes Pakistan—part of which is already Pakistan—the law of survival of Indian culture will be imperiled. Hence the urgent need for awakening, for organisation, spread of education, intense propaganda, defensive measures and instilling of new spirit of patriotism and nationalism into the minds of the communal-minded citizens of India, by implanting the seeds of strength and invincibility into the youth of the country. It is this new missionary work which the RSS is called upon to do in India, specially now when the hands and feet of our national leaders are practically tied to the helm of the Government, and they are fully engaged in the day-to-day administration of the country, in trying to solve the Kashmir tangle, rehabilitation of the refugees, solving the food problem, unemployment problem and various other difficult issues which our Government officials are confronted with today.

It is tragic that our country is losing the sense of her vocation and mission in life. Europe specialised in practical ordering of economic and political life. Asia has led the world in giving the historical religions to the mankind that today owes allegiance to Buddhism, Christianity, Hinduism and Islam as major religions. Parsism, Bahaism and such other minor religious systems also had their birthplace and cradle in the Orient. Among these various religious philosophies, the spirit of India, her culture and philosophy, remain to this day as the Mother of religions and philosophies. True, Buddhism, being but a daughter of Hinduism, took wider and more universal ethical aspects and spread almost to the entire Asian continent, even as out of the race, religion of the Jews there came out her all-conquering daughter, Christianity, that finally won the allegiance of the then Greco-Roman world and which today continues to be the religion that counts the largest number of adherents than any single religion in the world.

We believe that religion should not be the opiate of the people. If in many cases, religion serves as the morphine to deaden the intelligence and stem the creative drive of human beings, we are out to destroy it. It is for this reason that the most progressive and enlightened representative minds in India feel that we need to distinguish what is dead, outdated and dross in our religious traditions, which must be relegated to museums, and cling only to those forces and ideas which have power to resuscitate the people of India, inspire in them self-respect and human dignity, that will cement national and human solidarity among them and will pave way for national greatness and spiritual grandeur.

If that religion or philosophy—whatever name we might give to that doctrine and practice of health, physical well-being and mental and moral growth of human beings—preached by the *rishis* of the *Upanishads*, the ethical mastermind of Lord Buddha, the theistic practical faith preached by Jesus, the message of Kabir, Tulsidas, Guru Nanak, Hafiz, Rumi and by all those sages were to be dubbed as obscurantistic, then we would rather join the chorus of such obscurantists and part company with these illuministic wisdom men, the so-called secularists, rationalists and economists. We believe in human values, in imponderable worth of mental and moral life of the *Homo sapiens*, hence our faith and strength.

The clarion call of the RSS to the youth of the country, to foreigners who have adopted India as their Motherland, will be the call of nationalism. As watchdogs of national culture, as national guardians of Indian humanity, the RSS will see that the present unfettered and mischievous propaganda made by foreign residents in India in favour of selfishness against national interests be stopped. Foreigners who have married Indians and have settled down in the heart of Bharat should be helped and protected as long as their paper-press activities do not jeopardise India's national interests. If they are enamoured of Indian culture and want to absorb the vital limph of Indian tree of civilisation, they will be helped and enabled to do so, but they shall not be allowed to strike at the vital nationalist interests of the country any more in the guise of culture, religion, etc. and continue to serve the interests of Pakistan or their own foreign countries, while receiving the hospitality and kindness of Mother India.

The RSS has no other message, no other mission to fulfil but to see that India's accepted motto "सत्यमेव जयते न अनृतं"—"Truth alone triumphs, not untruth" (*Mundaka Upanishad III 1 5*) be made a living reality in the practical life of the people. It will be the message and mission of the RSS to see that India never ever becomes a political slave to any foreign country. The RSS will teach her people, her youth, her sons and daughters that death a hundred times is preferable to living like vanquished slaves. Herein lies the battle of Dharmakshetra, of the Kurukshetra, where the teachings of *Bhagavad Gita* are to be made glowing and living reality in the lives of Indians. Buddha has said, "Better to die in the battle for righteousness than to live as vanquished slaves." Netaji Subhas Chandra says:

"To my countrymen I say: 'Forget not that the greatest curse for a man is to remain a slave. Forget not that the grossest crime is to compromise with injustice and wrong. Remember the eternal law—You must give, if you want to get it. And remember that the highest virtue is to battle against iniquity, no matter what the cost may be.'"

—Subhas' Speeches to the INA

The ideal Rashtriya Swayamsevaks are embodiments of self-confidence and national self-sufficiency and hence their message is a pledge of hope in a world given to despair, of light in a society groping in darkness, of strength and power in a country of weaklings, with no imagination, creative drive and wider vision. The RSS, as successor to the grand old mother, the Indian National Congress, will see that the specific, power-giving message and mission of Mother India no longer remain a closed book, a piece of historic relic to be preserved in the archaeological museums of India, but a living reality, vitalised and energised, modernised and rationalised so that our youth can stand with confidence and dignity even before the most scientifically advanced countries of the West and of the East.

The message and mission of the RSS is the re-assertion and re-consecration of India's unbeatable soul, her perennial philosophy, her culture, her spirit, her civilisation re-interpreted and adjusted after the crushing weight of our political slavery for a thousand years, to arrest the weakening of the Hindu society, the growing menace of Islamic communal expansionism, Pakistan nightmare and its challenge and make the Indian intelligentsia to face the reality of scientific and rationalistic outlook of this Atomic Age. "While we re-orientate ourselves to the light of the twentieth century, as the law of survival demands, we shall not budge an inch from those eternal verities which are the cherished treasures of India's cultural heritage, our continued grip on the Vedanta philosophy, on the division of stages of life into *Brahmacharya, Grihastashrama, Vanaprasta* and *Sanayasa,* in the sense that we intend to get Indian citizens pass through the periods of self-controlled education for living, character-building and useful productivity, householder's life and service to the State, or vocational lifelong *Brahmacharya* for those who totally dedicate themselves to the service of the country, society and humanity, for its gradual emancipation and final liberation, passage from the *Karma yoga* to *Jnana yoga* of *samadhi*. We support the division of labour in society among intellectuals, the *vipra* or Brahmin class, the military and defensive forces of the State or the Kshatriya, the trader and businessmen, the Vaisya, and the peasant and the labourer or the Shudra. But birth and birth-privileges are not going to count in the new order in Free India with power and resources to develop her own people along her own national genius. Character, it is character, and character alone that counts. As the socio-economic factors change, the people, their mental outlook, interests, productive capacity, everything change. In this Socialist Age, the eternal ideal of *samya vad* will come true in India which, when materialised, will go a long way to strengthening the community life of a free people, with equal opportunities for growth, with equal duties and rights of citizenship. The Fundamental Rights of Man which, after the French Revolution and the American War of Independence, were extolled by man to the skies, India will learn not from the West, but from the logical implications which her philosophy and culture of Human Religion, *Manava Dharma,* envisage. Mere imports of foreign brands of Communism and Socialism will not satisfy the

Indian mind, but the best in Communistic and Socialistic ideology could be achieved by understanding and materialising the ideal of the RSS. In this matter also, says Shri M.S. Golwalkar:

"Socialists and Communists talked of an ideal society and ideal human relations. But I am sure the objects of an ideal social order and the maximum of human happiness could be achieved through following the RSS programme of nation-building. Bharat has gone through all the conflicts and clash of ideas that agitate the minds of Communists and Socialists and Bharat has also evolved out an ideal social order that meant contentment and prosperity to the people. We had in ancient Bharat experimented with planned and regimented society as well as an anarchical form of government but all through these experiments great care was taken by our forefathers to see that a united and Akhand Bharat was retained."

—Shri Golwalkar's speech at Matunga in February 1950

The resurrection and the national rejuvenation of India which the RSS heralds as the message and mission of the Sangh is historically based on the varied experiences and experiments India had in her long history. Its triple order is Unity, Humanity, Freedom. With faith in the destiny of India, with transparent, uncontaminated national character, with India's humanistic and rational philosophy, with order, discipline and iron sense of duty, Mother India, through her new Sangh, the RSS, is going to achieve her destined goal.

□

Part-II
ORGANISATION AND ACTION OF THE RSS

Chapter-5

The Constitutional Structure of The RSS

"The degeneration of India came not because the laws and customs of the ancients were bad, but because they were not allowed to be earned to their legitimate conclusions.

When you have men who are ready to sacrifice their everything for their country, sincere to the backbone—when such men arise, India will become great in every respect. It is the men that make the country."

—Swami Vivekananda

"There is strength in the patriotism born out of love and regard for our Bharatiya culture and tradition. We should have pride in our culture, our tradition, our society and our Motherland. Everyone must have the consciousness that he or she is the inheritor of that sacred trust and one's life is not for pleasures of drinking, eating and merry-making. One's life should be lived as a continuous dedication to one's society, one's culture and one's nation. One must be aware and alive to the fact that we are great, our culture and tradition are great."

—Shri M.S. Golwalkar

Constitution of any organisation or society has no strength and meaning save as the extension and expression of the inner spirit. The British people have no written constitution, yet their unwritten constitution is one of the best in the history of the modern world. Mere paper constitution is of little use. The present

Indian Government wasted crores of rupees to draw up a curious medley of the American, French and the British constitutions with some euphemistic clauses to suit the Indian conditions. Three brains with the cost of a few thousand rupees could have drawn up such a constitution. But then pomp and glamour are to be exhibited by the Government to show its authority. We consider Constitution only from the practical and utility point of view, not for its advertisements and publicity, glamour and glitter and the Government seal attached to it.

The RSS, the National Volunteer Corps, did not start with any written constitution. It originated as a new powerful idea, a movement, as a vital spirit and creative urge of Mother India at a particular historic period to meet certain vital needs. After the Government banned the RSS for eighteen months and the violent persecution from the secularists and advocates of material civilisation, as imported from foreign lands and foreign seas, were over, the RSS emerged stronger than ever.

It will be the spirit of a movement that determines its character, not the letter, of its constitution. Nevertheless, constitutional framework is not to be ignored, nay it is to be accepted, as a movement that needs orientation and efficient and effective canalised work. That is why, after the banning and persecution of the RSS, after intensified calumny and propaganda against the real nature, aims and ideals of the RSS, the nucleus of a draft Constitution has been issued with a view to dispelling the misconstrued fears and ungrounded criticism of the organisation. The written Constitution is not a new chapter in the history of the movement, it is merely partial putting in black and white the spirit and ideals which once give birth to the movement, which sustained it in the most bitter hours of trials and persecution, that give it the needed nutriment and inspiration to grow from within, stand on its own feet and then spread out as a country-wide network of youth centres, youth camps, training schools and a sort of missionary stations for the all-sided resurrection, *sarvodaya,* of India.

The Constitution of the RSS that was issued in September

1949 is the crystal-clear expression of the nationalistic character of the movement, its determination to achieve its goal, viz. regeneration, re-organisation and resurrection and renaissance of India for Indians. The preamble to the Constitution states:

"Whereas in the disintegrated conditions of the country it was considered necessary to have an organisation,

(a) "to eradicate the fissiparous tendencies arising from diversities of sect, faith, caste and creed and from political, economic, linguistic and provincial differences, amongst Hindus;
(b) "to make them realise the greatness of their past,
(c) "to inculcate in them a spirit of service (sacrifice and selfless devotion to the Hindu Samaj, as a whole),
(d) "to build up an organised and well-disciplined corporate life, and
(e) "to bring about an all-round regeneration for the Hindu Samaj.

"And whereas the organisation known as the Rashtriya Swayamsevak Sangh was started on the Vijayadashmi day in the year 1982, *Vikram Samvat* (1925 A.D.) by the late Dr. Keshav Baliram Hedgewar,

"And whereas Shri Madhav Sadashiv Golwalkar was nominated by the said Dr. Hedgewar to succeed him in the year 1997, *Vikram Samvat* (1940 A.D.),

"And whereas the Sangh had till now no written Constitution,

"And whereas in the present changed conditions, it is deemed expedient to reduce to writing the Constitution as also the Aims and Objects of the Sangh and its methods of work,

"The Rashtriya Swayamsevak Sangh hereby adopts the following Constitution—"

It is a sense of realism that has prompted the RSS to restrict their field of action, organisation and service to India, her people, her culture, her strength and to use precise words against the old vague universalism, cosmopolitanism and internationalism, which often promise mountains but achieve nothing. Liberalism is good, but whole-hearted dedication to the cause borne out of strong conviction, one-pointedness of mind alone achieves the impossible, the miracles of will-power, heroism and chivalry of character. There should be no more illusions left while appraising the balance sheet of our national life. The credit side will take care of itself; it is the liability, weakness, illusions and day-dreams that are to be protected against and remedied.

Too much tolerance, vague liberalism, over-doses of kindness may benefit the individuals, but national life can be preserved only through healthy tolerance of the strong, which, while leaving room for all-sided consideration, shall no longer make the country weak nor lack in that manliness, realism, resourcefulness and self-confidence, without which the rock-foundation of Indian culture may be destroyed. *Himsa* and *ahimsa* are the two sides of the same medal of Truth and Justice. Besides, the constitutional structure of the new RSS, will also free men's minds from hero worship and identification of a given movement with any single personality. Congress movement failed because it got identified with Gandhiji and the disappearance of Gandhiji from the national life of India meant the disappearance of the Congress also. But in countries like England, Gladstone, MacDonald or Bevin may *go,* but the party spirit and party discipline remain. In Indian history we see that societies and movements fall with the fall of great leaders and there is a big gap, a vacuum created after the disappearance of the leaders of the movement. This individualist tradition is now to be integrated with collectivistic and corporate philosophy. When one Rabindranath goes, Santiniketan should not be lifeless, but a hundred other Rabindranaths should grow from the fertile soil of Mother India and start so many Santiniketans and Viswa Bharati centres. When one Gandhiji disappears, the Congress organisation should not have gone to pieces, but many more Gandhis had to become Mahatmas and mobilise and organise the people all the more to strengthen and save the country. If one Dr. Hedgewar goes, the National Volunteer Organisation is not to fade out. Now Shri M.S. Golwalkar is piloting the RSS, the raft of salvation for new India and the constitutional structure of the movement focusses its main attention not on hero-worship, leader-worship, but in spreading out the ideas and ideals of the new nationalistic revival to larger and larger numbers of people, so that when one RSS leader goes, hundreds may be kept ready to shoulder responsibilities and maintain vital energy to face and solve the growing problems of the country. It is for this collectivistic *sadhana,* so miserably lacking in Indian tradition, that Shri Golwalkar's saying has become an accepted motto: "Individual salvation is to be abandoned and the cause of nation upheld."

Article 3 of the Constitution is a re-affirmation of the main objective which is to unite, strengthen and consolidate India through the universal and rational culture of the land, *Manava Dharma,* which is the real Hindu Samaj. The article states:

"The aims and objects of the Sangh are to weld together the diverse groups within the Hindu Samaj and to revitalise and rejuvenate the same on the basis of its Dharma and sanskriti, that it may achieve an all-sided development of the Bharatvarsha."

This all-sided development starts from the basic economic and social problems, for, all the thoughtful representative Indians have experienced and expressed clearly that religion, culture and philosophy are not and cannot be for hungry bellies. Now these shrivelled bellies and walking skeletons are legions all over India. Economics being the basis of all civilisation, food, clothing, shelter and education must be the four pillars on which we need build the superstructures of religion, culture and philosophy and all those imponderable ethical values in life. This should be the prime duty of all loyal children of Mother India who are intent upon safeguarding and strengthening the cultural heritage and the *elan vital* of Indian civilisation. "What is needed is," as Swami Vivekananda exhorts, "to build up strong bodily physique first, and then proceed to the fuller developments of mental and moral powers in man. The new Sangh will see that our people get the all-sided development and given the chance, restore the country to the maximum possible heights of economic self-sufficiency and the subsequent mental, educational and ethical advancement of the people."

Article 4 of the Constitution deals with the policy the Sangh will adopt to achieve its objectives. It states:

(a) "The Sangh believes in orderly evolution of society and adheres to peaceful and legitimate means for the realisation of its ideals.

(b) "In consonance with the cultural heritage of the Hindu Samaj, the Sangh has abiding faith in the fundamental principles of tolerance towards all faiths.

"The Sangh, as such, has no politics and is devoted to purely cultural work. The individual Swayamsevaks, however, may join any political party, except such parties as believe in or resort to violent and secret methods to achieve their ends; persons owing allegiance to such parties or believing in such methods shall have no place in the Sangh."

Herein the words 'orderly evolution' are used against the advocates of violent revolution. Evolution is 'law of Nature and not revolution'. What is achieved is violence which is maintained by violence and it prepares way to further and greater violence. The great principles of organised and systematic non-co-operation and non-violent methods can bring to knees even the most arrogant tyrants. But for this one needs greater discipline, orderliness, sense of humanity and righteousness. The sense of humanity, man's rational nature demands that man seek to right the wrong not by further wrong, but by greater righteousness.

The principle of tolerance, as enunciated in this clause, is the tolerance born out of strength, not the *laissez-faire* indifferentism of the weak. One may follow any religion or sect one likes, but such tolerance should not imperil national solidarity and the culture of the country.

Although the Sangh is not a political party as yet, it may not be far off when the leaders and members of the RSS may have to join politics in order to bring justice to the victims of socio-economic exploitation in the country and enhance the culture of the soil.

But the specific mission of the Sangh is not derived from its present or potential political and economic struggles, but most definitely from its cultural and spiritual roots. Indian history—

and for that matter the history of all nations—convinces us that abiding good has been done to society only when a given movement was radicalised in basic ethical values, in spiritual truths, in religion. The successes recorded in history from the annals of various violent revolutions have either petered out or were maintained through subsequent humanisation, spiritualisation of the movement. Hence it is that the French Revolution, to bear permanent fruits in the field of democratic freedom, the October Revolution in Russia to captivate the hearts of the people, had subsequently toned down its anti-religious drive and taken people into confidence and acquiesce to the inevitable natural hanker of human beings to be true, humane, virtuous, God-fearing, pure and such other imponderable values that make the desert of human existence an oasis of peace, a paradise on earth, that makes life worth living to the thoughtful and serious men and women everywhere. The RSS, then, will remain basically and substantially a movement upholding the quintessential of Indian civilisation, spreading it far and wide throughout the entire sub-continent of Bharat, throughout the two hemispheres of this planet.

The clause that excludes violent and secret agents from its rank is itself the refutation to the unfounded charges made by the merchants of hatred and sycophants of vested interests that the RSS is reactionary in trying to revive the essential and vital truths in Indian civilisation and that it is a violent and fascist organisation. If violence means the force of Truth, the invincibility of Humanity and Ethics, the tremendous discipline accepted by its members to subjugate their wild passions and make the animal in them entirely subservient to the ideals and spirit of Mother India, her Philosophy, Dharma and Culture, then there is no objection in calling the Sangh violent. But then the dictionary meaning of the term 'violence' is tortured and they have to compile new dictionaries to suit their own whims.

Article 5 of the Constitution is clearly demonstrative of the distinction between the political State and the religious 'Church' and that the separation of the respective jurisdiction in political and cultural life of the people is essential. The article states:

"While recognising the duty of every citizen to be loyal to and respect the State flag, the Sangh has its flag, the '*Bhagva-dhwaj*', the age-old symbol of Hindu culture."

In the history of the western nations the tussle between the State and the Church, since the separation of the political from religious life took place after the elapse of the Middle Ages, with the advent of Humanism, Renaissance and the Protestant reform, has proved to be necessary and healthy in so far as the high-handedness, thoughtlessness and gross and undiluted materialism of the political power of the State machinery could be checked and corrected through the religious organisation of the Church. In India, with the influx of modern scientific, industrial and political ideas, the separation and mutually integrating mission of the religious organisations and the State power is bound to come. While the *Asoka chakra* embossed on the national Tricolour will remain the symbolic representation of political India, the age-old '*Bhagva-dhwaj*' will be symbolic of the eternal spirit, culture, philosophy and Dharma of India. Healthy conflicts and tussles between the State and religion are always welcome, for, it is only in these struggles the really permanent values in life are brought to the fore and what is fittest in the State and religious traditions are enabled to survive, after having stood the test of the eternal law of the struggle for existence.

In the recent history of India, this struggle between the Church and State is found for example in the Hindu Social Disabilities Act, the Sarda Act, the Hindu Temples Endowments Acts, the Hindu Code Bill, etc. Only Truth can prevail and triumph, not vested interests, not subjugation of human beings by the rich. Hence the law of self-preservation demands eternal vigilance which is the price of freedom, which is also the purifier of all accumulated dross of centuries, the guardian angel and watchdog for the preservation of Righteousness, and for the defeat and eradication of the forces of Darkness and Death. Hindu society has showed enough elasticity and healthy adjustability in the past, and, given the necessary education, spread of gnosis or *jnana,* the social and economic ills could be remedied and the gold and pearl in the accumulated traditions of multi-millennial history of India could be preserved.

For this it is absolutely essential that we stress all the more on the fundamental unity of the Indian people, their culture, history and traditions. The present disease of provincialism, parochialism, caste and sub-caste isolations are detrimental to national unity. The Bengalis, Gujaratis, Maharashtrians, Malabarians, Sindhis, Madrasis, the Frontier tribesmen and the Himalayan races, the Dravidians and the Aryans, all are the children of the soil. If the Bengalis continue to condemn nationalism as represented by the RSS, it will be exposing their provincialism, for the RSS is not and cannot be merely a Maharashtrian affair, a Nagpur or Poona business. Such a narrow, walled type of provincialism is fatal. Similarly the Brahmo Samaj and the Ramakrishna Mission are not merely a Bengali-dominated affair. Its message and mission are for the whole of the country. It is to connote this all-India, essentially national character of the new movement that the Article I of the RSS Constitution starts by baptising the Sangh with its true national name. The article says:

"The name of the organisation is the 'Rashtriya Swayamsevak Sangh', which means 'National Volunteer Organisation'. The word 'Rashtriya' is not merely 'national' in the sense we understand this term in the West, it also means *wholehearted adherence to the* basic principles of the cultural heritage of the nation. Similarly, the other word 'Swayamsevak' not only means 'volunteer', but it also connotes the idea of self-help, self-confidence and self-certainty. 'Swayamsevak' means also 'to help oneself'. So the movement was born of the discovery of the national soul of India with the determination to help ourselves. For, even God does not help those who do not help themselves. The Americans and the Russians cannot and will not be *able to solve India's* food problems. The Europeans and the Asians will not be able to solve India's social problems. Only the children of the soil will solve them; they alone can solve the basic problems of the country. It will be up to us to remove with our own hands those social disabilities and anachronistic socio-economic order which was largely responsible for the internal divisions and cancers within the country, which made it easy for foreign imperialists and intruders to invade and subjugate the beautiful plains and graceful hills of Bharat. Now we need learn the lessons of history, the results and lessons of the bitter experiences we have had during centuries of our political slavery to foreigners. But these external fiends could not have subjugated us unless we were ourselves internally and domestically divided and weak. Now is the hour of grace, the hour of emancipation, to win our domestic freedom, Swaraj, that economic, social, cultural and spiritual freedom which, when once fully achieved, no power on earth can subjugate us anymore.

The RSS believes in organisation and discipline. The stronger the organisation the greater the chance of its survival in this world of strife and conflicts. The centre of the Indian peninsula is suitably selected as the headquarters of the Sangh. Article 2 of the Constitution says, "The Head Office of the Sangh is Nagpur." This central city of Central India is the cradle of the movement and the provincial-minded sectarians should not brand the RSS as an affair of 'pot-bellied Nagpur Brahmins'. The ancient ideal of a Brahmin is that of *vipra,* the sage, the intellectual. Anyone who is an intellectual with unsullied character is a *vipra,* the Brahmin. If any Indian intellectual, deeply rooted in the soil of India, true to the soul and spirit of India, heir to the lofty ideals and of unsullied character, then he is among the *vipra* group and he should be among those who will guide and lead the people, even if his name be a Karanjia or Karaka. But if he merely fights the RSS and other Indian nationalistic movements for fighting sake, writes merely for glamour sake, for advertising sensational news alone, then he becomes a Vaisya, a commercial man, without having, however, the ethics of the ideal Vaisya of Indian culture.

The constitutional framework of the RSS is small, business-minded and practical. The new characteristic feature of this movement is that it takes its stand on organisation, not as an end in itself, but as the materialisation of an ideal, the shadow of a movement, the body of a living soul. Wherever there are patterns of perfect organisation we will see them, study them, take what is best in them and graft them on to the national soul of India, deeply rooted to the tap-root and trunk of Indian culture. The new Sangh will learn what is best in the organisational wisdom from the Sangh of Buddha and Manu of old to the organisations of the Congress, Catholic Church, the Nazi and Communist parties of today.

□

Chapter-6

The Esoteric of Strength—Sex-Sublimation

यवक्षरं वेदविदो वदन्ति विवशन्ति यद्यतयी बीतरागाः।
यदिच्छन्नो ब्रह्मचर्य चरन्ति तत्ते पदं संग्रहेण प्रवक्ष्ये॥

Attainment of virile energy through Brahmacharya (sex-sublimation).

—Patanjali, Yoga Sutras 11 38

"That which is spoken of as the imperishable by the Vedic seers,
That wherein enter the sex-sublimated and the detached minds,
That for whose attainment men become Brahmacharis (sex-sublimates)—about that now I begin to declare in brief."

—Katha Upanishad I & II

सबै वेदा यत्पदम् आमनन्ति तपांसि सर्वाणि च यदवदन्ति।
यदू इच्छन्ती ब्रह्मचर्यं चरन्ति तत् ते पदं संग्रहेण व्रवोमि ॐ इत्येतत्॥
"That Adorable One about whom all the gnostic scriptures speak, for whose attainment are directed all sacrifices, restraints, Whom to realise the wise embark upon Brahmacharya (sex-sublimation),
That in brief I speak to you—That is 'OM'."

—Bhagavad Gita VIII 11

"Maintenance of perfect health should be considered almost an utter impossibility without the Brahmacharya leading to the

conservation of the sexual secretions. The sexual glands are all the time secreting semen. This secretion should be utilised for enhancing one's mental, physical and spiritual energy."

—Mahatma Gandhi

"He who has renounced his self becomes powerful as a thunderbolt, and with the power born of renunciation can work for the highest good of Humanity".

—Swami Vivekananda

"This organisation which aspires to endeavour for the national uplift, is the people's organisation. It is their patrimony. What is the object of this Organisation (RSS)? This country is Bharat, with crores of sons of her soil. This country has a claim on her sons and daughters. We put before our mental eye the full vision of the entire Free Bharat. In the world, in life there is strife everywhere. If we make our national life a success we must be strong. That strength cannot be merely brute force but must be pure and pious."

—Shri M.S. Golwalkar

The rest of the RSS Constitution, from article 6 to article 25, describes but the framework of the organisation. But the soul and life behind that constitutional structure will be the power of new ideas, strength that is born out of fulness of life which, an Indian, conscious of his Indian and human heritage, is expected to live. Life is more than theories and organisations. Power is born of idea. Ideas are power. Ideals are the dynamites that revolutionise the life of an individual, that change and transplant one from the life of the first-born to the life of the twice-born. The motive power behind the entire movement is not merely an emotional clinging to what is traditionally transmitted to an Indian; it is the unbeatable power is born of an idea, a conviction, a faith that urges one to take his stand and shelter on the rock of Truth, which alone gives freedom to human beings. Unless one is free oneself, he cannot free others. Unless one is strong oneself, he cannot make others strong. It is because of the lack of coherence between life and preaching that many well-placed and socially-big people remain weak, disintegrated and sterile. What a spate of lectures, writings and preaching and yet what a tragic scarcity of flowers of sanctity, holiness, purity, character everywhere.

The secret doctrine regarding power, the key of the kingdom of heavens, the esoteric of the philosophy of power, the quintessence of the orphic and oriental mystery religions, is to be sought and found in the sublimation of sex. The ancient ideal of *Brahmacharya* could be translated in the modern psychological term of 'sublimation'. Our first birth is the result of sex-subservience and our second birth comes from sex-sublimation. Sex is the quintessence of sense-pleasure, self or consciousness is the quintessence of spiritual joy and happiness. Sex is the gravitating force that generates, sustains and drives the life of the first-borns, self-consciousness is the alpha and omega of a life that is the unending creativity of human spirit. Sex is intense sense-pleasure, self-consciousness is refined idea-pleasure. Now the path that leads towards self-realisation, self-consciousness and self-unfoldment and the subsequent power derived therefrom, is sex-sublimation.

Repression, suppression and all other negative methods of controlling sex are not congenial nor desirable to achieve the positive results of acquiring and maintaining sex-sublimation, which is the condensed form of mental and moral energy, the source of inner poise and power, the motive force and dynamic energy to launch into action, to exercise in the vocation of *karmayogins,* to undertake the impossible tasks and make them materialise through sheer dint of will-power, psychic force, creativity of ideas and strength of ideals.

In a world given to an orgy of violence, to the insensate indulgence of unnatural sex-aberrations, the spirit of Indian culture, the philosophy of the Vedantic doctrine, the trumpet of the RSS, calls the youth of India to a life of vision born out of character, of character born out of purity, of purity born out of sex-sublimation. Indian philosophy, Indian yoga, Indian culture have never been negative. Indian thought is basically positive, essentially integrative, eternally fresh, adjusting, assimilative and vital. It is this philosophy of OM, of the supreme. Yes, that is taken out as the shield and sword in order to protect the basic culture of India, of the soil of Bharat, from further disintegration, falsification, adulteration and wholesale destruction.

While the ordinary Swayamsevaks will lead the common life of ordinary citizens of Bharat, the *Sanghchalaks, Pracharaks* and the active, full-time and life-long devoted souls, who stand at the top of the RSS hierarchy, must have their power born from within, maintained and intensified from within. Their mind and heart should be auto-charging batteries with active dynamos from within. Power comes from ideas; ideas, when systematised and translated into actual life, become ideals. Ideals or life-principles give clarity to mind and purity to heart. Thence come vision, invincibility, power and the active self-propelled drive to move forward and the irresistible urge to dedicate one's entire life wholly and fully for a big ideal, for a great cause, for a purpose.

It is for this reason that the pioneering leaders of the RSS have stressed on the hidden powers, the esoteric of sex-sublimation. In today's superficial world, where basic human values are discredited, distorting the great philosophic and scientific concept of relativity, when white is advertised as black and black is sold out as white, it will be absolutely necessary to re-affirm the psychological laws of self-knowledge, self-control, self-purification, self-confidence and transformation of sex and transcanalisation of sexual urge into the creative fields of human activity. For, sublimation is nothing but the pointing, directing and canalising of the sex in man or woman towards higher activities of life. The secretions of sex organs have bigger purposes for the strengthening of the nervous system, for re-invigorating the entire bodily system, notably of the spinal cord, the brain, the sympathetic nervous system and the sensory organs, than for mere indulgence and orgy of the reproductive functions. Mental and moral development in a human being is but the after-growth that takes place when the vegetative and sensitive life of man is outgrown. Sex is the source of creativity, growth and unceasing dynamism in the lives of those who have, through self-knowledge and self-control, sublimated and transcanalised sexual urge from procreative into creative channels. But sex becomes the *gravitating force*, dragging humans to the mire of obscenity, disease and death when such a mighty force within us is not controlled and guided by reason. Venus, the goddess of sex-beauty, has two faces—the face that smiles and bestows life to those who reach the self through sex, and then the face that curses and kills the victims of uncontrolled sexuality. Venus is the goddess of both life and death. So is Kali, the terrible goddess in Indian tradition. Kali and Durgha are symbolic of the two faces of the same *Maya*—Relativity of the universe, blessing and happiness to those who win the palm of life though sublimation, curse and death to those who fall and revel and perish in sex-aberrations, in the filth of sex-abuse.

The Gurukul, Santiniketan, Pondicherry, Belur Math, Sevagram and such other *ashram* centres, wherein the ancient ideals of Indian culture were sought to be revived, special insistence was always laid on *Brahmacharya*. For those who intend to serve this country with total dedication, total *Brahmacharya* is essential. Those who partially want to serve the cause of the RSS or any other renascent and nationalist organisation, India's advocate must observe conjugal *Brahmacharya*, compatible with monogamous marriage and family life. Those who have no other aim save serving their own sweet selves, they may dismiss *Brahmacharya* completely and live like swines and dogs and oxen. These form the lowest grade in the hierarchy of human beings, the strongest and mentally and morally the bravest being those who are the highest in understanding and practicing the ideal of *Brahmacharya*.

The psychic, occult and mental powers, derived from sublimation of sex, through the canalisation of sexual urge from amatory and procreative flirts to creative fields of literature, poetry, fine arts, philosophy, mysticism, social service and fighting for Righteousness, Justice and Truth in the *Dharmakshetra*, are known to be infinitely varied. The nervous system becomes more receptive to psychic impressions from myriad spheres of super-normal and supra-natural agents that surround us in both physical and mental planes. Clairvoyance, thought-reading, conscious telepathy, healing powers, bilocation, victory over all forms of diseases, transmutation of the physical body from grosser into finer, achievement of miracles at will, predictions and prophecy, omniscience and omnipotence and a rich variety of esoteric powers are conferred on the pure, chaste, virgin soul who has attained communion with the Over-Soul, has become one with the Cosmic Force, through the control and canalisation of sex urge, sex energy and sex drive. Not in oriental mystery books alone, not in the secret doctrine of the East, not in the teachings and lives of yogic philosophers alone, but also in the religious and secular literature of the West, throughout the world, abounds the unanimous teaching of sages on the powers that accrue to human beings when sex-sublimation or positive chastity is achieved and maintained for a few months or years. Milton says:

"...A hidden strength
'Tis chastity, my brother, chastity.
She that has that, is clad in complete steel,
And like a quivered nymph with arrows keen
May trace huge forests and unharboured heaths,
Infamous hills and sandy perilous wilds,
Where, through the sacred rays of chastity,
No savage fierce, bandit or mountaineer
Will dare to soil her virgin purity.
Some say no evil things that walk by night
In fog or fire, by lake or moorish fen,
Blue meagre hag, or stubborn unlaid ghost
That breaks his magic chains at curfew time,
No goblin, no smart fairy of the mine
Hath hurtful power o'er virginity.
Hence had the huntress Dian her dread bow,
Fair silver-shafted queen, forever chaste,
Wherewith she tamed the bounded lioness

And spotted mountain pard, but set at naught
The frivolous bolt of Cupid—
That wise Minerva wore, unconquered virgin
Wherewith she freezed her foes to congealed stone.
So dear to Heaven is saintly chastity,
That when a soul is sincerely found so
A thousand celestial angels befriend her
And speak to her things which no gross ear can hear.

—*Milton's Comus*

The Vestal Virgins of Rome, the Devadasis in India and the consecration of virginity to the gods and goddesses, the romance of the virgin birth are all corroborative and illustrative of this simple, psychological and scientific truth of sex-sublimated power which keeps up permanent values in life and asserts the infinite potential powers man, woman and mankind can draw forth from within themselves through sex-sublimation.

Sex-sublimation, chastity, virginity, *brahmacharya* and innocence are transcendental words of esoteric wisdom—wisdom in both East and West, in both the ancient and modern times. Man, a moat afloat in the infinity of Creation, reaches his identity with All, the All-in-All through purity. "Blessed are the pure in heart, for they shall see God," as Jesus says. Verily, purity is infinite power, incandescent innocence, transparent image of the Real in the universe.

Even in America where material civilisation and capitalistic merchandise have reached the most dangerous and menacing phases of pragmatic utilitarianism, there are minds that can appreciate the power, fragrance and irradiation of power and light emanating from purity, sex-sublimated innocence. Among the American votaries of esoteric wisdom there is one who wrote the following words in an American journal, few years ago, in praise of this angelic virtue, chastity, innocence, purity, *Brahamacharya*, sex-sublimation. He wrote:

"What is there in the world more beautiful than the innocence of the pure?" It is the fascination of a child, where is innocence and cannot help it; it is more fascinating still in an understanding girl or boy, in a grown-up man or woman," it is a pearl beyond all. Pure men recognise it when they meet it. They hardly know how and look back at it when it has passed them. Women know it by a kind of instinct, as if its possession were the object of their lives. The world itself, blind and soiled and sodden as it is, knows innocence when it finds it and either bows before it and suffers it to pass by unscathed, or else, in its devilish mood, lays itself out to despoil it; in either case, it sets up its external signs as the ideals and models for a man to cultivate.

"Nor is innocence only a thing beautiful, a delicate treasure to be kept safe from harm. It is also a thing secure and strong. Innocence will walk through fire and will not burn; it will fire amid refuse, and will not be stained; it will venture where greater so-called experience would not wisely dare, and will come away unscathed. It is its own defence; it believes because it itself is true and is believed in return; it trusts, because it has in itself no cause for doubt, and is trusted; it shows human nature at its best and receives in return the best and the worst of human nature."

"When, again, a noble deed is to be done, innocence is best capable of doing it. In the face of death, nothing is so fearless as the innocent hand and the heart that is clean, in the grip of physical torture, under the weight of heavy trial, at times when endurance is taxed to the extreme, there is no nature that blanches less than the nature that is innocent. O when action is called for, if one is bidden to do anything, great or small, for God or for man, to drag a poor soul out of the mire, to lift up one's fellow-men from their dead selves to higher things, to teach or to preach, to instruct or to counsel, to serve or to command, innocence will go where guilt may not venture, innocence will shy at no shadow where guilt will conjure up monsters, innocence will act and carry through where guilt will hang its head in confusion. While guilt will be content with a partial gain, innocence will bear all before it."[1]

1. Quoted by Dr. Valerian Gracias, *Heaven and Home*, pp. 32-33

The RSS is an organisation of strength. Its members, Sanghchalaks and Pracharaks are to be the children of Bharat, born of the *Shakti Sadhana* of the culture of the land. This worship of *Shakti,* the Primeval Power and Cosmic Force in the universe, can only be practiced by the sex-sublimates. All forms of *Shakti* or Power, whether physical, military, mental or spiritual, all are derived through the worship of the Supreme Reality, through the dedicated sacrifice of sex-excitements on the throne of Truth, Beauty, Good and Love derived from sex-sublimation. Sex is lust, sex-sublimation is love. Sex-gratification is blind; it is ignorance, it is *avidja*; sex-sublimation is light, clarity of mind, indomitable will-power and unending energy; it is knowledge, *jnana,* gnosis. Hence says Shri Ramakrishna:

"Sakti (Power) alone is the root of the universe. The Primal Energy has two aspects, Vidya and Avidya. Avidya, ignorance, deludes. Avidya conjures up 'sex and gold', which casts the spell. Vidya (knowledge) begets devotion, kindness, wisdom and love, which lead one to God. This Avidya must be propitiated and that is the purpose of the rites of Sakti worship."

—*Gospel of Shri Ramakrishna*

According to the Tantric philosophy, the tyranny of sex is to be conquered through control and sublimation of sex. This is the meaning of playing with the serpent and at the same time conquering its poison fangs through its own fangs. Poison is left aside, but the fangs remain, not any longer to bite and kill living beings but to cure and heal human wounds, maladies and miseries. The same unregulated seminal flow outwards, which caused nervous breakdown, headache, physical and mental neuroses of various sorts, diseases and weakness, when allowed to flow inwards, into the whole length of the spinal cord, into the medulla oblongata and the grey matter in the brain, the latent powers of mind are awakened, when not only the old diseases and neuroses are cured, but man also becomes the fountain-head of unending energy, ever-widening vision, incessant creativity, adamantine will-power and inflexible, unsullied personal character. It is this worship of Power, as symbolised in the sword of Lakshmi Bai of Jhansi, of Sivaji and Rana Pratap, which the RSS accepts as the source of spiritual and physical strength which are unfolded as the result of that *Sakti sadhana*, through which one conquers sex-thraldom and irradiates Love and Life to one's society, country and mankind.

The esoteric of power, the psychology of heart-purification, the knowledge of the awakening of *Kundalini* or 'serpent power' in the spinal cord and unbeatable strength arc necessary for the workers of the RSS, because the flames that burn their sacrificial offering are service, purity and dedication. The religious character and the cultural core of the Sangh can hardly be ignored while considering the social, economic or political mission which the Sangh is called upon to do in the new set-up of things in this country. Unlike the people who set out for worldly gains, such as power, career and fame, the Swayamsevaks will have nothing but the unending sacrifice and service to offer on this altar of their Motherland. Says the founder of the RSS:

"If it is this lure of office or rank which has brought you here, you will be sadly disappointed, for that you can find fertile field elsewhere outside the Sangh. Here it is selfless service and sacrifice, unqualified, ungrudging and absolute...Rashtriya Swayamsevak Sangh is the greatest Havana Kunda in which Swayamsevaks plunge themselves, like so many sandal sticks, unmindful of which burns faster or first. They all burn without sound and smoke. Here burning is the essence."

—*Dr. Hedgewar*

Discipline, self-control and self-confidence become all the more necessary when we see the growing misery and sad plight of the country. The more adverse the circumstances, the harder the battle, the stronger and more disciplined should be the soldiers. The RSS are the new National Army, with the discipline and idealism of men like Rana Pratap, Sivaji, Hedgewar, Netaji Subhas, Golwalkar, Tilak and all those who dreamt of a united, strengthened and purified India. It is for this reason that

Brahmabandav Upadhyaya, that intrepid fighter of *Swadeshi* days, while re-introducing Saraswati Puja among the students, said, "Purity of character, that is strength, that is national character through which is achieved the Swaraj of the sages."

Of this indomitable power born out of purity, the esoteric of strength, is now resplendently manifest in the life of Shri M.S. Golwalkar, the general servant of the Sangh. Whether as a teacher, professor, guru or leader, the power and fascination of the man is derived from the vow of *Brahmacharya*. Calumnies and detractions do not touch the fringe of his purity, saintly personality. Strength is nowhere to be found save in idea, thought, consciousness. The stronger becomes a man, through discipline and self-control, the higher he ascends the hierarchical ladder of sex-sublimation, purity, fineness and subtlety of spirit. It is out of this *sakti sadhana* that Narendra was reborn as Vivekananda, Gautama once became Buddha, Jesus once became Christ. Hence sang Swami Vivekananda the ode to Purity-God:

"Oh, when will dawn the blessed day
When Love will waken in my heart?
When will my tears flow uncontrolled
As I repeat Lord Hari's name,
And all my longing be fulfilled?
When will my mind and soul be pure?
Oh, when shall I at last repair
Unto Vrindavan's sacred groves?
When will my worldly bonds fall off
And my imperfect sight be healed?,
By Wisdom's cool collyrium?
When shall I learn true alchemy
And, touching the Philosopher's stone,
Transmute my body's worthless iron
Into the Spirit's purest gold?
When shall I see this very world
As God, and roll on Love's highway?
When shall I give up piety
And duty and the thought of caste?

When shall I leave behind all fear,
All shame, convention, worry, pride?"

—Swami Vivekananda's songs

While this Tantric philosophy of Power Cult is advocated through self-purification and inner discipline, we should only see that it never degenerates into popular Siva-Sakti pictorial unions. Power then only comes when individual self is become one with the Cosmic Self, when *the jivatama* becomes one with *paramatma,* the soul with the Over-soul, which is not sexual union, as the common herd interpret Siva-Sakti union and the Radha-Krishna romance. Shri Ramakrishna interprets Siva-Sakti union as follows:

"Yogic power is impossible if the mind dwells on sex and gold. The mind of a worldly man generally moves among the three lower centres those at the navel, at the sexual organ, and the organ of evacuation. After great effort and spiritual practice, the *Kundalini* is awakened. According to the yogis there are three nerves in the spinal column—*Ida, Pingal* and *Sushuman.* Along the *Sushuman* are six lotuses or centres, the lowest being known as the *Muladhara.* Then come successively *Svadhusthana, Manipura Anahata, Vishuddha* and *Ajna.* These are the st centres. The *Kundalini,* when awakened, passes through the lower centres and comes to the *Anahata,* which is at the heart. It stays there. At that time the mind of the aspirant is withdrawn from the three lower centres. He feels the awakening of the Divine Consciousness and sees Light. In mute wonder he sees that radiance and cries out, "What is this? What is this?"

"After passing through the six centres, the Kundalini reaches the thousand-petalled lotus known as Sahasrara, and the aspirant goes to Samadhi (ecstasy).

"When the Kundalini rises to the Sahasrara and the mind goes into Samadhi, the aspirant loses all consciousness of the outer world. He can no longer retain his physical body.

"And last of all is the seventh plane, which, according to Tantra, is the centre of the thousand-petalled lotus. When the Kundalini arrives there, the aspirant goes into Samadhi. In that

lotus dwells the Satchitananda Siva, the Absolute. There Kundalini, the Awakened Tower, unites with Siva. This is known as the union of Siva and Sakti."

—Shri Ramakrishna Paramahamsa

The purest and the most concentrated power is needed for those who are at the helm of the affairs of the RSS. This esoteric of Power, however, is not to be confounded or identified with manifold forms of superstition, black magic, witchcraft, priest-craft, idolatry and such weak and weakening practices prevalent among the masses of India. If there were not such weaknesses, Muhammed of Ghazni, Allaudin Khilji and the white plunderers could not have come and subdued the people of India and demoralised and degenerated them to such deplorable depths. Hindu Dharma, for its preservation, needs strengthening and collectivisation. When and where conviction, reason and commonsense fail to achieve and maintain unity, then and there should come the organisational rigour, discipline to maintain and preserve, to strengthen and expand, what is still left of the pearls like gems of Indian culture. Greater India, that lives today through the spread of Hinayana and Mahayana Buddhism, through the metaphysics of Zen, Taoism and Sufi Islam, serves as the basis for the conscientious and thoughtful Indians to explore deeper and find a stable basis for organisational union, national solidarity and invincible strength so that Indian culture may survive, not in the form of abstract metaphysics, dead books, polluted temples, caste-mongering, priest-craft, but as a source of power and strength to cement the country, to eradicate the weeds and accumulated dross of centuries of stagnation and slavery and revive and revitalise those doctrines and practices that generate power among the individuals, and help the society and nation to stand with their heads erect, with feets solidly on the soil and march forward to the destined goal of India, which is to be the Mother and Master of philoso-phic wisdom, yogic psychology, metaphysical ontologism and religious mysticism of the Self and Reality or God, plus economic self-sufficiency and social freedom.

It is collective *sadhana* that is now needed for our country. Individualism is good, provided the individual *sadhakhs* utilise their spiritual powers to the service of the society. But if they subordinate the vital interests of the society, country or nation to their own interests, then that individualism is condemned as fatal to the life and strength of the society. We are borne of the loving breast of Mother India, borne of her love, her seed, her soil, her culture, her spirit, which permeate and interpenetrate every pore of our being, every drop of our blood, every cell, every atom within. It is this debt to the country, to the Motherland, to the soil, that must be paid back through our service, born out of strength and enlightened consciousness, for which the only royal path and esoteric wisdom is purity, virginity, chastity, *brahmacharya*.

If a man fails, he crashes on this rock of chastity. If a man rises to Himalayan heights of valour, heroism and power, he rises on this rock of purity. It is for this reason that the ancient legislators demanded that the top-ranking leaders should be men of character, purity and power. The Spartan Constitution under Lycurgus (about 725 BC) was based on military and physical strength. The Athenian constitutional rudiments, beginning from Cecrops, the hero, and Athena the goddess, consisted in both mental and physical power derived from education, thought and philosophy. The Jews and Persians had their constitutions in the power of law, moral energy and ethical force, as embodied in the Mosaic Pentateuch and Zarathustra's Zend. Ancient Indians placed the Brahmins or the intellectuals at the top of their social hierarchy. The path of Brahmins to Brahman is *Brahmacharya.*

Wherever there is power that is the manifestation of the spirit. Buddha, being a Kshatriya by birth, became a Brahmin by life. So was Krishna who through his wisdom became a Brahmin. *Chandalas*, through the development of their mental power, through the awakening of *Kundalini*, can beat Brahmins in intellectual strength, the Kshatriyas in physical and military prowess and the Vaisya in trade and commerce ability, and the Shudra in service and labour. Everything depends upon the amount of energy one can generate as a result of sex-sublimation. But we may learn from the history of rise and fall of nations that such physical, mental, moral and spiritual powers are not released nor generations saved when individuals and societies are disciplined with the same elastic but iron discipline with which the Catholic Church maintains its hold on the Catholic Empire, the only non-political organised religious force that has stood the test of history and the challenge of militarists, royalists, critics and scholars. It is this disciplinary and doctrinal strength of the Church which Swami Vivekananda recommended to his disciples. Swamiji attempted to incorporate the disciplinary and ethical stability of the Catholic Church into his Mission with suitable changes made in the context of young nascent Hinduism. From the great monastic orders of the Catholic Church, Swami Vivekananda learnt the triple vow of obedience, non-possession and chastity as essential to the member of the Ramakrishna Mission. Certainly, there is no real lasting power without chastity or sex-sublimation.

Of the somatic, mental and spiritual realms in the human make-up the concentrated essence of sensuous pleasure is sex. Until this pleasure is transmuted through the touch of the philosopher's stone and is pleasure transmuted into Good, Happiness and Truth, there is no strength in man. As long as the mind and heart give way to the passing flux of sensuous perceptions and transient joys of sex-intoxication, there is no strength in man. Repression solves nothing; suppression solves nothing; but only sublimation of sex is the answer.

Power comes only through self-discipline, sense-control and sex-sublimation. The *Bhagavad Gita*, *Dhammapada*, *New Testament*, *Old Testament*, the Zen, *Masnavi*, Plato, Pythagoras, Yajnavalkya, all the cream of prophetic and scriptural wisdom teach the same truth. Those alone can serve the interests of the country who have acquired power, won power over the tiger and ape in them through the irradiant light and refreshing rays of sex-sublimation. Purity, *Brahmacharya* is the last and first word in the struggle for inward power, strength that is not vanity of the power-politicians, but valour that is mental light, indomitable will-power, unending creativity, selfless service and unceasing sacrifice on the altar of the Motherland, for the fulfilment of the great motto '*Alamno mokshartham jagat hitayacha*'—for the freedom of soul, for the good of the world, which Swami Vivekananda placed before Indian youth.

□

Chapter-7

The Organisational Discipline of The RSS

"Strike off thy fetters
Bonds that bind thee down,
Of shining gold, or darker, baser ore
Love, hate—good, bad—
and all the dual throng,
Know, slave is slave, caressed, whipped, not free,
For fetters, though of gold, are not less strong to bind."

—Swami Vivekananda

"It is evident Doctorji (Dr. B.R. Hedgewar) reached certain conclusions during this period. He had lived with the terrorists, he had worked with the Congress. He had contacted the then thinkers and leaders of the country. Not only that, having himself been brought up in poverty, he had opportunities of mixing with the common masses as well and he could closely study the people. He was aware of the potentialities of our race as well as the degeneration that set in due to foreign rule. He had carefully noticed where the strength of the British law lay and had unmistakably located the weak and vulnerable points in the administrative machinery. In quest of a solution he had laboured hard practically in all the spheres. The long and laborious search for the way out ultimately bore fruit. The solution was found out, the riddle solved. The doctor completed his diagnosis. He got light. He foresaw. He calculated what freedom would cost. He resolved and his mind became steady. He chose the auspicious day of Vijayadashami and founded the

Rashtriya Swayamsevak Sangh in the year 1925."

—Ekanath Ranade on the birth of the RSS

Out of pangs of the misery and from intense agony of Mother India was born the RSS which, while pledging to preserve and enhance the essentials of Indian civilisation, is now called upon by Providence to fill up the gaps and vacuum created by the outdated Congress organisation. It is precisely in this changing phase of Indian history that the Hindu Mahasabha has thrown open its doors to all Indian nationals, irrespective of religious labels to work and take part in the socio-economic and political life. Today nationalism, pure and simple, is the strongest asset and is the logical argument to defeat the forces of communalism, to undo the wrongs of partition based on communal claims and to unseat all the anti-national forces from the centre of national life. It is this strong, powerful nationalism that strengthens the RSS all the more to fulfil its mission in India during these critical times, when we are inundated by the deluge of this Iron Age. It is in this eminently national sense the word 'Hindu' is used and not in any communal and sectarian sense all throughout wherever the term 'Hindu' is used by the RSS.

Born of the sufferings of Mother India, fully conscious of the economic, cultural and social needs of the Mother, both Dr. Hedgewar, the father-founder of the RSS and the present Sarsanghchalak, Shri M.S. Golwalkar, knew the necessity of order, discipline and strict sense of duty among all the members and associates of the Sangh. A broad organisational structure and the basic disciplinary rules and canons of the Sangh are found in the Constitution.

About the Swayamsevaks, Article 6 of the Constitution says:

(a) "Any male Hindu of 18 years or more, who subscribes to the rules and regulations of the Sangh and takes its pledge, set out in Appendix (A), may be registered as a Swayamsevak."

(b) "A Swayamsevak shall be deemed to be an active Swayamsevak, if he attends a Sangh Shakha regularly or performs specific Sangh work duly assigned to him."

(c) "A Swayamsevak shall cease to be a Swayamsevak, if he resigns his membership or if expelled for misconduct or indiscipline or any act prejudicial to the interests of the Sangh."

(d) "Bal Swayamsevaks—any male Hindu below the age of 18—may be admitted and allowed to participate in the Sangh programmes. They will be classified according to their ages and given suitable training in accordance with the rules framed for the purpose."

"A list of Bal Swayamsevaks will be maintained in the units to which they are admitted."

Outside of the RSS, specially to those who like to depict RSS as a communal organisation, bent upon restoring a Hindu Raj, where non-Hindus will have no place, strict restriction of membership to born-Hindus, is a puzzle. But here one might say that not birth but Hindu character or strict monogamous nationalism would entitle anyone to be a member of the RSS, if not today, then tomorrow, when nationalism is firmly established. Any true Indian, heir to the *Vedas*, *Upanishads*, *Gita*, epics, the philosophy, culture and art of Bharatvarsha, is "Hindu". It is only when a born-Hindu repudiates his cultural past, or a born-Muslim looks exclusively to Koran, eradicating himself from his national tap-roots, or a born-Christian merely imitates the western *sahibs* and *memsahibs* without having national self-respect and roots deep down in Indian culture, that one ceases to be an Indian and thereby a true child of the Motherland. All that is intended by the term 'Hindu' is to revive and instil national pride in being heirs to such a rich heritage that is there for every child born of the sacred soil of Mother India. It is because of this connotation of the term 'Hindu' that recently under the leadership of Dr. Syama Prasad Mookerjee and Dr. B.G. Khare the membership of the Hindu Mahasabha was thrown wide open to any Indian national. Birth means little; character and spirit alone matter. There are many born-Hindus who are utterly ignorant of their cultural heritage, who have no pride in anything spiritual, who are only interested in defending their vested interests, or who are even positively opposed to everything Hindu, under the rationalistic and materialistic influence of western education. What is therefore needed is more education, enlightenment and propaganda of the quintessentials of the humanistic and spiritual faith and culture that form the core and rock-bottom of Indian civilisation.

A second objection that is often raised outside of the RSS circles is about the restriction of membership only to males, which they interpret as the continuation of the zero position of the fairer sex in any socio-cultural activities of the country. The critics of the RSS further state, "Even the RSS relegate Indian womanhood to the kitchen and bedroom. Hindu girls and women are excluded from membership and activities of the RSS." Even the RSS supports the Manu's saying:

पिता रक्षति कौमारे भर्ता रक्षति यौवने।
रक्षन्ति स्थाविरे पुत्रा न स्त्री स्वातन्त्र्यमर्हति॥

"A woman is not worthy of freedom. Her father protects her in her childhood, her husband in her youth, her children protect her in old age." First of all, the ideal of Indian womanhood, as enshrined in the healthy Indian traditions is the highest, although after centuries of political slavery, internal divisions and weakness, the menfolk have exploited the grace and patience of the fairer sex and have degraded them from the heights they were placed by our ancient rishis and legislators. Says Vivekananda:

"Oh India! Forget not that the ideal of thy womanhood is Sita, Savitri, Damayanti; forget not that the God thou worshippest is the great Ascetic of ascetics, the all-renouncing Sankara, the Lord of Uma; forget not that thy marriage, thy wealth, thy life are not for sense-pleasure, are not for thy individual personal happiness; forget not that thou art born as a sacrifice to the Mother's altar; forget not that thy social order is but the reflex of the Infinite universal Motherhood; forget not that the lower classes, the ignorant, the poor, the illiterate, the cobbler, the sweeper, are thy flesh and blood, thy brothers. Thou brave one, behold, take courage, be proud that thou art an Indian, and proudly proclaim,—"I am an Indian, every Indian is my brother". Say,—"The ignorant Indian, the poor and destitute Indian, the Brahman Indian, the Pariah Indian, is my brother". Thou too clad with but a rag round thy loins, proudly proclaim

at the top of thy voice, "The Indian is my brother, the Indian is my life, India's gods and goddesses are my God, India's society is the cradle of my infancy, the pleasure-garden of my youth, the sacred heaven, the varanasi, of my old age". Say brother, "The soil of India is my highest heaven, the good of India is my good", and repeat and pray day and night—"O thou Lord of Gauri, O Thou Mother of the Universe, vouchsafe manliness unto me! O Thou Mother of strength, take away my weakness, take away my unmanliness and MAKE ME A MAN."'

—Swami Vivekananda's Inspired Talks

The answer to the critics is already there in the above quotation. The ideals of Sita and Damayanti, of the Upanishadic women teachers, of Lakshmi Bai of Jhansi, of Mira Bai and others are there to refute the charge against the RSS, reducing Indian womenfolk back to the kitchen and bedroom. No, the ideal of Indian womanhood is always the idea of *Prakriti*, the *Mahamaya,* the relative, visible God on earth. Man is *purusha* and hence approximating the impersonal Absolute. But woman is the image of the Universal Mother whence the Creation sprang, the Queen of Creation, the Mistress of the Home, the comforter and inspirer of man, his guide and friend in every walk of life. There is no question of inferiority or superiority, but only different functional status, beginning from purely biological plane, right up to their common ventures into the cultural, social, economic and political life of the country. So there is no question of excluding women from the Sangh, much less does the RSS support the idea of reducing woman into merely a chattel at home, instrument of pleasure for man or a child-producing machine. Woman remains the visible image of the Universal Mother, equal partner of man in facing the problems and undertaking adventures in life.

These two main objections exploded, it is necessary to see the enormous strength that has accrued to the RSS after it has deployed bands of well-disciplined and organised young men on the battlefront. The question of organising girls and women of the country along the same lines will arise in the near future, and when that need arises, the RSS will add new clauses in the same article, or draw up a separate constitution for the Swayamsevak *balikas* and The Constitution is not the last word and rules and constitutions are there only to help the work and achieve the target, national unity and solidarity.

The efficiency of the organisational structure, the steely discipline and above all the selfless service of the Swayamsevaks have been acknowledged and praised by our present Congress leaders. Shri Bhayaji Dhani, General Secretary of the RSS, stated at the Sivaji Park rally in October 1949 about the growing appreciation of the work of the RSS and the acknowledgement from our Congress leaders in these words:

"In private conversations and their talks with me, some of the leaders have admitted the fact that the RSS is a well-knit organisation that has a creditable record of patriotic and nation-building activities to its credit."

"They also admit that the rank and file of the RSS is free from corruption and profit-motive, and that some of the best patriotic elements in the country have joined our ranks."

"After making these confessions, these leaders say, 'It is all right that the RSS has a mass following but has no leaders. Our party has many leaders but no following. Let us therefore join hands.'"

—Bhayaji Dhani

This recognition of the services and the untainted spirit of the Swayamsevaks would not have been echoed unless there was inner discipline, organisational efficiency and true, permanent character of *bharatiyata* among the Swayamsevaks. *Bharatiya* culture is unique for India and it is an intelligent appreciation and pride in that culture that forms the basis of the new national resurrection which the RSS envisages. This is not merely an emotional attachment, but is a solid philosophical and metaphysical ideal also. For the Advaita, or the philosophy of monistic idealism, as developed in India, is the basis of the assertion that India is one country, one people, basically of one racial and cultural features, which Shri M.S. Golwalkar puts so tersely and philosophically in these words:

"The aim of the RSS is to spread the message of Bharatiya

culture which seeks to instil feelings of service and sacrifice for the community. According to our culture, all human beings are one and equal, being the limbs and parts of the body of the Lord. When we serve the weak and the poor amongst us, we only serve God and do not give anything in charity. This world is only the manifestation of the Almighty and we should strive to live here only as his trustees. We should work hard and produce material wealth, no doubt, but our aim should be to utilise only that which is most necessary for us. I appeal to my Swayamsevaks not to fritter away their energies in trivial matters but to concentrate on the fundamental task of National Regeneration which is the need of the hour. We should not be distracted from our path under any circumstances just as the normal temperature of the human body does not fluctuate, whatever be the atmospheric conditions."

—Shri Golwalkar's address in Delhi before the Swayamsevaks and the women volunteers of the RSS Samiti

The keynote of the organisation is that one great phrase 'unity in diversity'. Not a mechanical uniformity that is desired, but the unity of spirit that is maintained, although uniform to wear and drills, military bands and marches, etc. are not thereby excluded. This all-unifying thread is Indian nationalism, the common denominator not only between the various sects and sub-sects within the born-Hindus, but also among all the castes and creeds of India, who have the courage and pride to see and cling to the life-giving sources of Mother India. Herein again the words of Shri Golwalkar ring true:

"We believe that in this country the people known as the Hindus, in spite of their various religious persuasions or panths, have got common substratum—a common heritage and this common heritage can serve as a unifying factor. We have tried to bring about this unification."

—Shri GolwalKar's first press conference in Bombay since his release

The new imprint of the RSS movement is its adherence to certain well-defined principles and ideals of national resurrection and national survival, and subordination of individuals and leaders to those ideals to be translated and lived in life. In this land of hero-worship, it is necessary to bring eternal Truths and Principles back to the hearts and minds of the people. It is these eternal verities that transform the first-borns into the twice-borns, into the *dwijas* and our people should be taught not to worship the twice-borns but the Eternal Truth whose manifestations or embodiments are the sages, seers and *rishis*. In this connection there is an interesting episode that is recorded in the life of Dr. Hedgewar, which is as follows:

In the year 1927, Doctor Hedgewar arranged a *Guru Puja Day*, quite in keeping with the tradition of the land. But on this occasion it was not the traditional guru in the form of a human being that was worshipped, but the Eternal Principle, Truth, as symbolised in the national flag that was saluted, worshipped and adored. The story goes:

On the eve of the great Guru Puja Day, Doctor told his Swayamsevaks, "Tomorrow we shall celebrate Guru Puja festival. Every Swayamsevak should bring flowers and *dakshina* (offering in the form of money or kind) according to his faith and capacities." The Swayamsevaks were wondering who this guru was going to be. Some Swayamsevaks had thought that the guru may be the instructor who was conducting the Officers' Training Corps of the RSS. In fact, in the Indian tradition that would have justified the Swayamsevaks to think that their preceptor might be the guru of the day, but some others couldn't believe that and suggested, "Of course not. It must be Shri Anna Saheb Sohni. For, was he not the architect of the whole system of the physical education of the Sangh?" After all these speculations, the next day Swayamsevaks assembled when they saw that not a human being but the *Bhagva* flag was their guru to be worshipped. On that occasion, Dr. Hedgewar said:

"The Rashtriya Swayamsevak Sangh reveres *Bhagva* as its 'guru' and not any individual man who, however great he may be, is imperfect and fallible. How can we make an imperfect and fallible being our 'guru'? Individual man may seem perfect today, but he may not remain so tomorrow. That is why our flag and none else is our 'guru', our conquering *Bhagva*, which symbolises Bharatiya culture based on sacrifice. The inspiration we shall receive from this sacred flag will be definitely greater than the inspiration obtained from any individual."

From this one episode alone is clear the ideological strength of the RSS. Unlike those mushroom sects that spring here and there under the inspiration and fallible guidance of a *sadhu* or guru—genuine or spurious—the RSS had its birth in an idea. It is strong enough to stand the test of the severest progressive critics outside. The organisational machinery of the Sangh is nothing but a mere framework to preserve this idea and make it grow, expand, permeate every nook and corner of the land and bring about the needed socio-economic changes, based not any longer on the concept of class-struggle—which is so fundamental in the Communist: philosophy—but on the concept of class-cooperation. The RSS has struck the golden mean between the two extremes of foreign-imported, materialistic, exclusively economic Communistic ideology and the orthodox, all-defending, uncritical Hindu Mahasabha. It is for this that the organisational structure of the RSS is strictly disciplined without, however, thereby impairing the growth of the individual, as it often does with various political and religious organisations. This vital fluidity, combined with disciplinary rigidity, is possible when such a movement is grafted on to the main national and cultural trunk of the Indian Kalpataru tree. This is the magic, this is the mesmerism, hypnotism and enchantment of the spiritual culture that is India—India that is the Mother of spiritual culture.

It may interest the reader that the *Margashirasha* number of the astrological magazine of Bangalore gave the following description about the organisational discipline of the RSS. It said:

"In whatever he (Shri M.S. Golwalkar) does, he will be generally confronted with obstacles and delay, but the ultimate objects will be realised. His organisation is marked out for efficiency, discipline and concerted work, and he will be surrounded by friends pure-hearted, fortunate and learned."

Whether one believes in astrology or not, the facts mentioned in the article appeared in the magazine, edited by Shri B.V. Rama

Raman, are proved to be correct. It becomes now increasingly clear that our national identity, Indianism, Bharatiyata, and the entire cultural, racial and biological features cannot, and will not, be preserved, enhanced and transmitted to posterity without organisation, discipline. Once the rigid rules of caste system preserved the traditional culture of the land, now that system has fallen because, instead of attending to the inherent qualities and inborn tendencies of the individuals, the *varnashrama sanatanists* base their doctrine on accidents of birth. So a new, democratic, up-to-date organisation is to be built up as the bulwark of the national soul of India. Now there is every chance that the RSS can become the one single India-wide organisation to fulfil that task and shoulder that burden of safeguarding Indianism or Bharatiyata from further disruption, division and degeneration. Hence the ideal of Sangh is not a mechanical organisational engine, but a strong, well-knit, free, co-operative unit that leads a corporate life and absorbs and transplants individuals to the bigger life of India as a whole.

After the moral victory gained by the RSS after the Central and state Governments banned the organisation from 4th February, 1948 and various persecutions suffered at the hands of the first National Government, the RSS emerged stronger and far more united than ever. This only confirms the golden adage, 'The blood of the martyrs is the seed of the Church'. The united and well-knit organisational front of the RSS was born not only out of external circumstances, but more so due to the genuine, realistic national core, patriotic love and sacrificial fire of the Sangh. For it is so true that we often equate freedom with license and politics with power and nationalism with communalism. It is precisely in these fields that the RSS has steered the road straight and has set the pattern of nationalism as a force for organised unity, stern purpose and clear voice of duty to the children of the soil. Here again, says the RSS leader:

"We lack that feeling of love for our nation which is the basis of life in other nations. We must always feel that this nation is ours, that we will guide and control our thoughts and activities so as to contribute to the good of our nation. This is the essence of freedom. But falsely enough, we have come to think that freedom and licence are one and the same thing. This misunderstanding of freedom is a grave question. It is same as the lack of discipline in our national life and this is also the cause why our national plans fail."

—*Shri M.S. Golwalkar*

To the present mad rush of the empty blockheads for winning power for power's sake, there stands the challenge of the RSS to seek service without power, achieve substance without size, rain graces and services without thunders and lightning. At a time when the foreigners are laughing at the present state of impoverishment, famine conditions, economic exploitation by both foreign capitalists and domestic black-market magnates, when our present leaders are puffed up on their cathedrals of power intoxication, fully self-satisfied and self-complacent about their 'achievements and past sufferings', it is good that a new organised and powerfully and closely-knit body should arise from the lap of Mother Earth, even as Sita was born of the furrow of the agonising Mother India's soil, to atone for the sins of commission and omission of the pseudo-nationalists and bring back the smile of life and cheer of love to the uprooted, famished, despondent and dejected citizens of the Motherland.

This is the reason why the RSS begins training of the youngest and most pliable children of our country, boys and girls, before they have reached their later teens, to whom training, discipline, patriotism, nationalist pride and manliness are all infused. The *Bala* and *Balika* Swayamsevaks will have all discipline and courage as the old Bahia groups of the *Gaventi Italiana del Litono,* minus their fascist totalitarianism and imperialist dreams and militarist pride. For, the entire RSS hinges upon power and discipline borne out of the culture or *sanskriti* of the land, and not on the military might or myths of the twentieth century injected into the blood-streams of the tender and uncritical youth.

With regard to the registration of the Swayamsevaks, Article 7 of the Constitution provides for jurisdictional authority. It says:

"Each village, town, city and provincial centre having a

Shakha, shall constitute a primary unit of the Sangh. Every Shakha shall maintain a register of all its Swayamsevaks—active or otherwise."

"For organisational purposes the country shall be divided into provinces. (b) Every province may further be subdivided, according to their order of subordination as indicated in the table as in Appendix."

The procedure of elections within the Sangh is definitely democratic and elections are held after every three years. Qualifications and method of voting are laid down in the next Article of the Constitution. Then the hierarchical order of the various constituent units and authorities is laid down in Article 11, whereas Articles from 12 to 19 deal with the office-bearers and officers, beginning from the Sarsanghchalak down to Prantiya Pratinidhi Sabha. Article 12 about the Sarsanghchalak reads:

"Late Dr. Keshav Baliram Hedgewar, the founder of the Sangh was the Adya (first) Sarsanghchalak. Shri Madhav Sadashiv Golwalkar was nominated Sarsanghchalak by him in consultation with the then Kendriya Karyakari Mandal. He is the Sarsanghchalak since then. The Sarsanghchalak will nominate his successor, as and when the necessity arises, with the consent of the then Kendriya Karyakari Mandal.

"The Sarsanghchalak is the Guide and Philosopher of the Rashtriya Swayamsevak Sangh. He may attend, summon or address any assembly of the Swayamsevaks, Prantiya Sabhas and Karyakari Mandals severally or jointly."

The Sarsanghchalak, then, is not only the constitutional head, but is also the guide and philosopher, which in Indian parlance, amounts to the concept of guru partly due to the conceptual implication of the words 'philosopher and guide' in the Constitution, partly due to the inherent qualities of self-controlled, self-purified and self-realised dynamism of Shri M.S. Golwalkar, from his days as a professor at the Benares Hindu University down to this day. The present Sarsanghchalak is known as Guruji Golwalkar. In India's cultural traditions, guru is the supreme embodiment of enlightenment, the torch-bearer of Life Divine, the signpost and lighthouse for the wayfarers to forge ahead and reach the pinnacles of spiritual perfection, to gain power through the psychic control of animal nature and live as human beings with dignity and freedom of the twice-borns. In a world given to superficiality and spuriousness of life, the real gurus arc so few, and from among those few gurus, those who could lead an organisation, especially with such a lofty mission and message as the RSS are fewer still. The Sangh and the country are blessed with such a simple, great, humble, energetic, self-realised 'philosopher and guide', as Shri M.S. Golwalkar, the Guruji of millions.

As such an India-wide organisation needs its ideas and ideals to be spread to the remotest village, the RSS envisage a network of propagandists and preachers, called "*pracharaks*". Every great movement in history, as we know them, were not the outcome of writing and academic lecturing; they were the outcome of speakers, preachers and propagandists. The apostles of this new movement, even as Swami Vivekananda envisaged it, must be men of iron will and steely character, who will become the living embodiments of the spirit of Vedanta and will spread the ideals from place to place," Swamiji says.

"Before flooding India with socialistic and political ideas, first deluge the land with spiritual ideas. The first work that demands our attention is that the most wonderful truths confined in our Upanishads, in our scriptures, in our Puranas—must be brought out from the books, brought out from the monasteries, brought out from the forests, brought out from the possession of selected bodies of people and scattered/broadcast all over the land, so that these truths may run like fire all over the country, from North to South and from East to West, from the Himalayas to Cape Comorin, from Sindhu to Brahmaputra."

—Swami Vivekananda

About such apostles of national resurrection, of nation building, along the best of Indian traditions, the Constitution of the RSS lays down the following canon:

(a) (i) "Pracharaks shall be full-time workers selected from amongst those devoted workers of high integrity, whose mission is to serve the society through the Sangh, who, of their own free will, dedicate themselves to the Cause."

(ii) "They will receive no remuneration.

(b) (i) "The Akhil Bharatiya Pracharak-Pramukh will appoint Prant Pracharaks with the consent of the Sarkaryavah and in consultation with the Sanghchalaks concerned.

(ii) "The Prant Pracharak will appoint the Pracharaks for different units in the province in consultation with the Prant Sanghchalak.

(c) "The ultimate authority for the appointment, transfer or discontinuance of the services of the Pracharks shall vest in the Sarkaryavah."

—Article 17

Full-time dedicated souls alone can perform the duty of preachers and propagandists of a great idea. One-pointedness of mind and single-hearted devotion to the cause are essential. Hence those who reach nearer the ideal of Pracharak will be farther and farther removed from the worldly life of householders, whose prime concern is to employ all their time and energy to rear up their family, almost to the exclusion of any other wider interests of nation and country. To these dedicated souls no question of remuneration or lucrative job stands in their way, provided their basic essentials and needs are met. But the Sangh and the RSS authorities will provide for those needs, even as Providence clothes the lilies of the fields and feeds the fowls of the air.

The ideal, discipline and the organisational structure of the RSS, all tend to build up character and such dedicated souls for the cause of Freedom, Country, Culture and Life of Mother India. The uniform, dull, discipline, songs, marches, classes, studies and manifold fields of social services are all directed to imprinting national character to the Swayamsevaks and Swayamsevikas. The Article 20 of the Constitution among other things says:

"Physical training will be given by means of exercises and games organised at a convenient hour every day. Occasional talks and lectures will be arranged for imparting intellectual training and inculcating love for ideals of Hindu Dharma and culture. Periodical classes for Swayamsevaks to be trained as instructors and workers will be arranged. Festivals of cultural importance will be celebrated and members of the public may be invited on such occasions. Agencies and institutions may be established to disseminate knowledge of the ideals and activities of the Sangh and to educate the people generally. In general the Sangh may do all such things and carry on any other work capable of being undertaken in connection with and calculated, directly or indirectly, to promote and achieve any of the objects mentioned in Article 3."

It is because of this organisational discipline, training and idealism that the Sangh had been able to achieve so much during such a short period of twenty-five years and forge ahead in the teeth of opposition. During the partition and after, the vigilance, the nationalist apostolate and mental alertness of the RSS saved the Indian Union from many political and social traps, which the protagonists of communalism had prepared for the people. The Gestapo of Hitler and the Intelligence Service of the British incarnated—as it were—in the vigilance section of the RSS to detect tricks and traps of those who partitioned the country to serve their own interests. Kashmir would have been raped overnight by the Pakistani Pathans had not the vigilant and disciplined RSS sentinels given information, clues and joined action to defend the Kashmir hills, the Indian Switzerland.

There is, however, so much more to be done so that the RSS organisation may be rooted in knowledge, reason, education, discipline and not on pure sentimentalism and cheap popular religious prejudices. But once education of the masses is rooted on nationalistic idealism, when the present deplorable divisions and distinctions between creeds, castes and sub-castes are removed, the battle for national unity and solidarity will be won. It will tax the brains of the most thoughtful, the character of the noblest sons and daughters of Mother India. In this new uphill job of nation-building on the unalloyed gold and priceless gem of nationalism, rationalism and humanism of the Indian culture, the foremost role will have to be played by the RSS, the ideal RSS which will be the ideal haven for all the children of the soil of Mother India, the symbol and substance of that Swaraj which the prophets of modern India dreamt about, the martyrs of the Indian National Army fought and died for, the ideal Indian Republic which the true children of the soil herald, long for and welcome.

□

Chapter-8

The RSS Action for The Economic Swaraj

"My heart is too full to express my feelings. You know it, you can imagine it. So long as the millions live in hunger and ignorance, I hold every man a traitor, who, having been educated at their expense, pays not the least heed to them. I call those men, who strut about in their finery, having got all their money by grinding the poor wretches, so long as they do not do anything for those two hundred millions who are now no better than hungry savages. We are poor, my brothers, we are nobodies, but such have been the instruments of the most High."

—Swami Vivekananda

"Everything in the world is in motion. Life changes, productive forces grow, old relations collapse. It is not the consciousness of men that determines their being, but, on the contrary, their social being that determines their consciousness."

—Karl Marx

"Social relations are closely bound up with productive forces. In acquiring new productive forces, men change their mode of production and in changing their mode of production, in changing the way of earning their living, they change all their social relations. The hand-mill gives you society with feudal lord, the steam-mill, society with industrial capitalist."

—Karl Marx

The main problem in India today is to build up such an economic and social structure that can make the culture of India not a morbid, moribund verbiage, but a living force in the lives of the largest possible number of the citizens. Social life is the outcome of the economic structure and the cultural and political activities are but the manifestations of the healthy economic-social order of a given people. Now as the economic-social factors change, it is clear that the cultural and political forces also must change. Nothing is destroyed, annihilated, but changes are necessary for the survival of the permanent values and verities in the culture and heritage of a people.

Those alone are the realists and real benefactors of modern India who work for the preservation of the culture and spirit of the country not by merely shouting and advertising the empty slogan 'Hinduism in danger', as against its communal counterpart 'Islam in danger', but by working with their own hands to lay solid foundations for the economic freedom and social Swaraj of the people of India. We have to admit the fact that the economic-social degeneration of the larger part of the Indian people is today so deplorable. Merely gloating over our ancient glories and culture—whatever be that glory and culture—is no remedy to the crying needs of the people of India. This stern reality, this staggering iron law of economic slavery, is to be driven home to the minds of every social worker, politician, student, agriculturist and men and women in every walk of life in India. Economics is the basis of all right social relations, of culture, philosophy and religion.

India's past isolationism and separatism from the main world currents have been largely responsible for her political, economic and social slavery. Mere sentimental attachment to Ravana's air-chariot cannot in any way help us from modern aeroplanes. The former is a myth of luxuriant tangled imagination, the latter is a fact. Ganesh and Hanuman may still have some sentimental meaning to those who cannot look to the broad daylight of that humanistic and metaphysical philosophy which is the essence of the *Upanishads* and Vedanta. Similarly the old caste-system, priest-craft, idolatry and manifold social injustices will go the moment the illuministic humanism of Ram Mohun Roy, Vinoba, Ramdas, Kabir, Dayanand, Chaitanya, Nityanand and others reach the remotest corners of the country. As the practice of *sati* can no longer be revived, because we cannot put the clock back, so the weakening, obscurantic, anti-human social practices, specially child marriages, slavery of our womenfolk, are to be removed if we have to survive as a united, solidly-knit people with the economic basis laid sure and social relations made healthy.

We have now to be honest with ourselves. There is no need of mincing words and beating about the bush. We have to be stern realists. In the modern world we have to be modern if we mean business and survive. But this modernism does not mean a thoughtless imitation, uncritical acceptance and disgraceful surrender to the glamour and glitter of foreign civilisation. But this modernism does mean acceptance of those principles and facts without which our life would be anachronistic, and we, as a people, as a nation, as a country, will be slaves of others who are stronger and more up-to-date than ourselves.

In the economic struggle, the challenge of Marxian thought is not to be minimised nor ignored. In some form or other, socialist economy is today a living fact in the majority of nations of the world. Let us be honest. Let us not be deceived by the flavour of the phraseology like spiritualism, God, culture, etc. Let us face facts and answer the straight question, how much are we prepared to accept of the socialist economy in Indian life? There is no need to take recourse to Marx-Engels, Lenin-Stalin version of socialism. There is the socialist tradition in the Indian village *panchayat,* in Guild Socialism in Syndicalism, in the modern types of social security schemes as in England, Switzerland, Scandinavia and corporativism of pre-war Italy. There is socialism in the philosophy of the *Upanishads* and Vedanta, in the books of Plato, in the New Testament, in the writings of Aquinas, Thomas More and Rousseau, Fenelon and Mazzini, in the socio-economic reformism of William Godwin, Henri de Saint-Simon, Charles Fourier, Robert Owen, Louis Blanc, Lassalle and Proudhon. If these foreign socialists wound our nationalist pride, then we may turn our eyes to the greatest children of Mother India, beginning from Lord Buddha, Mahavir and Sankara down to Raja Ram Mohun Roy, Vivekananda, Dayanand and Ramakrishna Paramhamsa, whose economics was essentially socialistic.

Are we brave enough to face facts and surrender to nothing but Truth? Then, what is this bogey about materialism? Does one need so much philosophy and speculation to see that intellectual, moral and spiritual powers are but the outgrowths and after-growths of our physical well-being? *Shariramdyam khuladharma sadhanam*—this Sanskrit proverb corresponds to the other well-tuned English proverb, 'A healthy mind in a healthy body'. This bogey about materialism in economics is the same as the bogey of atheism in religion. But Lord Buddha was an atheist, pure and unalloyed atheist and materialist. The orthodox defenders of vested interests may argue and say "Well, then, that is why Buddhism failed in India and died out." No, Buddhism has not faded nor died out of India. It is Buddhism that created Greater India and became the all-conquering daughter of the racial and national religion of India, even as from the physical confines of Judaism in ancient Palestine, there arose Christianity that spread to the Greco-Hellenistic world and became a universal factor in the history of human civilisation. As Vivekananda said, "Atheists and materialists are more often honest, whereas the theists and spiritualists very often fumble and are hypocrites."

Economic materialism only means that food, clothing and shelter, productive labour, value and material conditions of production come first in human life and that the imponderable ethical values, intellectual speculations and spiritual realisations are the after-growths. This is no denial of spirituality, but only putting philosophy after economics. Here we must be honest and see how far we are prepared to accept this socialist economy, both in its dystopian form as represented by Fourier, Owen and Saint-Simon, and in its scientific form as expounded in Marxism and Fabianism. The materialistic concept means nothing more nor less than placing body as the base, economics as the foundation of spirit and philosophy. Says Karl Marx:

"The materialist conception of history starts from the principle that 'production, and with production the exchange of its products, is the basis of every social order', that in every society which has appeared in history the distribution of the products, and with it the division of society into classes or estates, is determined by what is produced and how it is produced, and how the product is exchanged. According to this conception, the ultimate causes of all social changes and political revolutions are to be sought, not in the minds of men, in their increasing insight into eternal truth and justice, but in changes in the mode of production and exchange, they are to be sought not in the *philosophy* but in the *economics* of the period concerned."

The economics of this century is definitely socialistic. As feudalism has outlived its utility, so capitalism today is practically extinct in most countries, giving birth to modified types of socialism. But socialist economy in India will be definitely Indian and not the sort of socialism of the Labour Party in England or the wonderful social security schemes materialised in countries like Switzerland and Scandinavia. The present economy in our country is both feudal and capitalistic. The inherent contradictions of such economic systems in this period of history will sound the death-knell of the old order of things, giving birth to new societies, new productive forces.

In a world that is sharply divided between socialism and capitalism, where will be the role of the new nationalist force like the RSS? Many have asked the present writer where precisely stood the RSS in the tug-of-war between capitalism and socialism? The writer confesses that he is not a formal member of the RSS, but the ideal RSS, which he envisaged as the successor to the Indian National Congress, as the heir to the reform and renaissance movements like the Brahmo Samaj, Arya Samaj and the Ramakrishna-Vivekananda Mission, must strike the right note and gravitate more to ethical socialist side than to heartless capitalist cruelty.

But there is a vast difference between the socialist leanings of a super-eminently cultural Sangh like the RSS and the political parties like the Labour Party of Great Britain or the Communist parties of the Soviet Union or the Red China. The type of socialism which the Rashtriya Swayamsevaks would support is that economics which is based on the principle of human dignity, social equality and national solidarity. It is true that there are inherent differences among individuals, but an ideal economic and social order should create conditions of equal opportunities for those who are prepared to work and create their own destiny. Indian tradition is definitely democratic and, as long as this democratic spirit is maintained, any government that undertakes the great task of bringing the economic Swaraj to the people is welcome.

To the question put to Shri M.S. Golwalkar: "What form of Government do you prefer—democratic, dictatorial, socialist or communist?", the leader of the RSS replied, "Well, as long as the representatives of the Government are elected by the people, we must be loyal to the Government. I would accept any type, of responsible Government which allows Sangh to work unhindered."

When problems of starvation, hunger, famine and capitalistic exploitation are solved, the next problem will be how to bring about that economic-social order wherein human beings shall not be mere cogs in the machine, but will maintain their dignity, freedom and humanity. Here is the place of libertarian socialism as opposed to totalitarian or dictatorial communism. But which of the two types could deliver goods to the famished and walking skeletons is to be known and judged from the practical realism with which the respective ideologies work. Excepting a few giant individuals, the common man cannot sing the song of freedom, nor can he pronounce the ABC of culture before he has his belly cared for. The painful realities in Indian life will compel any all-India organisation to build culture and philosophy on the basic trinity of food, clothing and shelter. Grinding poverty of the masses is the prime problem which both the ministers and citizens of the Indian Union have first to tackle.

The history of the RSS during the last two decades has shown that not merely academic culture but more primarily service of the people, in its most elementary and basic needs of food and clothing, is most vital. The victims of partition of the country, whether in the Punjab or Bengal, found a ready helping squad, a veritable Indian national army of service in the RSS. During the worst days of the refugee influx from East Pakistan, the RSS did not remain purely a cultural body, but it became a veritable National Volunteer Corps to tend the sick, to feed the hungry, clothe the naked and meet and minimise the material miseries of the children of the soil. At the Sealdah station alone, the RSS volunteers were handling over 1,500 displaced persons a day, feeding them with milk, barley and fruit, with medical attendance to the sick and diseased. About the RSS activities in Howrah station during those days, a report says:

"At Howrah Centre, the Samiti has been daily supplying three chataks of rice, three chataks of atta, potatoes and vegetables with 4 annas per head to nearly two thousand displaced persons daily. In addition over 1,500 are treated medically, clothed and given light refreshments daily. This Centre has also to its credit the rehabilitation of many families by securing jobs for the bread-winners."

—National Guardian, May 14th, 1950

Another feature that became conspicuously clear in those days of refugee relief and rehabilitation is the absence of any trace of provincialism or casteism. If the RSS is merely a Maharashtra affair for the benefit of the Maharashtrians only, why should the youth of Maharashtra raise a fund of several lakhs of rupees to be devoted exclusively for the benefit of the East Bengal refugees? It is the gravitation of the Motherland that is there as their driving force. All those who claim India as their Motherland are Indians, are 'Hindus', whose loyalty is towards their country, to the best of Indian traditions and to the broad basic cultural heritage of India and the wider world outside.

This Motherland of ours today is a land of paupers, ignorant, illiterate, physically debilitated and morally weak millions. The question, then, that is often asked is, "What does this political freedom mean? Does it bring about any real change in the lives of Indians?" Political freedom which we have achieved since the British withdrawal, subsequent upon the living vivisection of indivisible India, has brought us but modicum of *swaraj*, freedom. But the real substance of freedom will only then come when we have solved the economic slavery and brought economic and social *swaraj* to the dumb millions of our people. This *swaraj* is still to be fought for, laboured for and it will be in the price of rivers of sweat, tears and blood. If *Bhagavad Gita* is the spiritual, military and social Constitution of India, then broad-based socialism is the gospel of the economic *swaraj* of the country.

In this economic *swaraj*, the wealthy and powerful *ut sic (few)* will no more gain leadership, but only those who are leaders of productive labour and real service to the people.

Once the kings were autocratic despots. Today our governors are nominal heads, who do not serve but adorn occasions and hardly have any pattern of service to set to the people, save their pious exhortations and sermons to be good, when they themselves in their lives contradict their teachings. They draw an enormous salary, quite out of proportion to their service and the average income of an Indian citizen. To mention but one instance, look at the West Bengal Governor's budget for the year 1949-50. It is as follows:

Governor's salary sumptuary allowance	66,000
Military Secretary	30,000
Secretary	1,21,200
Doctor, furniture, carpets, etc.	1,50,000 16,000 35,500
Cars, servants, etc.	1,34,500
Travelling allowance	90,700
Total (Rs.)	**6,44,000***

** The sum total is found incorrect, may be some typo: Ed.*

This is the amount a governor, a disciple of Gandhiji, Dr. Kailash Nath Katju lavishes. How can he then feel for the people? His ornamental post is reduced to self-advertisement in journals, in manifold items of vanity which will buy him many material blessings of earth through public money that is collected for public good. The rich and the aristocratic class must lend their lip-service to God and priests, to idols and caste, out-caste and sub-caste systems, for it is on these baits their victims fall and the huge masses are held under their sway.

In the new economic *swaraj* that is to be brought about the old order of privileges and positions will not count, but only the democratic test of intrinsic charter, productivity and capacity to serve. This is the *sanskriti,* this is the culture of India, as it is the basic culture of humanism everywhere, at all times. There are times when recitation of beads and passion for individualistic salvation are to be abandoned and the cause of people, nation, country upheld. We are now passing through that stage in Indian history. The skill, tenacity, character, sincerity, truthfulness and the right intentions of the men and women of the country are on trial. If we fail this time to make use of the Dharma and culture of the land as a dynamic and creative force to solve the basic economic and social problems of the country, we will have lost our golden chance to set our house in order and pave way for the real unity, solidarity, prosperity and happiness of the Motherland. Let us have no illusions about it.

The present Government has forfeited the trust and the mandate of the people by vivisecting the country without consulting the people or their cultural representatives. The present Government forfeited the trust by continuing to be the appendage of the British Commonwealth, by devaluing Indian currency to suit the interests of the foreigners and their yes-men here, by continuing the appeasement policy towards Pakistan, by failing to lay solid foundations of a new economic and social order which, the Nehru leadership, while fighting the British, had pledged to give to the people. Now they forget that time is of the essence. They are issuing paper schemes after schemes, reiterating promises, repeating their pious exhortations. All their plans and schemes have proved to be mere size without substance. In the meantime, the plight of the people in the land goes from bad to worse. Instead of taking the side of the have-nots, of the dispossessed and expropriated millions, of the toiling labourer and the peasant, the present leadership has predilections for the money-lords, for the vested interests and forces of reaction in the country.

If historical developments take place according to fixed laws, if the laws of the philosophy of history are correct, then we may know for certain that we can only survive in so far as we are prepared to hasten the wheels of economic development of the country, taking adequate measures, either to curtail the population of the land within the limits of our economic resources, or to increase the economic resources to such an extent that the productive forces keep pace with the present population flood. If birth-control is immoral, then there is self-control which is part of Indian culture. If, however, self-control cannot be practiced due to the ignorance and weakness of our people, then the other alternative is to substitute bullock ploughs with modern tractors and maintain handloom industry only as a supplement to the mechanised, electrified forms of this super-industrial age.

We have to admit that the general masses of our people are idle, indolent, ignorant and weak. This is a fact which we must recognise so that based on facts of our actual life, we may forge ahead to the great task of nation-building that awaits us. Then again in our self-conceited isolation and nationalist pride, let us not close doors to the outside world. India's culture, her philosophy, is a great achievement in the history of human civilisation, but as Swami Vivekananda said, "The West has excelled India in political and economic and scientific fields. We need both. No greater calamity could obstruct the cause of healthy Indian nationalism than by getting ourselves self-imprisoned within the meshes of our own country and ignore, or still worse, close our doors to the world outside. If we do this, then the sort of economic-socio-political slavery, which we may have to face so grimly will be even worse than what we have been experiencing for the last several centuries.

Merely shouting against the triumphant advance of Communism will solve no problems. Communism thrives and triumphs in those countries where there is too much talk of God, religion, priests and idols, but in fact, the vast majority of the people, the 90 per cent, the *Demos*, are left illiterate, ignorant, victims of manifold economic, social and religious exploitation. That is the reason, quite against the predictions of Karl Marx, the Communist revolution did not take place in industrially and, scientifically advanced countries like England or Germany, but in the intensely religious, but illiterate, poverty-stricken, exploited countries like the Soviet Union and China. Pious talks and pious friends do not solve problems of hunger and famine and where the axe of poverty grinds hard, there is the fertile field for Communism. That is why the most practical American observers in the Far East, in South-east Asia and the Middle East are convinced that the answer to the Communist challenge is not merely bayonets and atom bombs, but more food, healthier living conditions and higher standards of life. The bite of hunger is the same everywhere, whether one is a European, Asiatic or African, a Christian, Hindu or Muslim. It is this basic human fact that should be taken into consideration. It may also be mentioned that long before Karl Marx or Communism or any other Communist thinker had propounded his doctrines on economics, the Upanishadic sages put food on par with *dharma*. They went even still higher and identified food with Brahma. Says the *Upanishad*:

अन्नं ब्रह्मेति व्यजानात्।
अन्नंध्योव खल्विमानि भुतानि जायन्ते।
अन्नं न जातानि जिवन्ति।
अन्नं प्रयन्ताभिसं विशन्ति।
अन्नं न निन्त्यत्। तद वृतंम। प्राणे व अन्नं।
अन्नं न परिक्षितां। तद् वतंम। आपो व अन्नं।
अन्नं बहु कुवित। तद् व्रतमं। प्रथिविः व अन्नं।
न कञ्चन वसतौ प्रत्यचक्षित। तद् व्रतमं॥

This Upanishadic dictum may be paraphrased as follows:

"From food are born all beings in this world and by food do they live, and after death, they become food again for other beings. Food is indeed Brahman. We should not speak ill of food. We should produce plenty of food. Let no one be turned away who comes hungry."

—Taittirya Upanishad, HI 4, 9,10,12

Food, as the main sustenance of physical body, is given such importance in the Upanishadic teachings because those dispassionate and clear-minded sages knew that mind is the product of a healthy body, as spiritual powers are the after-growths of healthy body and healthy mind. They had insisted on "grow more food" campaign far more rationally than our political propagandists. These senseless power-mongers and career-seekers are merely content with slogans. While the 'grow more food' campaign is in paper, the grow-more-children is a fact that threatens to exhaust the fertility and resources of Mother India. We today stand as a beggar nation before the resourceful countries and we do not find people outside to fill our begging bowls. The rich Mr, Miss or Mrs Bombay and Calcutta may hoard up, store and dance in mirth and joy, but the average man in the deficit provinces and regions of the Union famish, fade away and die by inches.

The significance of the labour movements that fought for the dignity of productive labour over and against the vested interests of monopoly capitalism, birth-privileges and stereotyped forms of slavery should be recognised by any movement that aims at the cultural, political, educational or social uplift of a country like India. The labouring loyal children of the soil are the true citizens and not the vociferous defenders of vested interests of the monied-idle class. The test of democracy is only character, the intrinsic merit of the individual and not the time-honoured traditional worship of the rich and the privileged.

The task of providing jobs for the citizens, to guarantee them their basic minimum living conditions, the ways and means of developing the economic resources, the mobilisation of the entire manpower for the task of building up and cementing a united, democratic republic, when the present Congress Government collapses, will devolve over the RSS, if the official and non-official members, admirers and sympathisers of the movement are conscious of their mission. If they could read the writings on the walls, it will become all the more clearer that a new political organisation, with cultural and eminently nationalistic spirit, with the ideals of service and sacrifice, must be there to take the place of the present decrepit Congress. This eventuality is not excluded when Shri Golwalkar replied to the question:

"Supposing the Congress disintegrates and there is anarchy in the country, would you still confine yourself to cultural activities?"

To which question Shri Golwalkar answered, "If the Congress completely disintegrates and anarchy rules the country, and there is nobody to take over, and if everybody presses me, in that eventuality I may sacrifice a part of my spiritualism and accept the responsibility." Now this is more than a mere eventuality. And we need men and women to shoulder responsibilities. Unlike in many other civilised countries, we are more hero-worshippers than sustained soldiers of clear-cut ideology with the result that when the leader goes, the throne remains vacant. None has yet replaced Gandhiji or Subhas. True, Hedgewar was replaced by Shri M.S. Golwalkar. But we need men to replace also the present political leadership of the country. Vacuum cannot be the basis of nation-building, specially when confronted with such huge economic problems, for, as Shri Golwalkar says, "The first thing with us is culture which includes food."

□

Chapter-9

Hindu Cultural Renaissance and Communist Challenge

"I believe that Sangh ideology can act as a corrective to the Communist mode of thinking in Bharat. In the beginning he may remain a Communist as well do the Sangh work. But I feel eventually he will secede from the Communist Party."

—Shri M.S. Golwalkar

"The word Hindu State is nowadays unnecessarily misrepresented as a theocratic one, which would wipe out all other sects. On the contrary, I want to state today that this State or country which has been made over to us is a Hindu State, and it is also a secular State, and all those who are now non-Hindus have equal rights to be here as Hindus do. From the point of view of what is considered a democracy, i.e. rule by the majority, when the vast majority of people are Hindus, the State is democratically Hindu, but the State cannot exclude all those who live here to occupy any position of honour in the State. During those days when the Muslim League was carrying on propaganda, they said that Congress was a Hindu body. We may deny it but that was in a sense true, and though a Hindu body, it did not exclude others, but on the other hand, all those who thought alike with them, were occupying positions of great respect and honour even in those days. These are all only qualifications and it is unnecessary to call it a Hindu State or a secular State. In other words, it is not necessary to say anything about it. We never qualified our State by the word 'Hindu'. That was misreporting of one of speeches by some paper. I was sorry that such misreporting should have been then."

The main political and socio-economic force in the world today is Communism. In most countries, it works as part and parcel of an international movement for the emancipated working and peasant class to wrest all political power and subject all the non-productive idleness to the productive forces everywhere. The claim of Communism for a new world order cannot be easily dismissed. Whereas the challenge of Communism is against the anachronistic set-up of the modern socio-economic conditions of the working class and therefore so real and vital, the remedy often offered from various quarters is academic, or sheer propaganda of the power of the moneyed class. Another group of militarists intend to fight Communism through the atomic explosions and on the point of bayonets. Nothing is more puerile than all these toy-fights by the beared babies against the giant of world Communism.

The added strength of Communism in the world today is its religious zeal and a sort of missionary fire. Communism fights God, scriptures, religions of the traditional types, but it speaks of justice, social and economic equity, of brotherhood and peace. In the modern world we may dispense with words like God, Bible, Koran, *Vedas*, priests and ceremonies and idol worship, we can never dispense with words like justice, truth, righteousness, character, etc. and it is on these words most of the social revolutions of history hinge. This shows that mankind, in its onward struggle for social justice and progress, could dispense with almost everything save humanity. There is nothing higher or greater than humanity. Had it not been for this humanistic appeal, the major part of the world would not have today owed allegiance to Communism. The international link of Communism today is second only to the Catholic Church. In fact, international Communism is the major rival to international Catholicism of the Roman Catholic Church.

Yet, there is something that is so miserably lacking in the Communistic philosophy of life. It is not its violent revolutionary character that is found to be as wanting as its lack of faith in the imponderable values of human spirit. If Communism seeks justice, it seeks it only for the industrial labourer and the peasant, for a particular class, but not for the theologians, philosophers and mystics. Even the most sympathetic students of Communism have felt the need of some corrective to the one-sided drive of the Communist parties all over the globe. In India, Shri M.S. Golwalkar says that the RSS, as based on the best cultural patrimony of the Indian sub-continent can offer the needed corrective to Communism.

None can today underestimate or ignore the drive of international Communism led by Moscow. It spreads like the new religion of the twentieth century. The prophecy of Karl Marx himself that the most advanced nations like Germany, England and America would be the countries where Communist ideology would triumph proved a failure. It was in the illiterate, poverty-stricken, economically-backward countries, outstanding victims of economic-social injustice like the Tzarist Russia and corrupt Chiang-Kai-Shek's China that the Revolution swept over triumphantly and brought about a sigh of relief and a glow of material happiness to the have-nots and poorest sections of the people. It is so obvious to anyone who could diagnose the causes of Communism that it is *grinding* poverty, socio-economic injustice, canonised and sanctified under the name of legions and blessed by an ignorant priesthood that offers incense and is prepared to bless the vested interests of the rich and look down upon and ignore the pangs and tears, sweat and blood of the common people that become the fertile ground for Marxism to germinate and glow. Revolution in history is known to have taken place only when the common man, the have-nots and the victims of socio-economic injustice have been grounded down, pulverised under the feet of the rich and the society could not go any further without volcanic eruption.

The propertied and moneyed class, oblivious of their duties to serve the people, invoke authority and police to defend their ill-gotten wealth, close eyes to the infernal sufferings of their fellow-beings, tear the golden strings of mercy, compassion and charity asunder and continue to indulge in their death-dance of sex and wine, until the flood of revolution overtakes them unawares, when the socio-economic order is turned upside down. The French Revolution has not ended. It survives today in Communism. True, the common people of India are meek and mild, long-suffering, patient and non-violent. But injustices perpetrated by the glamorous rich and the powerful towards the dumb millions cannot go on forever without crying to Heaven for justice, if not for vengeance. The crimes of injustice, accumulated through indolence, indulgence and indifference of the plutocrats are to be cured in time lest the seeds of injustice germinate, and the country is caught in the fires and flames of revolution that purify the accumulated debris and filth of centuries of economic slavery.

Today in India there is only one major force that can meet the Communist challenge, and that is the ideal RSS. Congress has grown decrepit and, although Pandit Nehru and Co. could prate and boast that the Congress is today as "strong as an elephant", we know Congress is a spent force in the life of the nation today. The Hindu Mahasabha has outlived its purpose for which it came into existence at the time of the League as its communal rival. Today the neo-nationalism of the RSS, rooted in the neo-Vedantism and strong organisational and disciplinary strength, is the main national force. On this strong nationalism, all citizens of India can unite to fulfil their patriotic mission as common children of Mother India.

"More than that, the RSS is a crucible in which caste, class and provincial angularities melted away and the fire of national love harmonised the intents, purpose and the ways of the Swayamsevaks."

—M.S. Golwalkar

In this burning crucible of self-sacrificing service will melt away the remnants of communalism, hypocrisy, pauperism, injustice, indiscipline, indifference, duplicity and such other weak points that have kept us divided, degenerate, disorganised and have made India a laughing stock to foreigners. The embryo, the nucleus that is there in the form of the RSS for the national resurrection still needs tending, watching, ordering and organising until India is built up anew on the foundations of

Vedantic humanism and socio-economic justice restored to the common man. Culture is no culture that cannot provide bread and butter to the shrivelled bellies and walking skeletons. That culture that has no practicality for the heartening and re-animation of the paupers of the land; that cannot educate the illiterates, clothe the naked and house the houseless is mere arm-chair philosophy and academic verbiage which are of no avail. If we indulge in mere culture-phrases without removing with our own hands the glaring injustices which the common man of India has fallen a victim to, we have thereby betrayed our trust and another chance of arresting realistically the Communistic flood, we will have thereby missed.

Indian philosophy, Indian social system and, above all, the new upsurge of creative and dynamic nationalism can teach that not class-struggle, as the Marxian Communists uphold, but class-co-operation is the right method and the royal road to lasting peace. This new co-operative way for co-operative peace is what the world at large is sighing for. India has a philosophy, an attitude, a culture and system that can help this co-operative way and in that way put up the strongest bulwark and answer to the Communist challenge that is based on the theory of class struggle. Man is essentially co-operative than competitive.

"A new type of thinking is necessary if man is to survive and move to higher levels. In previous ages a nation's life and culture could be protected to some extent by the growth of barriers in national competition. Today we must abandon competition and secure co-operation. This must be the central fact in all our international affairs, otherwise we face certain disaster. Past thinking and methods did not prevent World War. Future thinking must prevent wars."

—Albeit Einstein

The RSS believes India can become the *jagatguru*. The Communist challenge can be met through the cultural soul of Mother India when she could show practical methods of class-co-operation. Nothing is impossible. Nothing is too late in life. All that are needed are grit, courage and conviction.

The supreme test of realism of any political or cultural organisation that emerges out in India today as the saviour of the country will be its earnestness, seriousness and practical sense in tackling the problems of country-wide unemployment, illiteracy, ill-health, grinding poverty, public immorality and such other material and ethical needs of the common man. The Asoka wheel, the national flag, the *Bhagwa* flag of the RSS, all are to be symbols to awaken and arouse the youth of the country to come forward in their hundreds of thousands to tackle these basic problems. At the *Guru-Puja Utsava* of the RSS branch at Cuttack towards the end of August 1950, Shri Raghunath Swami Acharya of Vrindavan, presiding over the function, said,

"This flag is the traditional Hindu flag. Our national heroes like Sivaji, Guru Gobind Singh, Banda Bairagi, Rana Pratap and others fought under this banner. With a great national spirit your organisation is working and that is why it could do great work in Punjab and Delhi where there are great difficulties. It is this organisation which has saved our capital a few years ago in September 1947 from fanatical outbursts."

"Three things are required for national uplift, viz.—(1) Self-development, (2) Physical development and (3) National development. Under self-development comes the development of individual, under physical development comes the development of the power factor of the nation, while under National development comes the development of nationality, culture, upkeep of the Swaraj."

To save the country not only from the communalism of Pan-Islamism of Pakistan but also from senseless slavery of economic materialism is the paramount task that lies ahead of young India. Then the maintenance of Swaraj, not merely the political, which they say we have got after the vivisection of India and the British withdrawal, but more so of the economic and social *swaraj* of the country, is not possible unless and until the country has a network of national volunteers, of disciplined and patriotic youth. Mercenary soldiers will not be able to withstand the onslaughts of modern armies from outside, nor face the economic-social slavery from within the country. It will be the attempt of the RSS to mobilise the entire country and canalise all the manpower, the youth resources and assign to each and every son and daughter of Hindustan the duty that is his or hers by vocation and innate tendencies.

Now is the hour of action, the hour of grace. Now is the time for Indians to wake up to the hard realities and stem the tides of anti-national forces through strengthening of the RSS, which is, if properly catered for and nurtured, the natural heir to the best of Indian cultural heritage, the only force that can offer corrective to Communistic inrush and bring back unity, solidarity and strength to beloved Indian nation. If we do not strengthen such a selfless and nationalistic force as the RSS, the other alternative is either chaos and disorder, further division and despondency in the country or the triumph of Hammer and Sickle in place of the *Bhagwa* flag. Herein comes the importance of that memorable warning, call and exhortation, all combined, given by Shri Golwalkar, to the people of India. He says:

"The work of the Sangh should claim the first priority of the attention of every true son of Bharat for the future of our nation and the future of generations yet unborn depends on it. The revival of Bharatiya culture and the building of national character are the true foundations of a bright future for our nation and not the spate of paper plans and schemes. Have you ever thought of the paradox of a nation 34 crores-strong wallowing in the slough of despondency and under the heels of foreign invaders? From the Himachal in the North to Kanyakumari in the South there is one unifying force, ennobling, though to the superficial observers there are diverse people and races in the stream of Sanatan Bharatiya culture and tradition based on high spiritual values. And yet today we see a babel of tongues and welter of clashing interests eating into the vitals of this Bharatiya society of 34 crore sons and daughters. This deplorable state of affairs is due to our forgetting our Bharatiya culture and tradition that bind the people from the North to South in one organic whole. In one word, we have forgotten our ancient Dharma—our obligations to ourselves, our nation and our society.

"We have what Westerners would call, lost our social

conscience. It is this lack of social conscience, or I, as a Bharatiya, would put it, our turning away from the ancient Dharmic path which is the root cause of our national degradation, cultural bankruptcy and economic ruin. The British have gone but have we sufficient national character to defend our freedom and prevent any future invasion from any quarter? The Western nations enslaved the East by sending first missionaries, traders and then finally politically and economically dominated the countries of the East. The same process in different form is going on in the world. The lesson of China should be a sufficient object lesson to us. China as an individual with its ancient culture and tradition are things of the past. The fissiparous tendencies and the clash of ideologies have been the undoing of China. No true Bharatiya would wish China to be repeated in our country. In the context of international set-up of today, we have to evolve out such a social and national order in our land that every Bharatiya forms an important unit of Bharatvarsha and that unity and community of ideas could only be built on the rock-bottom of our ancient culture and tradition and on nothing else. The Sangh is quite confident that once our people are brought together on the eternal platform of Bharatiya culture and tradition, the strength of Bharatvarsha could be built to resist all the onslaughts of foreign invasion and foreign ideologies. But mere wishing has no meaning unless actual work is done The Sangh by preaching the message of love and brotherliness among the sea of humanity of 34 crores hopes to achieve this laudable object. And for the consummation of this happy end, the Sangh expects the loyal and loving co-operation of every son and daughter of Bharatmata and who believes in our Sanatan culture and tradition."

—Shri M.S. Golwalkar's address in Saurashtra on the role of the RSS

These are words with deep significance in the present context of Indian history. Communistic typhoons sweep across countries and continents swifter than an eagle's flight across the air. But those countries alone survive which are true to the ethical values, imponderable human verities enshrined in the cultural heritage of their nation. Man is not merely food, clothing and shelter. The most we admit is that spirit is an after-growth of the basic essentials of our physical needs. But man is man through his mind, his ideas, his ideals. In proportion as we are prepared to reach this invisible and invincible realm of human mind to that degree we realise and preserve the gems and treasures of our spiritual heritage. Revolution can only overtake a country when the patriarchs of spirituality prefer to dwell self-complacently in their celestial mansions without caring to descend to the solid earth, and tackle the manifold economic and social problems of the country It is in this sense we believe that the RSS is not going to get enshrined in the niche of glory after fame, and remain self-satisfied in popular applause and vainglorious isolationist touchmenotism. The RSS, as the spirit of its founder and the message of the best interpreters and spokesmen of the Sangh testify, means business and by facing the basic economic problems of the country, make the Communistic challenge either superfluous or unreal. But before facing the Communist challenge, we must liquidate this satanic capitalism in all its exploiting phases and by founding Co-operative Commonwealth Corporativism based on economic and social justice, rooted in the dignity of labour.

It is this sense of urgency and realism towards facing the economic problems of the country that the RSS is keenly aware of. On the Republic Day, January 26th, 1950, the RSS chief said:

"Time marches on. Some parts of the glorious picture of a happy Motherland envisaged by all patriots and martyrs have been translated into reality. But despite that the picture remains incomplete. To complete it, we must temper our joy of new-won rights in the Constitution with the realisation of the problems that face us today. One crore hungry, homeless, unemployed, sorrowful refugees are in our midst today. Problems of poverty and misery face us on every side. To solve them we must co-relate every right with duties and responsibility."

—*M.S. Golwalkar*

Yes, our political freedom is of little avail without achieving the economic *swaraj* for not only the displaced persons and victims of partition, but also for the many crores of the have-nots, unemployed illiterates of the country. If healthy and true nationalism, as represented by RSS fails to do it, we may have to go through the agony and birth-pangs of a new socio-economic order, as it happened in China. If we do not want repetition of China in India, then we should shoulder responsibilities to face economic problems courageously and solve them realistically. अन्नं ब्रह्म:—Food is Brahma.

Communist challenge is basically economic. On this basis the inrush of Communistic forces should be met. Besides the economic cancer, there are various other factors that make the Communist vessel sail fast in the agitated sea of life today. The Western democracies are still languishing under their white superiority complexes which have not grown lighter or weaker. Their past imperialist holdings, their subjugation of the coloured continents, their racial pride and arrogance still continue to infect the still politically enslaved countries like Malaya, Indochina, South African Union, Belgian Congo and a good many other countries, still under the white man's heels, and which still are the living patterns of racial discrimination and white man's burden. In South Africa, the Africans, Indians, coloured races and mixed races are treated with contempt and scorn by the whites. In America, the Negro problems continue to be the white man's sore in their land. These racial humiliations, political subjugation and economic exploitation by the white races have been another factor in making the Communist fires burn high and consume those countries which were hitherto politically enslaved or economically backward, and bring them back to a state of power and self-respect, economic self-sufficiency and military invincibility. The world forces work in favour of Communism. Let us not forget that, let us not live in an illusory world.

When we know that India's soul is Truth and Freedom par excellence, it will become clearer that the passion for bringing justice to the common suffering masses, serving the downtrodden, humble and the lost, is the practical philosophy in consonance with the letter and spirit of Vedanta. The RSS itself was born not as an academic and exclusively cultured society, but as a mass movement to emancipate the paupers and illiterates of Mother India, win political, economic, social and all-sided freedom, *mukti,* emancipation, not any longer by shouting slogans or through cheap political propaganda, but through service, through holding firm to the essential culture of the soil. The life of Dr. Hedgewar was itself a lesson of service, sacrifice, purity embodied. He did not wear the *gerua* colour nor he put ashes and sack clothes around him, but he was a *sanyasin* without these external paraphernalia, which more often are being utilised by the sycophants to deceive the ignorant and serve their own selfish ends. Similarly today Shri Golwalkar is at heart and spirit a *sanyasin* and teaches a practical *vedantin,* and yet there is no show and glamour about him, for his eyes and heart are firmly fixed on the rock of Indian culture. "Culture, which", he says, "that includes also food."

Young Keshav Baliram Hedgewar will ever remain in Indian history as a supreme pattern of patriotism, political realism and social justice and one of the boldest soldiers who fought the battle of righteousness and fell to consolidate the defences and inner resources of young India. His short life (1890-1940) is the argument and proof of a dedicated soul who lived but for one sole purpose—the resurrection of Mother India. Because he sought and fought to revive Bharatiya culture, there is no justification whatsoever to charge him of the sin of communalism. For the fundamental thesis all sane nationalists hold is that India is their Motherland and the culture and spirit of the soil, prior to the Muslim or Christian domination, is the spirit and culture of every true Bharatiya. It matters not who is a caste Hindu, outcaste, or sub-caste, whether one is born of Hindu, Muslim or Christian parents. All those who stuck to the gun and defended the culture of the soil of India and built his or her future on that solid basis is a Bharatiya, a Hindu, an Indian. It is in this sense Gandhiji, Rabindranath, Vivekananda, Hedgewar, Golwalkar and all genuine patriots and nationalists continue to be the pointers to the way.

The destiny of 381 million of Indians, plus the mutilated parts of India, called Pakistan, may be held in the hollow of one single man, if that man is sufficiently representative of the spirit of the people. Mahatma Gandhi was one such man. Subhas Chandra Bose was one such man. Golwalkar is one such man. The life of a Gandhi or Subhas was the most eloquent commentary to the type of economic and social *swaraj* the people of India, remaining true to their traditions, can and must build up. Their life spoke out that the present gulf between the possessing few and the dispossessed many should be bridged. Their eminent and unsullied character was the supreme challenge and expiation to the vices of over-indulgence, indolence and indifference of millions of their own countrymen whose veritable God is nothing but Venus and Mammon. Their lives show that the country's salvation is more in internal discipline, personal and individual character than in slavishly imitating the glamorous machine civilisation and the dazzling rays of industrial progress. Their life taught us that scientific and industrial progress is of no avail if there is not corresponding progress in the ethical stature of man. If then, we in India fail to understand the significance of the lives of the prophets and reformers and revolutionaries of renascent India, and adjust and orientate the country to the principles of the economic and social swaraj which they taught us and bequeathed to posterity as their permanent legacy, there is every chance of India going the Communist way. But action and steps should be taken without delay. Time is of the very essence of the much needed economic and social revolution, which alone gives meaning to the political freedom.

Communism is the easiest and cheapest road to achieve economic swaraj. But the RSS, working patiently to arouse the people to their sense of personal responsibilities, is working for the economic freedom on the humanistic way. Hence its fruits are more lasting. It is the unity based on national culture that is being sought by the RSS as different from-if not opposed to the cheap slogan: Workers of the world unite! Progress is then only progress when the progressists build their temple of Man on Humanity, and not on the shaky sands of expediency and an exclusive appeal to our animalish nature alone.

It is "culture that includes food" that is the basis of unity and strength; and to work for that ideal to be realised more progressive methods than ruthless instigation to the workers to rise in revolt are needed. Education and not sword is the more progressive path for the humans.

"In the present welter of contradictions and divisions, the realisation of the fundamental unity of Bharatiya culture itself may be considered as progress. Any persuation that diverts the people from unity to fission must be considered retrograde. Today we find fissi-parous tendencies to divide into absurd and hopeless divisions. Are we going back to the times when people of our country, because of lack of transport and communication, did not realise this fundamental unity and fell prey to foreigners? Now that the Britishers have left our country, say, by our good fortune, the same tendencies continue to exist even today."

—M.S. Golwalkar

Communists divide people into the working class, the new Israel, the chosen people of God, and the bour-geoisie. The communalists divide the people still further. It is only nationalism and humanism that can be corrective to these divisions and pave way for unity and solidarity. It is precisely herein that the new young movement initiated by Dr. Hedgewar could stem the tide of soulless material industrialism and machine civilisation which popular Communism upholds. If the RSS or any other Indian cultural movement undertake the task of solving the economic and social problems it will be with the vision and power of the Absolute, based on that ethics and philosophy that is the unique patrimony for us in India. Here again warns Shri Golwalkar:

"The question now is how we cannot understand the country's interest? The reason is that we have not cultivated that spirit of service which the greatest exponents of Bharatiya culture, like Paramahansa have propounded. He saw God even in the destitutes and worshipped them as 'Narayanas'. SOCIETY IS GOD. We should worship the Almighty manifest in the nation. But today social service has become more a bargain than sacrifice. This is because we are trying to imitate others, though we have got our own inheritance of knowledge and culture. By imitating other people we would be making a compendium of these ways of life. We do not want to be

mere 'carbon copies', lacking originality. We will be looked down as those who take inspiration from others. Can we stand on our own legs and lead the world? Can we at least lead Asia? It is a very good thing to lead; but on what basis? Once we did lead the whole world. Unless we have got something original and unless we study and incorporate these ideas in us, we cannot give any lead. We think that we raise ourselves only by repeating. That only brings us into spiritual subjection. It is for this reason that we should revive our own way of life; our own culture and revitalise our society on the basis of this cultural oneness. Revitalising is often dubbed down as reaction. But the revival of a truth or the revitalisation of a permanent order cannot be and is not reaction".

—M.S. Golwalkar

To the communistic challenge, then, there is the Bhagava Flag of the RSS that rises high up in the air with the call to the people not to lose heart, not to abandon themselves to the disruptive forces of foreign, imported and exotic ideologies, but to stand firm on the rock of India's eternal cultural soul, to get indissolubly united as one people and nation and one race, and lay the foundations of a new economic and social order that will not only render Communism superfluous, but also will give a stronger, healthier and nobler ideal to live by and die for the children of Mother India.

This then is the new call, the new urge and apostolate of the RSS in the new order that Free India is looking ahead to bring about. The trumpeters and workers of the RSS sound the clarion call to the country, heralding that the economic and social *swaraj* which Free India is wanting to create must spring from the tap-root of India's own culture, her philosophy, her way of life, her sociology and not merely grafting imported boughs to the tree of Indian civilisation. It is this tree of knowledge and wisdom that India grows the real Kalpataru, the tree that fulfils all healthy desires of human hearts.

Self-respect, self-confidence and sure footing of Indians demand that they should on no account fall a victim to the momentary dilatation which foreign undigested ideologies give. Ours is the ideal world made real, the impossible of the weak and fools made possible and tangible, and embark upon and fulfil the nation-building task that is before us. Unity, national solidarity, human warmth and rational torch will guide us on amidst this encircling gloom, yonder to the shore of *swaraj* which looms in the minds of many nationalists, but still remains unborn in India today. It will be the target and task of the nationalist and cultural organisations like the RSS to lead the people of India to that promised land of our dreams.

□

Chapter-10

Neo-Hinduism, The RSS and The Indian Republic

"I have practiced all religions—Hinduism, Islam, Christianity and I have also followed the paths of the different Hindu sects. I have found that it is the same God towards whom all are directing their steps, though along the different paths.

"The tank has several *ghats*. At one, Hindus draws water in pitchers, and call it *jal*, at another Mohammedans draw water in leather bottles, and call it *pani*, at a third, Christians call it *water*. Can we imagine that the water is not *jal*, but only *pani* or water. How absurd! The substance is one under different names and everyone is seeking the same substance. Every religion of the world is one such *ghat*. Go direct. With a sincere and earnest heart by any of these *ghats* and you will reach the water of Eternal Bliss. But say not that your religion is better than that of another.

"Different creeds are but different paths to each and one God. Diverse are the ways that lead to the temple of Mother Kali at Kalighat in Calcutta. Similarly various are the paths that take men to the house of the Lord. Every religion is nothing but one such path.

"The mind and intellect can comprehend and put in terms of language the range of thought up to the Vishishtadvaita and no further. In its perfection, the Absolute and the manifestation are seen to be equally real—the Lord's name, His abode and He Himself are found to be composed of this one spiritual substance. Everything is spiritual, the *varna* being only in form.

"The Advaita is the last word in realisation. It is something to be felt in *samadhi*, for it transcends mind and speech."

—*Shri Ramakrishna Paramhamsa*

The above-quoted saying of Ramakrishna is the epitome of the essence of Neo-Hinduism, and is the foundation on which to build the new Indian Republic. The masons and builders are the soldiers of the RSS, the brave sons and daughters of India who know their country, loyal to the essential spirit of Indian civilisation and are devoted and dedicated to the cause of serving India and Mankind.

All quarrels about religions are quarrels about straw. The old religions divided man against man, caste against caste, creed from creed; the new religion of the twentieth century proclaims aloud the fundamental unity of all religions and the basic identity of Self-realisation or God-consciousness in every religion. This is the new light which irradiates from India, thanks to the great experiments made on the phenomena of religions by such sages like Shri Ramakrishna, Vivekananda, Shri Aurobindo, Ramana Maharshi, Anandamayi Devi and other spiritual giants of Modern India. Gandhiji, Netaji, Rabindranath and all other moderns confirm this central truth and bold assertion that religions and sects are but paths to reach the same goal.

If religious values are set aside, if ethics are discarded, then the only gospel for the modern world is the Marx-Engels-Lenin-Stalin versions of Materialistic Communism and economic determinism. But if the message of Christs and Buddhas, Sankaras and Ramanujas, Laotzes and Confutzes, of Platos and Rumis are to persist in this world, side by side with economico-social progress of mankind, then it is absolutely necessary to harken to the claim of the Neo-Vedantic revival, as initiated through the God-intoxicated life and dedicated service and sacrificial offerings of the two great prophets of Modern India, Shri Ramakrishna Paramahansa, the Seer, and Swami Vivekananda, the St. Paul of Neo-Vedantism.

India's message through the ages has been the gospel of strength, of power born out of Self-knowledge and Self-realisation. In fact, today more than in any other period in Indian history, it is this gospel of strength and power that the Young India needs. But this power and strength are not the weakness based on the armed forces of the country, but the power based on the self-discovery of every son and daughter of Bharat of the roots from which he or she sprang, the core of her physical and psychical make-up, the source of his or her perennial inspiration and the powerful dynamite that is the Philosophy and fact of Self-realisation. God is nothing save the highest ideal of perfected man. God is strength; God is Power. There is no God other than Truth and Perfect Humanity. It is this gospel of strength born out of self-confidence and self-mastery that is to be spread.

Weakness in all its forms has to go. Strength and strength alone pays. Religion is strength. God is strength. This spiritual strength is invincible and unbeatable even with the most violent militarist war machines of the world. The soul-force, of which the latest exponents were men like Vivekananda and Mahatma Gandhi is the specific qualification of Mother India and this soul-force is her invaluable and priceless gift to the world at large. Then only India has fulfilled her mission when she has given this message to the world. Vedanta shines anew under the new light which Science sheds to the world. Vedanta is the Everest in the history of both Eastern and Western Philosophy. Its heights cannot be climbed, save by those who have realised their Self. Vedanta is the philosophy of Power and Strength which India today so badly needs, not merely the strength of Nazi Germany, Atomic America or Soviet Union, but the Power that is born of the strength of the discovery and realisation of the Self. There is no weakness, all are manifestations of the Self, Power and Infinite Strength.

"Vedanta recognised no sin, it only recognises error, and the greatest error, says the Vedanta, is to say that you are weak, that you are a sinner, a miserable creature, and that you have no power and that you cannot do this and that."

"The old religions said that he was an atheist who did not believe in God. The new religion says that he is the atheist who does not believe in himself..."

"Strength is life, weakness is death; strength is felicity, life eternal, immortal; weakness is constant strain and misery. Weakness is death. Let positive, strong, helpful thoughts enter into your brains from very childhood..."

"Weakness is the one cause of suffering. We become miserable because we are weak. We lie, steal, kill and commit other crimes, because we are weak. We suffer because we are weak. We die because we are weak. Where there is nothing to weaken us there is no death, no sorrow."

—Swami Vivekananda

India is going to remain India. Bharat will remain Bharat as long as there is but one single son or daughter of the country who is conscious of the message of the *rishis*, of the power of Vedanta, who is receptive, universal, humanistic with all-sided catholicity. Germany may beat India in military prowess; Rome and Athens may beat India in Law and Humanistic culture, but India remains the unique Mother of Philosophy and Religion. Today, however, with the growth of population, far beyond the economic resources of the country, the same religion and philosophy which once soared to the meta-physical heights of contemplative religion and speculative philosophy, today calls her people to call "religion" that zeal and enthusiasm with which the children of India would bring social and economic justice to the common man. For, social justice delayed is social justice denied. Economic justice side-tracked is economic justice killed. Religion is not for empty bellies. There is no more room in India for arm-chair philosophy and that religion which serves as a camouflaged defence of the vested interests of both priests and mammon-lords.

The new life which the Indian republic is looking forward will be the reformed, purified and fortified form of Hinduism, as lived and preached by sages like Ramakrishna, Vivekananda, Ram Mohun Roy, Dayananda Saraswati, Khesub Chunder Sen, Lokamanya Tilak, Mahatma Gandhi, Ramana Maharshi, Netaji Subhas Chandra, Annie Besant and such other leaders of modern India. It is in the light of these champions and soldiers of Modern India that the educational, social and economic life of the country is going to be modelled and re-built. The present imitation system of education, with its denationalising and degenerating influences, is to be radically changed. The present profit-motivated monopoly and black capitalism is to be replaced by mutualism and co-operativism between the producers and consumers, wealth and labour. The present birth-privileges of priests and maharajas, zamindars and the landlords are to be abolished in favour of the toiling millions. Wealth and productive labour alone entitles one to the good things of the earth, equitably distributed among the citizens. There is no question of equality, but only of equity in which system alone socio-economic justice could be administered to the people.

The new socialist education of new India, the new economic pattern of the young Indian Republic, will rise on the philosophy of the Bhagavat Gita, the Ethics of Dhammapada and the Sermon on the Mount, the Meta-physics of the Vedanta, the psychology of Patanjali Yoga. National character alone is the test of our new national economy. Here, Santiniketan, Gurukul, Sevagram, Pondicherry Ashram and such other nationalist lycea and educational institutions will be the corrective to the foreign-imported education through the medium of English in the land of Bharat. The new system of life which free and nationalist India envisages is to build up the super-structure of socialistic economic and cultural order on the core of Upanishadic wisdom, which is the torchlight for the Indian youth, the source of strength to the people of the country. It is this culture of the Vedic and Upanishadic wisdom that teaches that a man who identifies with his mind and spirit becomes by that very fact all-powerful, even as a man who identified himself with his bodily ego becomes weak, mortal and ephemeral. Man becomes as he thinks. Thought tends to materialise in action. Hence the new gospel says: "Control your character and life through your thoughts; control your thoughts through your mind and spirit."

In a world abandoned to the blind forces of violence, Mother India teaches her children and says: "Violence is no answer to violence, hatred is no answer to hatred even as more fuel is no answer to the burning flames." It teaches the path of all rishis and prophets which is the path of knowledge, *gnosis, janana*, the path of education, of love, compassion. But this is not weakness; this is strength of the supreme type, the power that controls the movements of the planets and stars and the solar systems, the infinite power far beyond the release of atomic power and the destructive forces of radioactive rays. Spirituality is the Supreme Reality and in the hierarchy of beings and becomings, there stands at the apex the Prime Mover of all, the Pure Act, Consciousness Pure. Nor Mother India is escapist nor merely speculative, for she equally teaches that the Supreme Reality appears and presents itself to the hungry in the form of bread and butter, to the naked in the form of clothes, to the diseased in the form of curative laws of Mother Nature and medicine. And to the *rakshasas*, the perpetrators of injustice, Reality Supreme, the Cosmic Power appears as the flashing sword, clenching fist, the lightning that destroys evil becomes more poverfully than hydrogen bombs.

No, India is not purely a mystic country. Her philosophy which is the Advaita Vedanta is the most dynamic and power-philosophy that has ever appeared in the history of human civilisation. The highest Platonic Monism is but the Monte Bianco compared to the Everest of Sankar's non-dualistic Monism. Science and society only confirm in the most tangible form the wisdom, truth and practicality of the Philosophy of India. The fault lies not in the system of our philosophy, but in our weakness and stupidity in clinging to the mere shells and overlooking the kernel in religion and philosophy. Not Ganesh, but the knowledge of the Absolute is the dynamite that can revolutionise India and the world. Not Hanuman but Patanjali Yoga that can make men fearless, powerful, self-sufficient and pure. It is the hour of national self-discovery for every son and daughter of India, at least for those who are to be the living patterns and embodiments of the spirit and culture of this land, that eternal India whose philosophic wisdom remains to this day as solid as the rock of the Himalayas, as pure as the snows above her peaks, that India which through Buddhism spread far and wide and built up Greater India far beyond the confines of the geographical indivisible India, now cruelly mutilated into Pakistan and the Indian Union-that India that is still the most receptive and assimilative mother of all cultural and scientific achievements and economic progress of other nations.

New Bharat with reflorescent and renascent culture today

stands out fearless, bold and brave, self-confident of her power and also fully determined to remove weakness in every walk of life. True, that under Pandit Nehru's regime India stands like a begger nation with her begging bawl before the rich Americans. But nationalistic Indians and militant soldiers of Mother India are not going to take their hats off before any nation, however mighty or plutocratic they may be. We consider death far more preferable to dishonour. We shall bend our knees to none save God. Yes, in the atheistic material-ism Mother India still teaches her children to affirm spiritual values, the ethical code of human unfoldment, the Ultimate Reality variously called as "God", "Para-matman", "Allah", Dieu, Tao, Deus, Theos etc.

Darkness encircles us everywhere. But light also shines, though amidst darkness. It is darkness that does not acknowledge Light; it is death that recognises not Life. But Light and Life are there, and to every child of India the path of light and life shown by India is the basis for her national resurrection and for international give-and-take co-operation. "*असतो म सत गमय, तमसो मा ज्येतिर्गमय, मुश्योर्म अमूर्त गमय॥*

—Lead us from untruth to Truth, from darkness unto Light, from death unto Immortality", was the prayer of our forebears, and it shall continue to be the prayer of Indians of today and of all the children of the country for future ages. The Gayatri Mantram is not the mono-poly of the Brahmin priests, it is the symbol and substance of the spiritual and cultural heritage of every child of the soil, the most naturalistic, rational and humanistic culture in history. We are out to remove the dross and present the unalloyed gold to our countrymen. This is what the best of the Indian Nationalists think and work for, among whom today the vanguard is being formed and held by the Rastriya Swayamsevaks.

The RSS or the National Volunteer Corps is the van-guard of the new Indian National Army, no longer led by Netaji Subhas but by a hundred Netajis, leaders not in leading but in serving and sacrificing for the real and lasting happiness, prosperity and unity of the nation. It is this RSS, that held the helm in the most turbulent period in Indian history, when in the wake of partition, -veritable vivisection of Mother India that Pakistan was held at bay and the capital of the Indian Union, New Delhi, did not become the first target of attack. Those who have information of the quick and vigilant activities of the RSS know that the coup d'etat was averted and conflagration of New Delhi did not take place mainly through the sentinels and soldiers which the RSS has given to the land. In this connection Dr. Bhagavandas says:

"If those high-spirited and self-sacrificing boys of the RSS had not given the very timely information to Nehruji and Patelji, there would have been no Government of India today, the whole country would have changed its name into Pakistan. Tens of millions of Hindus would have been slaughtered, and all the rest converted to Islam or reduced to stark slavery, and the super-orthodox and fanatically bigoted Pandit-gentlemen would have either been dead or would be eating cow's flesh with gusto".

—Dr. Bhagavan Das of Benares

In Kashmir, since the pirates invaded the graceful queen of the Himalayan range, it was the heroic boys of the RSS that stood the test of character and formed the behind-line and became the mainstay of the soldiers of the Indian Union to repel the bandits, and those who divided the country on communal basis, and have temporarily acquiesced to Pakistan, which is conceived as a mere springboard for rebuilding their old Moghul Empire and making Pakistanised Bharat, the centre and heart of the Pan-Islamic movement. There are several episodes of the brave boys of the RSS who have silently and reverentially given up their lives in trying to defend inch by inch the sacred land of Bharat. These unknown soldiers are the names that are recorded not in the pages of Indian history but in the unrecorded and undescribable hearts of Indian patriots. In the rehabilitation of the Refugees from the West and East Pakistan, in combating natural calamities like flood and famine, in spreading education and national self-respect the apostolate of the RSS is beyond description.

The dignity and forbearance with which the RSS stood when the interested parties were incriminating the Sangh for Gandhi murder is one of the most interesting episodes in the annals of the history of the movement. The money-madness, power-intoxication and careerism of the Congressmen, of even the most trusted lieutenants and right-hand men of Gandhiji, had already broken the heart of Mahatmaji, long before the bullets from Naturam Godse's revolver pierced his body. It was the moral bankruptcy of the people who were with him in the Congress, after they had taken possession of the Governmental ghadi from the British, that was the thorn in the flesh for Gandhiji. He wept and sighed and sobbed for all, and his prayer towards the end was that God may deign to remove him from this world instead of seeing the country deteriorating, and his own Congressmen falling short of those ideals of sacrifice and service on which was so painfully built up the Indian National Congress.

Brave men die but once. But the cowards and the weaklings die every day, nay many a time a day. The brave never die, for even the physical death is nothing but the laying off of their mortality, even as the worn-out garments are removed by the body-dweller. Such are the heroes and martyrs like Gandhiji and Netaji in the history of India's freedom struggle. As the Gita puts it:

न जायते म्रियते वा कदाचि
न्नायं भूत्वा भविता वा न भूयः।
अजो नित्यः शाश्वतोऽयं पुराणो
न हन्यते हन्यमाने शरीरे॥२०॥
वासांसि जीर्णानि यथा विहाय
नवानि गृह्णाति नरोऽपराणि।
तथा शरीराणि विहाय जीर्णा–
न्यन्यानि संयाति नवानि देही॥

Which means, "the soul is never born, nor does it die. It is not that not having been born, it comes into being. This is unborn, eternal, changeless, ever self-subsisting. The soul is not killed when the body is killed.

'He that knows this to be indestructible, changeless without birth, and immutable, how is he, O Son of Pritha, slay or cause another to slay?

'Even as a man casts of his worn-out garments and puts on new

clothes, so the embodied self casts off worn-out bodies and enters into others that are new and tender."

—Bhagavad Gita, II 20-22

Gandhiji became Mahatma when he realised his Self. It is the great lesson of self-realised action that Gandhiji has taught us and thus reminds us forever of the Father of Indian nation. True, politically Gandhiji made Himalayan blunders, which, had he continued even after August 15th, 1947, Pakistan would have already been established in the entire Indian Union. Giving 52 crores of rupees to Pakistan by fasting is nothing, but to persist in identifying politics with religion and religion with politics was the fatal blunder. It was Netaji Subhas who believed and practiced that religion was religion and politics was politics and lived up to the teaching, "Render unto Ceasar what belongs to Ceasar and unto God what belongs to God."

Whereas the RSS will learn life-wisdom, ideals of service and sacrifice from prophets like Mahatma Gandhi, Buddha, Sankara and others, they will learn politics from men like Netaji Subhas Chandra, Shri Aurobindo, Tilak and such others who have kept up continuity with practical statesmanship and realistic politics in world history. The RSS owes much to Gandhiji's inspiration and guidance. Only there is not going to be any exclusive hero-worship to the detriment of the integrative and complementary mission of the rivals to Gandhiji in Indian politics. In fact, it was not the RSS that distributed sweets at Gandhiji's martyrdom, but it was the black-marketers and many Congresswalas who felt secretly happy because the old saintly man, Bapu, would no longer preach to them about *Brahmacharya, Asteya* and *abaya*. Naughty children are always glad when their judicious and saintly father is gone. Now Pandit Nehru has no more a guide and moral check when both Gandhiji and Patel are gone, save the inner instincts and rational dictates in him, which, unfortunately are at times emotional and not firm, solid and clear enough to steer the country straight amidst the raging gales and burning flames, that try the character and practical realism of the first Indian National Government.

When the present country-wide languor, self-seeking and suicidal internecine divisions are remedied, the country will arise like one man and that unity and national solidarity will be the surest guarantee for Indian's political freedom from any further foreign invasion and the guaranteed pledge for the nation-building and all-sided economic development and social reforms. Mercenary soldiers and the paid armed forces of the country cannot defend India from foreigners, but India becomes impregnable and invincible when the country is defended by the people, by every son and daughter becoming the watchdog and soldier of Bharat, now no longer disorganised and indisciplined, but solidly knit into one compact and cohesive body of national volunteers for a healthy corporate living, working, struggling and dying like heroes and heroines:

It will be this new generation of disciplined and organised men and women of India, this new National Uniform, that the RSS has made its symbol and substance of the new patriotic awakening, that will make India once again the land worthy of the wisdom of the sages and rishis of old, a country receptive to any new light that may come from any quarter of this planet. The freedom which the RSS envisages is the freedom of the culture which India gives, freedom to be good and better, freedom to live and die like free men and women, freedom to develop our society and country in the way we think best, consonent with the best of our traditions. Says Golwalkar: "There can be only one true freedom, the freedom to be good. I want that freedom for every son of Bharatmata, nay for the whole world".

The RSS and all the patriotic forces in the country want that the new patterns be set to the Youth of the country, but not any longer a slavish imitation of the glamorous west, but the natural blossoming and flowering of the culture of the soil, of that eternal wisdom of Vedas, Upanishads and Yoga, of the literature and social sciences born of the soil of Bharat, that culture and wisdom which is symbolised by Saraswati, who is for Indians more sacred and meaningful than the Greek Sophia or Diana or Athena. Saraswati is the Eternal Virgin Mother of wisdom, the Parthenon, on which cultural India is built. Of the mythological lore we will preserve only those that are vitally linked with the growth and the national development of the people. In detecting and discerning gold from dross, wheat from chaff, substance from shadow, all the nationalist and illuministic forces in the land should work together. Culture, Thought, Idea, enlightened consciousness, these are the bases on which to raise the new socialist India.

"After long and deep thinking, I am confirmed in my view that we can live and rise only on the basis of our common great national culture. We can eliminate our weakness and augment our strength only by rooting our lives in the fertile field of culture. I shudder to think what would happen to this great society if people continue to be petty and selfish".

—Shri M.S. Golwalkar

The world may grow more scientific, the military weapons ons may be improved to the highest pitch of efficiency and destructiveness, but the law of Ethical Man remains unchanged. The ideals of self-sacrifice and renunciation, of self-knowledge and self-control, of self-confidence and self-realisation, will not change, cannot fade, as long as man remains man. Crucifixion of the homo sapiens is the necessary prelude to the resurrection, and the pivot on which all religions and the philosopher's stones revolve is this central truth of the effacement of every trace of selfishness and the new life that thence is born in the heart of man, which alone forms the lasting code of healthy social living, the highest peak of philosophical Anarchism, which Buddhas and Christs envisaged and left as their parmanent legacy to the nations of the world. If Asia is the classical land of philosophy, mysticism and religion, then India remains Asia's heart-beat and brain. These imperishable riches of our patrimony should be preserved, defended, enhanced and propagated, for they are the eternal sources of invincible strength.

"The Hindu social ideal is that state of society where the state has withered away, where there are no police and no armies, no jails and no slums, where individuals are so much human and so very cultured that each thinks of others before himself".

—Shri M.S. Golwalkar

But today we are still so far away from that ideal. As Feudalism was replaced by Industrial Capitalism, and the Capitalistic period is being succeeded by Communistic Age, so this Communist wave of history also is bound to pass and prepare the way for that Anarchism where brotherhood of Man and Fatherhood of God will de established, at least among those who mean business in life and are rooted in the ethical core of human existence.

"The logic of Marxism must inevitably lead Mankind to Mutualism and co-operativism, where alone, on the foundations of humanistic ethics, strong individuals can arise. Thus on that group of human beings arise a society, not any longer roboted by machines and totalitarian statism, but on the true human solidarity and co-operative instinct of man.

"War is a political affair; co-operation is an economic affair. The co-operative method provides for supplying people's needs. Among their needs is peace. Co-operative Democracy is when state makes no provision for a war department. It assumes that a people well supplied with necessities of life do not need to attack any nation".

—P.J.P. Warbasse in Co-operative Peace

When monopoly capitalism, whether individual-owned or state-owned, is gone there can be only the full play of free economy with free land, free trade and free money as the basic economics to build up a healthier and more humane society. This will no longer be the old classical *laissz-faire* capitalism, but cooperative economics of a really and truly free people, emancipated from the clutches of totalitarianism and monopoly capitalism. In this new economic order money will have no more power to enslave people. Money shall no more have the purchasing power of man and human values. Money will remain purely and simply as means of exchange for our material existence, for the produces that sustain our somatic life. Not paper or gold money, but values alone will be the standard for gauging human progress. Money for matter, values for spirit is the rule.

But individualism, that has been the curse and cause of so many internecine divisions in the country, can only be tolerated as long as it does not conflict with the social good and the corporate life of the nation. Subjectivistic individualism, the dominant principle and the cardinal heresy of Protestantism, if uncontrolled and unchecked by sound dictates of reason and common sense, can lead the country to chaos, and weakening of the social ties among the citizens. There is an old Sanskrit proverb that says that individuals should sacrifice for the family, that the family should sacrifice for the society, and the society should sacrifice for the welfare of the world and that world also should be sacrificed for Atman, the Absolute.

त्यजेदेकं कुलस्यार्थे ग्रामस्यार्थे कुलं त्यजेत्।
ग्रामं जनपदस्यार्थे ह्यात्मार्थ पृथिवीं त्यजेत्॥

In this hierarchy of values, although individual is subordinate to the society, even as part is partial to the whole, the ideal social order demands that the individual realises himself in and through society. There need not be any necessary conflict between individual freedom and social authority. But it will always tax human reason, practical sense and humanity to harmonise and integrate the freest individuals in the strongest society, and the most compact and cohesive society with the most free and receptive individuals.

In this science of human adjustment, in this new ecology of the twentieth century, the philosophy and social structure of India could contribute her bit in solving the human problems of the world. The quintessentials of Indian culture, which, under the communalistic challenge of Islam or any other exotic religion, may be called 'Hindu', are to be the mainstay for Indian citizens while embarking upon the gigantic task of nation-building. The ancient Mother is awake and the children of Bharatmata are called upon to respond to this new renaissance and rejuvenation of the soul of India.

The new Republic of India will eschew all traces of communalism, separatist factions that weaken, dwarf and deaden the spirit of national solidarity. Only pure flames of patriotism and the radiant lights of nationalism will be the unshakable rock of the new cultural efflorescence under the most enlightened and spirited prophets of modern India. In this neo-Hindu revival, all free and patriotic children of the soil are welcome. Labels are often liabilities. Only character, life and ideals count in the new economy of the national life of India. In the sacrificial fire offered at the altar of the Motherland will rise the new apostles of service. In sacrifice is power and light, whether it is in the East or in the West, in ancient times or in modern times. There is no going back from this law of our existence.

"Be great. No great work can be done without sacrifice. The Purusha Himself sacrificed Himself to create this world. Lay down your comforts, your pleasures, your names, fame or position, nay even your lives, and make a bridge of human chains over which millions will cross this ocean of life. Bring all forces of good together. Do not care under what banner you march. Do not care what your colour, green, blue or red, but mix all the colours up and produce that intense glow of white, the colour of love. Ours is to work. The results will take care of themselves."

—Swami Vivekananda

The much-need energy comes with the re-rooting of our nation on the rock of Indian philosophy, on the power of Truth that is God. India at present is frustrated, despondent, inactive, unimaginative and inert, and that, not unfrequently, in the name of God, religion and *satva*. But the real energy is lacking, the real *rajasic* power, enlightened by *satvic* life. Here again says Swami Vivekananda, the apostle of neo-Vedantism:

"*Rajas* is badly needed just now. More than ninety per cent of those whom you may take to be men of the *satva* quality are only steeped in deepest *tamas*. What is now wanted is an immense amount of *rajasik* energy, for the whole country is wrapped in the shroud of *tamas*. The people of this land must be fed and clothed—must be awakened—must be made more fully active, otherwise they will become inert as trees and stones."

Unfortunately the vast majority of our countrymen, whatever be their religious titles and labels, are on the vegetative level. The standard of life is to be raised. All forms of barriers and social ostracism are to be removed. Caste barriers and communal cancers, untouchability and all other inhumanities are to go, to be ruthlessly uprooted if India is to survive as a strong, united nation.

"As long as 'touch-me-notism' is your creed and the kitchen-pot is your deity, you cannot rise spiritually", says Swami Vivekananda.

It is no good merely shouting about our ancient glories unless those romantic and vital truths of our culture are translated in our every day life. Buddha is not old. Christ is not old. Krishna is not old, nor Bartrihari nor Yajanvalkya. But they need be lived and on their ethics and spirituality is to be raised and a new culture and a new organisation.

"The spiritual life of Europe belongs not to Caesar and Napolean but to Christ; the civilisation of the East has been more influenced by Buddha than by Ghengis Khan or Akbar. It is this truth we have to learn, if we are to survive. We overcome hate by love and evil by good; baseness begets a progeny like itself", says Mahatma Gandhi.

There can be no freedom, no power, no new India save when there is self-confidence born out of self-know-ledge and self-respect. This auto-redemptive character of life is to be hammered into our hearts and minds. All outside dependence is weakness, all self-confidence is power and freedom.

"Each one must be a lamp unto himself holding fast to the truth as refuge, and looking not for a refuge to anyone but oneself", says Buddha.

What is today needed is no longer paper schemes and lip-service to culture, but embodiments of the spirit of India, whose life will irradiate the essentials of the message of the land. This spirit of the country in the words of Rabindranath Tagore, is roughly as follows:

"India's special genius has been to acknowledge the divine in human affairs, to offer hospitality to all that is imperishable in human civilisation, regardless of racial and national divergence. From the early dawn of our history it has been India's privilege and its problem, as a host, to harmonise the diverse elements of humanity which have inevitably been brought to our midst, to synthesise contrasting cultures in the light of a comprehensive ideal. The stupendous structure of our social system with its intricate

arrangement of caste testifies to the vigorous attempt made at an early stage of human civilisation to deal with the complexity of our problems, to relegate to every class of our peoples, however wide the cleavage between their levels of culture, a place in the cosmopolitan scheme of society. Ram Mohun's predecessors, Kabir, Nanak, Dadu and innumberable saints and seers of medieval India carried on much farther India's great attempt to evolve a human adjustment of peoples and races; they broke through barriers of social and religious exclusiveness and brought together India's different communities on the genuine basis of spiritual reality. We must not forget that in modern times this emancipation of our manhood has been made possible by the indomitable personality of Ram Mohun Roy.

He paved the way for this reassertion of India's inmost truth of being, her belief in the equality of man in the love of the Supreme Person, whoever dwells in the hearts of all men and unites us in the bond of welfare."

—Rabindranath Tagore

There is no need any further to cling to anything and everything in India purely because they are Indian. Our critical and rational faculties are to be followed, the laws of human evolution and progress, if we have to survive. Caste and sub-castes and superstitions have to go in order to build up purified and perennial culture of the land, based on humanity, rationality and progress.

"I regret to say that the present system of religion adhered to by the Hindus is not well calculated to promote their political interests. The distinction of castes, introducing innumerable divisions and subdivisions among them, has entirely deprived them of patriotic feeling, and the multitude of religious rites and ceremonies and the laws of purification have totally disqualified them from undertaking any difficult enterprises. It is, I think, necessary that some change should take place in their religion at least for the sake of their political advantage and social comfort."

—Ram Mohun Roy

It will need Herculean efforts on the part of all nationalist forces, specially the RSS that is today in the vanguard of Indian national life, to achieve this ideal, rational and human solidarity in the country. All sectarian and isolationist tendency has to go. India's soul, that is the Vedanta, and the *Upanishads*, the spirit of the *Mahabharata* and *Ramayana*, in so far as they help us to grow from within and cement national solidarity to be adhered to and defended. India's expansive and universalist mind is not to be lowered nor degraded by any narrow partisans of casteism, creedalism or communalism. Indian spirit is the most universal and catholic that has appeared in human history. Neo-Hinduism in the new Republic of India recognises this widest possible catholicity and humanity of Indian culture. On this basis shall be laid the foundations of a strong, united India, whose doctrinal catholicity is as wide as the universe, perennial beyond time and space.

"God's temple is this wide universe, Wisdom is the pure land of pilgrimage; Truth is Man's everlasting Scripture, Faith the root of every religion; Love is the true spiritual culture; Destruction of selfishness is asceticism."

—Khesub Chunder Sen

India can be united and strengthened only on the rock of Truth. Pakistan is a lie. This lie of Pakistan will be automatically rectified when true nationalist forces are detected and strengthened and unified. Truth alone is strong and powerful. Politics of expediency can stand only on shifting sands. We have accepted as our motto, the ideal of Free Indian Republic, the Upanishadic saying: "सत्यमेव जयते न अनृतं—Truth alone triumphs, not Untruth." Jesus also says: "You shall know Truth and Truth will set you free," There is no Freedom, no power, no unity save in Truth. Truth is that which is. This universe subsists on the force and power of Truth. Mortals by knowing and identifying themselves with that Truth become Immortal, Invincible and Eternal.

Pakistan has recently allowed a new party to come into being, a party called "Hindustan Hamara Party," which aims at the "liberation" of the entire Indian sub-continent. They want to Islamise the entire country. Now the only answer to this challenge is strengthening Hindu fold, not as a communal counterpart of Muslim communalism, but as the unshakable rock of Indian nationalism, where all the children of the soil can join and form a united front. Hinduism is not a religion in the accepted sense of the term. It is essentially a spirit, an attitude of the children of the soil of India towards life. This spirit is to be preserved and maintained, stregthend and fortified through diffusing and defending the teachings of the Upanishads and, above all, through the living patterns of service and sacrifice.

What the nation wants is pluck and scientific accuracy. We want great spirit, tremendous energy and boundless enthusiasm. No womanishness will do. It is the man of action, the lion-heart, that the goddess Saraswati favours and blesses.

Hindu nationalism is Bharatiyata or Indianism. This is an all-pervasive spirit, eluding definition and yet something so tangible and definite, more transparently and lucidly clear than the most rigid dogmatic and crystalised religions of the world. It is this spiritual and philosophical acumen that the world needs. We shall learn the science of economics, chemistry and termodymanics from the West, and in this international trade and commerce of cultures, India remains the Mother of Religious Philosophy and Philosophic Religion.

The RSS, and what is still left of the Congress, of the Brahmo Samaj and Arya ya Samaj, the Ramakrishna-Mission and various reformist and patriotic movements in the country should now unite to form one solid block, and face the common perils and common problems of the country, and form the bulwork of national solidarity and cement human brotherhood and citzenship in the country. Any ray of light that may come from any side must be accepted. Broad-mindedness is not weakness. Only indolence, indifference and selfishness weaken the individuals and nation. Under the able leadership and enlightened guidance of Guruji M.S. Golwalkar the youth of the country can rightfully expect the fulfilment and flowering of all that are best in the cultural heritage of the country, duly wedded to what is best and congenial in other cultures, so that India may grow into a veritable strong and united Republic, that the communal factions and social divisions may end, that the sin of Pakistan may cease, that the economic, educational and social problems be realistically and bravely faced and solved, that India become once again the land where it will be the privilege and happiness for humans to be born, the eternal punya bhumi, the sacred land, where will remain enshrined the Himalayas of Philosophy, Mysticism and Religion, Godliness and Character, Creativity and Loving Service.

May Mother India grow united and strengthened through the unity and strength of her children! May Mother Nature and Father God lead us to the ideals of HUMANITY, FREEDOM, JUSTICE and BROTHERHOOD!

ॐ भूर्भुव: स्व: तत्सवितुर्वरेण्यं भर्गो देवस्य धीमहि।
धियो यो न: प्रचोदयात्॥

—Gayatri, Rigveda III. 62 10

□

Chapter-11

Secularism, The RSS and The Indian Youth

Compared to the young and energetic nations of both East and West, Indian youth is today disorganised, despondent and dejected. There is no concentric force to unify them, to give them an ideal, a dream to live by and die for. Merely by shouting "Secularism," the basic cultural problems of the country cannot be solved. Where there is no culture there can be no idealism; where there is no idealism the Youth is as good as dead.

Of all the various political and non-political organisations existing today in the Indian soil, there is no other organisation that can inspire the Indian nationalistic youth to get themselves united into one single compact indissoluble organic whole as the RSS While the veteran Congress leaders, with Pandit Nehru at the top, continue to shout from the housetops in and out of time about their new fad of pseudo-secularism, it is the conscientious and thoughtful Youth of the RSS and allied patriotic forces which work and worry, strive and strain to preserve the quintessentials of Dharma, Culture, Religion, Philosophy, which are inestimable gifts of India to the world at large. In fact, Indian Philosophy and Religion, in its basic essentials, is the fountain-head of that secularism which representative modern Indians like Ram Mohun Roy, Dayananda Saraswati, Vivekananda, Rabindranath and Gandhiji lived and taught. But the religious secularism and nationalistic patriotism of those bygone prophets and architects of modern India have little, nothing in common with the protagonists of pseudo-secularism of the type which, unfortunately, such an eminent scholar like Shri Nehru who continue to repeat his pet secularism ad nauseam in and out of season.

No amount of cathedra proclamations of the so-called secularists can convince anybody that Gandhiji, the Father of the Nation, would have anything to do with the sort of secularism which the Nehru Government is advocating. Gandhiji was, of course, against untouch-ability and caste discrimination between man and man on the ground of religion. But that does not mean that Gandhiji was a secularist in the sense our veteren Congressmen of the Nehruan wing understand. Gandhiji taught also the spirit of prayer, practice of the presence of God, practice of voluntary poverty, minutest details of observing the angelic virtue of Brahmacharrya, etc., which also should be taken into consideration by those who would drag in the great name of the departed prophet to confirm their secularist thesis. Gandhiji was bigger than the whole Congress and the Congressmen he moulded. Gandhji's essential greatness is religious and not secular; no, not the Nehruan humbug.

Now, ethical religion, humanistic and nationalistic Dharma, is bound to survive in some form or other; and it is on this great truth the organisation of the RSS is based. Not only the RSS, but all the sane-thinking nationalist and patriotic youth have to admit this. On this great issuc was fought the Tandon-Nehru fight and, although Pandit Nehru captured the Congress chair by defeating Purushotamdas Tandon, events would prove that the cultural and spiritual hold of Tandon was impregnable and invincible. This superiority of religious realisation over pseudo-secularism was proved when Shri Nehru declined to serve on the Working Committee to maintain the prestige of his fashionable secularist creed, while the "communal and obscurantist." Tandon, in national and patriotic interests, agreed to serve on the very Committee reconstituted by his political opponent, thus practicing the religious principle, as formulated by St. Paul: "Do not be overcome by evil, but conquer evil with good." Anti-religious secularism is indeed an evil, more so in a country like India.

Let's leave it. But India in South must base an ideal which unfortunately the Congress has failed to give. There are two potent ideals alive in this world today. One is undiluted materialistic, Marxian Communist ideal: the other undiluted Idealistic pattern. Today, however, there is a great deal of idealism infiltrating materialistic Communism, and there is a great deal of materialism invading the domain of ideals. So the clear-cut dividing line is next to impossible, although to describe the leanings of the youth of a nation, of a people, whether it is more on to the Marx-Engels-Lenin-Stalin versions of Communism or the Kroptkin, William Morris, Kautskey, Trostsky or Mao type of Communism. Today both materialism and spiritualism transcend their traditional frontiers and encroach upon each other and balance and integrate the new outlook on life in this super-industrial Atomic Age.

We have now to choose which ideology is to be presented to our youth so that they may arise from slough and despondency and work for the much-needed socioeconomic and cultural revolution in the country. It is at this juncture that the RSS offers the youth of India an ideology, a dream which is not the undiluted materialism of orthodox Marxian Communists, but the saving leaven of centralised discipline and highest self-sacrifice based on the idealistic patrimony of Indian culture. Because the RSS base their stand on the Philosophy of the Upanishads, the Ethics of the Sermon on the Mount, the Psychology of Buddhism, the Metaphysics of Vedanta, the so-called secularists say: "These are Hindu revivalists, let's put them down." These secularists have no philosophy, no ideals to build up Indian youth, nor their own sweet selves.

Experiments in Europe and Russia have proved beyond doubt that positivistic pragmatism, amoral and anti-religious scientific materialism, have failed to make man out of mere mud, to give stable principles of life and orientation to the youth. Our secularists have seen and studied but the surface-layers of Western ways of life, not the deeper depths of the Greco-Roman civilisation, of the Catholic Church and the inner core of Protestantism. These secularists have roots neither in the East nor in the West and they would like to drag the rest of the country into their miserable plight. What they really ought to have done is not to shout for a colourless secularism, but to reconstruct themselves and their country on the basis of ethical principles, on the basic elements of self-restraint and sense-control, whereby the higher powers latent in human nature are manifested, where virtue is respected, where Truth is lived to its logical implications. "Religion is but manifestation of divinity already in man," says Vivekananda. "Virtue is spotlessness of mind; all else is mere noise," says Tiruvallur. "Truth is God," says Gandhiji.

So, then, the RSS is in the fore and sides with me. Forces of ethical, humanistic and rational religion, as preserved in the broad Indian cultural heritage. The RSS uses words when fully conscious of their meaning. They do not preach secularism to their adherents and friends, simply because secularism would mean downright denial of India's past history, of the great names in Indian history. Just imagine Buddha, Asoka, Sankara, Chanakya, Manu, Yajnavalkya, and in our own days Gandhiji, Tilak, Rabindranath, Subhas Bose and others, all to be classed among the Nehruvian secularists!

If secularism is power, then ethical and humanistic religion, metaphysical and mystical realisation, is a thousand times more power. If secularism is the means of cementing human brotherhood and national solidarity, then anti-communal religious realisation is thousand times more adamantine power for unifying peoples of this sub-continent on the solid basis of Humanistic Religion. But if any politician or statesman thinks that he could wipe out religion and reinstate his secularist fad on the throne of Dharma, which such leaders like Buddha, Christ, Muhammed, Zoroaster, Krishna, Rama and Ramakrishna taught, then they are sadly mistaken. They will fall and fail, being *Dharma* or religion the nutriment, inspiration, *raison de'tre* and life of the noblest specimens of humanity, of many strongest personalities of history and, indeed, the source of solace and strength to the broad masses everywhere.

While the RSS and so-called Indian nationalists are against all forms of communalism, they are open to any new light which may be shed from any side, thus through their lives and deeds refuting the charge of closed-door, stereotyped orthodoxy. Certainly religions also survive through continuous adjustment and change, being part of the very life itself, which is continually changing. Supreme Reality alone is impermanence, everything else is transient flux. We shall learn the lessons of equality and Social Democracy, as was learnt by Ram Mohun, Rabindranath and Gandhiji from Islam. We shall learn charity and social uplift from Christian religion; but at core we remain Indians, fully rooted in our Bharatiya culture embracing other sources of light and life only to strengthen and enhance what is already implanted in our lives, that is alive in our life-blood, innate in our racial instinct.

So, then, the religious ideal, in its purest non-sectarian form is placed by the RSS to the youth of the country. They are taught that the purpose of life is not mere economic security nor social decorum, but inner poise and power and integration that can only be the outcome of Self-realisation. They are taught to appreciate the imponderable values in life, to stand erect with human dignity and spiritual invincibility, being heirs of Immortal Bliss, *अमृतस्य पुत्राः* They are taught the path of acquiring real Freedom through self-restraint, self-knowledge and self-unfoldment. Spiritual Freedom is placed as the highest form of Freedom to the Youth of the country, as has been taught by our Rishis and bequeathed to history as the permanent legacy of India down to the days of Gandhiji. When passions are controlled, sex-sublimated and mental poise acquired, then individuals become powerful, unbeatable and invincible from every side. As the Upanishads say:

यदा सन्वें प्रभिद्यन्ते हृदयस्ये ह ग्रन्थयः ।
अथ मत्र्योऽमृतोभवत्येतावदनुशासनम ॥

"When all the fetters that tie the hearts of man down are torn asunder, then the mortal becomes immortal, then he attains Brahman."

—Brihadaranyaka Upanishad, IV 4.5-7

It is not the secularists, but sages, saints and philosophers that teach that man is part of the Whole, and that it is in identifying the individual self with the Cosmic Self that real power comes, and the country becomes strong. It is religion that sanctifies and gives higher purposes to social institutions, notably marriage, which otherwise is nothing but a biological and animalish affair, with no ideals of fidelity, sanctity and means of self-realisation. Marriage is a fall even as our birth on this planet is. If life, death, disease and miseries and sins could be got over, that is the royal path which mortals cannot set aside so lightly. This we call "Dharma", religion. These basic essentials of *Manava Dharma* are at the root of both the Semitic and Aryan groups of religions. It is this humanistic man-making core that gives power, vitality, significance to religions. "Without these man-making constituents, religions are sources of division, quarrel, persecution and communalism, which the prophets of Indian Renaissance tried to remove from the life of India. It is to this basic essential core of religion, the Humanistic, Rational and Ethical quintessence of the religious lore of India that the RSS continues to cling. Communal cancer is cured the moment we realise that all Indians, whether Hindus, Muslims, Brahmins or *Chandalas,* are all children of the same soil, flesh of our flesh, blood of our blood, bone of our bones. Being tarred with the same brush, germinating from the same seed of the proto parents, evolving from amoeba to the highest species of *homosapiens,* this *Manava Dharma*, anti-communal religion, has a lasting value. It is this the RSS in India represents; it is this the Indian patriots uphold.

While the RSS subscribes to the highest possible ideal of what is best in the Indian cultural heritage, it is a well-disciplined army of boys and girls who will not only defend their culture, but also their land and country which gave birth to such an eminent culture and civilisation. Here must come political realism, specially since the vivisection of the country. The League communalism has already done mischief and the Indian leaders, at the time of the British withdrawal, had to reconcile themselves to the moves the Tory politicians had made on their political chess-board in India. But now it is up to us to minimise the evils of partition and not allow partition to be a time bomb to explode and ruin our Motherland. For this we need political realism, iron discipline among our youth, love of our culture, our language, philosophy, ways of life without which we will easily glide down to colourless secularism, or a vague dazzling machine civilisation, which will weaken us in our minds and hearts. It is the soul of a civilisation we have to preserve, if we mean business in the life-battle and survive and transmit what is best in our heritage to posterity, keeping vital continuity with such names as Asoka, Chandragupta and Akbar who were truly children of the soil. Akbar's *Din Ilahi* was born of his greater loyalty to Indian soil than to Koran or Arabia.

It is for this purpose that the RSS took in its hands the task of moulding the youth, a task so miserably neglected by our first secular government. Unity, discipline, patriotism, ideals, *Dharma* and ethical values are being instilled into the life-blood of the Indian youth. In a broad nationalistic sense, any individual, group or organisation that is true to the basic cultural heritage of India pursues the same ideal as the RSS. The opening of membership to anybody, irrespective of birth-religion, to the Mahasabha, Jana Sangh, Benares and Aligarh Universities are all welcome signs. Abdul Ghaffar Khan, the Frontier leader of Kudhai Khidmatgar is a true Indian patriot, an informal member of the ideal RSS, than many Hindus who merely happened to be born Hindus, but have no culture, discipline, purity, progressive outlook to see beyond their nose. Birth-privileges are dying, for, as Vivekananda said, we are having the age of Shudra revolution, where only Labour, Character and Life alone will count and not birth-privileges. In fact, it is life and character alone, spirit of discipline, self-sacrifice, ideals alone, which should determine who is a patriotic Indian and who is not. By being a true patriotic Indian, rooted in the unshakable Himalayan rock of Vedanta, one has thereby become a true citizen of the world also. The modern trends in world culture and world outlook entitle thoughtful and open minds to be world citizens.

So we welcome all nationalistic movements rooted in the basic cultural heritage of India. This is the very denial of communalism, as the divine word 'patriotism' is antithetical to communalism. Mother India needs the new renaissance of her ancient culture, the re-florescence that will not reject but absorb and assimilate what is best in other cultures and religions that have come from abroad, but are being naturalised in India. In modern times, the Brahmo Samaj, Arya Samaj, Theosophical Society, Ramakrishna Mission, Marxism, the Shia and Sufi survival, were powerful waves of this renaissance, of which once the Congress was the heir, specially under the leadership of Tilak, Subhas and Gandhiji, of which all true nationalist organisations are heirs. Nationalism displaces all forms of communalism. It is in this sense the RSS presents the patriotic ideals to the youth of the country, fight against communalistic contamination and inject the life-blood of Indian culture, *Bharatiyata*, plus what is best in foreign cultures, to her youth.

Today in India there is no other organisation that has given such disciplined, solid, patriotic and humanistic training for citizenship as the RSS. The Congress has lost hold on the people and they have no living gospel to bestow to the new generations who consider Congress romance to be a thing of the past history of Gandhian days. The Communists and Socialists have left aside the culture of the land and they look mainly to Marx-Engels-Lenin-Stalin versions of socialism. Hence the youth organisations under their auspices lack the vital link with the tap-root of Indian culture. But the RSS from the very inception of the movement hoisted the *bhagwa* flag, *Dharma chakra* and *Satyameva jayate,* as their symbols, and have grown around these patriotic ideals. Hence the RSS youth, given more favourable circumstances, can be in India what Hitler was to the youth in Germany, fascist youth in Italy and what the Mao's youth is in China today.

"But then are not the RSS youths fascists?" asks our pseudo-secularist. This bogey of fascism and communism are quarrels about straw and the might-fever caused by seeing a ghost at a distance which, from near, however, is nothing but a scarecrow. If discipline, organised centralisation and organic collective consciousness mean fascism, then the RSS is not ashamed to be called fascist. All hallucinations and sophistication about name and form. This silly idea that fascism and totalitarianism are evils and parliamentarianism and Anglo-American types of democracy are holy, should be got rid of from our minds, if we want to approach problems realistically and bring in solutions for them. Did they not condemn Subhas Bose as a fascist? And yet it was Netaji who was the most realistic politician among the Congress trinity of Gandhiji, Nehru and Subhas.

So, then, one need not be afraid of calumny and slander of calling intense iron discipline and corporate living as fascism and branding fascism itself as an evil nowhere to be brought near the holy sanctuary of the parliamentarian democracy, which in England works smoothly and for the good of the people, being the result of their natural historical evolution, but in India is becoming a big mockery and imitation, all size without substance, debates without deeds.

It was some brave RSS boys who helped many youth organisations in villages and towns along the best nationalistic traditions. In this connection it may be usefully recalled that in Bengal it was the brave RSS, quasi-RSS and pro-RSS youths and propagandists who started the Indian National Youth Movement since Independence. Many of the later associates of the Indian National Youth Movement were not formal members of the RSS organisation, but they were definitely intense nationalists and patriots. They had started camps for imparting ideal youth training. There is no publicity nor prominence given to such youth movements, because there is no government support for them, no backing of money-power, and, not unfrequently, they are being decimated by the Government and the reactionary vested interests through sheer jealousy and high-handedness.

A resolution of the Youth Workers' Conference held under the presidentship of Shri Niharendu Dutt-Mazumdar, the Hon'ble Judicial Minister, West Bengal Government, on Sunday July 16th, 1950, had passed a resolution entrusting the present writer with the task of drafting a Manifesto for the Indian National Youth Movement. Accordingly, on 30th July the manuscript of the Manifesto was submitted to the youth leader, Shri Niharendu Dutt-Mazumdar. The youth workers further decided to publish the Manifesto on 15th August, 1950 as their souvenir of the third anniversary of Indian Independence and the 78th birth anniversary of Shri Aurobindo, the late prophet of Pondicherry. On 15th August, 1950 the Manifesto appeared on the scene. While presenting the Manifesto of the Indian National Youth Movement to the Youth of Free India, Shri Niharendu Dutt-Mazumdar, the youthful, enthusiastic and super-idealistic political student of

Saklatvala, the late Indian Communist MP in British Parliament, the genial disciple of Deshbandhu C.R. Das and the right-hand man of Netaji Subhas Chandra Bose, specially at the historic Tripuri Session, wrote in his foreword:

"The privilege of presenting this Draft Manifesto of the Indian National Youth Movement to the public, specially to the youth of Free India, falls to my lot and it is, indeed with real pleasure, I undertake to fulfil this patriotic duty to the generation of my youngers in India and abroad."

"The present moment of supreme agony and crisis of the soul, through which partitioned India, hardly after three years of her political Independence, is passing, calls for superhuman efforts on the part of her youth to combat despondency, frustration and a general sense of country-wide helplessness of the common man. The people of India and the Government today are confronted with so many grave national problems. Upon our realistic approach and successful solution of these manifold problems, that beset our path, will depend the march of our Motherland to peace, prosperity, and progress.

"At this historic juncture of India's political life a special duty has fallen on the shoulders of India's youth. They are to be the vanguard in the country's march towards fulfilment of the great task of nation-building. After the withdrawal of the British we have yet to consolidate the country internally and cement into one single mosaic of diverse lines the entire nation, tackle her manifold economic and social problems with a sense of realism and make our country strong, a mighty power, proof against any possible aggression in the future. We must build India as the strongest bulwark of peace and human brotherhood in the world, based on the power of her ancient genius for universal humanism. Only humanism can break barriers and build bridges not only among varied religious communities and systems of thought in India, but also between the East and the West."

The youth of India are heirs to the rich, varied, catholic, all-sided spiritual heritage of India's cultural achievements of the past, handed down to them through an unbroken chain of seers, thinkers, saints and martyrs. In modern times martyrs with their sacrifices fertilised the soil for the growth of freedom in India—martyrs, beginning from Khudiram, Jatin Das, Bhagat Singh, Surya Sen, Chandrashekhar Azad down to the leader of the nation, Netaji Subhas Chandra Bose, not to mention the Father of Free India, Mahatma Gandhi, whose influence lives in the lives of men like Khan Abdul Ghaffar Khan—still languishing, alas, to the shame of Free India, in prison in the land of his birth and love. Mahatma Gandhi's influence lives in the lives of Pandit Nehru, Dr. Rajendra Prasad, Maulana Azad, Sardar Patel and other elderly fighters at the helm of affairs of our nation today. It is now up to the youth of India to ponder over their own responsibilities, as heirs of a glorious heritage, as worthy children of Mother India, still bleeding from the partition wounds. The country is confronted with increasing problems on her domestic front and the youth of India shall have to solve them, as torch-bearers of the new light which the Free Republic of India is destined to shed not only to the nations of Asia but to the world at large.

"The crying need for organising Indian youth along the best nationalistic traditions of the Congress has been felt throughout the country and some scattered efforts were made to this end, since India achieved her Independence. The efforts at organising such a Youth Movement have continued now for about two years and a half, since the All-India Youth Convention and Rally was held at Jaipur on the occasion of the first session of the Indian National Congress, held after the transfer of power took place from the British to Indian hands, on the historic day of the 15th August, 1947.

"The Manifesto now is an attempt to present the broad ideas and ideals of our National Youth Movement, to state clearly its central ideology and the general outline of its practical programme of work. It endeavours to state with utmost frankness the case of the Indian Youth and seeks to survey the nation-wide issues and problems connected with the Youth Movement in the perspective of India's historic past. It will now be up to the reading public to judge how far it has succeeded in seeing and interpreting the vital needs of the people of the country.

"The main ideas, sought to be presented in this Manifesto, were discussed more than once in various meetings and conferences of Youth workers, specially in Bengal, whose youth, in common with the youth of Sind, the Punjab, the North West Frontier Province and Kashmir, are passing through the most bitter agony of soul, as a result of the partition, the never-ending nightmare and crucifixion, as it were of the two arms of Mother India brutally cut off from the main trunk. At this time when discussions for a programme were going on, it was singularly fortunate that Anthony Elenjimittam, the author of this Manifesto, hailing from Cochin State, Malabar, after over a decade of peregrinations in Europe in his searchings after Truth, re-discovered his own national soul in the poems and songs of Rabindranath, in the sacrificial fire of Subhas Chandra, in the Sadhana of Sri Aurobindo, Vivekananda and Ramkrishna and made Bengal his spiritual home in the service of Mother India and her Youth. He undertook the task of drawing up a programme and fulfilled it in the form of this Manifesto.

"This Manifesto is, however, only a draft meant to serve the basis for discussion before it is finally adopted by an all-India National Youth Convention. Criticism, corrections, suggestions, etc., from our readers are most welcome, nay, necessary, for the Manifesto to serve its purpose of mobilising, canalising and organising the youthful forces for the positive programme of nation building."

"We embark upon our task with undying faith and optimism that hopes for the best, but prepares also for the worst. The youth of India are inexorably on the march. I hail them and wish them all success to the glory of the Motherland." Thus wrote Shri N. Dutt-Mazumdar, the nearest heir to Netaji Subhas in Bengal."

Hardly two weeks had elapsed when the public in-terest in the Manifesto called for its Hindi translation, which was done by Shri Mohun Singh Senger, an RSS apostle and the editor of the Hindi monthly, Naya Samaj. The programme and policy of the Indian National Youth Movement, as outlined in the Manifesto caused some headache to veteran Congressmen, some of whom violently opposed certain passages in the Manifesto. A high Government Chanakya, successor to Lord Mount-batten and Sardar Patel, advised us to delete the quotation from Shri Aurobindo's message on the Independence day, which says: "India is free, but she has not achieved unity, only a fissured and broken freedom But by whatever means, the division must go," printed on frontispiece of the book. The Youth Workers then decided to hold an all-India Youth Conference at Nasik on the 16th and 17th September, synchronising with the Congress Session. Shri Sankar Rao Deo, the then General Secretary, opposed this Youth Convention, and it was unfortunate that he made some derogatory statements about this Manifesto and the Youth Workers, which was broadcast throughout India by the Press Trust of India Reuter agency. This made Shri Niharendu Dutt-Mazumdar and the present writer to reply the Congress boss in public in their capacity of being the President and General Secretary of the Preparatory Committee for the All-India Youth Convention. The press controversy and the wide publicity the PTI-Reuter gave to it prepared our way to hold the proposed Youth Convention at Nasik in the teeth of the opposition from the Congress bosses, who denied the use of Gandhinagar Pandal to us. The story of that controversy, opposition and trials at the Nasik Youth Convention was something like the Haripuri Session in miniature, when Subhas Bose was outlawed and humiliated by the big Congress guns. At any rate, we stood our ground and the Convention was held, as was scheduled, at the Municipal Hall, Nasik, on the 16th and 17th September, 1950, when the youth delegates and workers adopted the Manifesto with some modifications in the light of various suggestions and criticisms received by them from various Government, non-Government, Congress and anti-Congress circles, from many a friendly and also hostile quarters.

Ten months after Nasik, at the All-India Youth and Students Convention held in the Senate Hall, Calcutta, under the presidentship of Dr. Kailas Nath Katju, the West Bengal Governor, the same Manifesto was adopted as a workable programme of ideals and actions for the youth. In parts of West Bengal there are various youth organisations and youth camps which are implementing the programme and policy of youth action along the lines suggested in the Manifesto.

There is so much in common between the training imparted

to the RSS youth and the workers and missionaries of the Indian National Youth Movement.

Many RSS youths of Bengal found in the Manifesto a mirror of their own ideals, specially of their iron discipline, unflinching loyalty to the Motherland and burning missionary zeal for the all-sided regeneration of the country. Several youth workers and selfless missionaries of new India have suggested to bring out a Bombay edition of the Manifesto to popularise its ideals in western India. It is not therefore without reason that the Manifesto is published as an appendix to this book, that deals with the philosophical basis, cultural roots, organisation, discipline, youth training and action of the RSS for the achievement of the ideal Hind Swaraj, where there will be economic freedom, social justice, national solidarity, patriotic love and human brotherhood, the ideal Hind Swaraj which Netaji Subhas, Dr. Hedgewar, Rabindranath, Mahatma Gandhi, Ram Mohun Roy, Vivekananda, Tilak, Aurobindo and Vallabhbhai Patel and many a prophet, seer and soldier of modern India, fighters of national freedom, heralds of New India, *Nava Bharat,* dreamt, worked and struggled for, and laid down their lives at the altar of the Motherland.

"Lead, kindly Light, amid the encircling gloom
Lead Thou me on.
The night is dark and I am far from home,
Lead Thou me on.
Keep Thou my feet, I do not ask to see
The distant scene, one step enough for me."

—John Henry Newman

वन्दे मातरम्। वन्दे मातरम्।
सुजलाम् सुफलाम्, मलयज शीतलाम्
शस्य श्यामलाम् मातरम्।
शुभ्र ज्योत्स्नां पुलकित यामिनीम्
फुल्ल कुसुमित द्रुमदल शोभिनीम्
सुहासिनीम् सुमधुर भाषिणीम्
सुखदां बरदां मातरम्॥

पञ्चत्रिश कोटि कण्ठ कलकल निनादकराले
द्विपत्रिश कोटि भुजैः घृत खर करवाले
के बले मा तुमि अबले
बहुबल धारिणीम्, नमाभि तारिणीम्
रिपुदल वारिणीम् मातरम्
वन्दे मातरम्।

□

Appendix
Manifesto of The Indian National Youth Movement

I. Lessons from History

Historical past is not dead enumeration of dates and events, but it is a living reality influencing and explaining the present and preparing the way for the future. What we are today is largely the result of what we were yesterday and our today prepares us for our tomorrow. If man is forgetful of his historical past, he becomes all the more oblivious of that philosophy and psychology that explain and interpret history, those immutable natural laws that shape the destiny of men and nations, that account for the rise and fall of empires and peoples, that maintain the vital continuity between the old and the new, the ancient and the modern in the history of civilisation.

As on the trinity of food, clothing and shelter were raised the proudest, the most ancient and the mightiest cultures and civilisations of history, so it is equally true that all progressive steps, onward strides, upward marches in history were the result of creative thinking, new ideas, high ideals which have the power to infuse new blood into the youth of the country, that can revolutionise the static, stagnant, unproductive, unimaginative and reactionary socio-economic forces of a people. These ideas forge ahead to change the order of things and create a better society, a better economic system, a better political ideology. The martyrs who created new era bequeath the fruits of their labour and worries of their blood and' sweat, to their posterity. They sacrifice, they die in the battlefield, so that their people, their country, their culture, their humanity, may live, live forever.

Long before the Pharaohs raised the pyramids in Egypt, the Vedic hymns were sung in the Indo-Gangetic Plain, Homeric songs were sung in Athens, the Chinese walls were raised, long before Zarathustra, Confucius, Laotze, Buddha, Socrates, Plato, Jesus and Muhammed delivered their message of freedom to the world, the eternal law of struggle for existence, of the never ending tug-of-war, between the forces of justice and injustice, of light and darkness, of love and hatred, of duty and indolence, of character and cowardice, is clearly traced back to pre-historic days. Jinmu-tenno, Xerxes, Pericles, Hannibal, Pompei, Caesar, Constantine, Joan of Arc, Lakshmi Bai of Jhansi are mere names. Mohenjo-daro, Harappa, Hastinapur, Carthage, Thermopylae, Marathon, Athens, Rome, Patliputra and Alexandria are mere places, 2500 BC, 500 BC, AD 318 and sixteenth century AD are all mere dates but the flesh and blood, the nerves and sinews, the heart and brain—nay, the entire living soul animating the human drama in its historic past, continuous present and infallible future, in so far as the history of the world is being staged in our own individual lives, in the history of a country, a race or a nation—is the idea, the ideals, which release new energy, create new horizons, instil new hopes and impel the people to march forward, on and on, to their dreamland of an ideal society, always better and nobler than the past and the present, well-adjusted and suited to the vital urge, requirements and the general spirit of the changing times.

We have it in the history of the modern world how European Renaissance and Reformation took place. It is the new learning, the rediscovery of the eternal soul of the ancient Hellenic and Roman civilisations, the meeting and mating of the West with the creative forces of the East after the Crusades, which brought about that mighty intellectual and moral economic and political earthquake in Europe in the sixteenth, century. With the advent of modern scientific and industrial civilisation, it was again the diffusion of new ideals of modern democracy and freedom that brought about the French Revolution. It is again the spread of new ideas that brought about freedom struggle in the politically-enslaved countries. Washington's America fought and won the great War of

Independence. Asia, long subdued by pirates and imperialists, is today awake and is mostly politically free. Then came the struggle for economic and social justice which was fought and won in England where the altar of constitutional Democracy was raised in the consecrated temple of the Fundamental Rights of Man. The old anachronistic feudal and infernal economic order was turned upside down in the Soviet Union where the first and largest experiment was made of the socialistic political philosophy, where the proletarian revolution resulted in the overthrow of bourgeois vested interests and the Socialist State of workers and peasants was firmly established. Today the entire world is divided between the economic-political philosophy of Marx and Lenin on the one side and of capitalist democracy on the other.

Ideas are based on legs and feet. Ideas are stronger than men and armies more powerful than bayonets and bombs. The ideas of one Kemal Pasha of Attaturk have metamorphosed the fate of entire Turkey beyond recognition. The ideas of one Hitler built up an iron Germany out of the ruins of war—the devastated, despondent and dejected German people whom the clever Anglo-Saxon diplomacy and atomising super fortresses could defeat. The power of ideas and an indomitable spirit built up a disciplined, militaristic and imperialistic Italy which, even in the clear light of twentieth century, attempted at reconstructing the old Roman Empire. New ideas created the young and strong Japan that defeated Czarist Russia, ideas that made the Japanese once the terror of the Asian continent to the Western powers.

Ideas make and unmake history. War and peace originate in the minds of men. Man is his mind. As a man thinks, so he becomes. The character of a nation is that of the aggregate of its individual citizens. If the majority of the citizens are brave, the nation will be brave; if the majority are cultured and dutiful, the nation will be cultured and dutiful. But if the majority are victims of poverty, disease, ignorance, blind faith and superstition, then the country goes down, the people fade away, the nation is in danger of being obliterated from the pages of history. We need to learn realism from history and the infinite power new ideas have in order to resurrect the people from their tomb of death or lethargic slumber, to give them wings to fly, to give them energy, inspiration and conviction to move forward, onward.

II. Millennium of Political Slavery

The dense, tangled and chaotic pictures in Free India could not be understood without the light of historical past being thrown upon them. As we are today the children of our historical past, so we are the children of the soil of India. But patriotism and national self-respect, to be useful and operative, must be enlightened and pure, critically and historically correct. From the days of Mohenjodaro and Harappa, the days of Rig-Vedic civilisation, *Ramayana* and *Mahabharata*, the *Upanishads*, Vedanta, yoga and other monuments of India's perennial philosophy, running through the Buddhist, Islamic and British periods of Indian history, right down to August 15th, 1947, there are certain fundamental, clear-cut and vital truths emerging out of the chronicles of India's national life. While we may rightly feel proud of our past cultural achievements, it will be criminal folly to ignore, side-track or whitewash the causes that made India politically enslaved for over a thousand years and internally divided for over two millennia.

Political slavery is the worst form of slavery a people, race or nation could suffer. It degrades, degenerates, dwarfs and darkens the general masses of the people. That is the reason why the civilised nations of the world, beginning from the most ancient peoples like the Egyptians, Chinese, Greeks and Romans, fought out their way back to political freedom when their country fell a prey to and was dishonoured, exploited, pillaged and ruined by intruders, invaders, empire-builders and plunderers. In India, in spite of various invading tribes penetrating and establishing their empires, the united all-India-wide passion for political freedom was not as conscious as we see it in the case of other freedom-loving peoples of the world. While India specialised in Indian culture and inner freedom, she largely neglected social and political cohesion, community-comradeship and nationalist pride. The nemesis was that foreign invaders like the Siahs, Kushans, Huns, Turks, Arabs, Moguls and other rapacious and greedy conquerors could, without much serious resistance, descend into the fertile plains and graceful hills of India, establish their empires, exploit India's wealth and resources and then leave the people of the country disorganised, economically poor, collectively inoperative, socially bankrupt and politically enslaved.

After the glorious days of Asoka and Kanishka, all along the Gupta, Mauyra, Sunga and Harsha periods of Indian history, it is always this lack of all-India united political front that made India weak and made her helpless victim to ambitious, energetic invaders who, from the days of Mohammed of Gazni to the establishment of the French and the British suzerainty, came to dominate and exploit the country for protracted centuries of political slavery. The coming of Mohammed-Bin-Kasim in 711, of Mohammed of Gazni in 1025, and the rapid, Islamic conquest of the larger part of Indian territory, and the subsequent creation and consolidation of the Mogul Empire, not only deprived the Indian people of their political freedom but, what is far more delicate, significant and fraught with graver consequences, it also uprooted a large proportion of our countrymen from their national, cultural and racial tap root. Considerable sections of those who embraced the religion and customs of their Muslim conquerors became not only exotic plants but also enemies of their own erstwhile kith and kin. The change of religious label thus became one of the darkest blot and liability on the Indian nationals. But the sterling characters like Abdul Gaffar Khan, Rafi Ahmed Kidwai, Sheikh Abdullah and Maulana Azad expiate the sins of Muslim communalists.

While there was somewhat a give-and-take policy between Indians and their Muslim rulers after the Mogul Empire got settled down—a policy, wisely accelerated by the greatest of the Grand Moguls, the Great Akbar—the European political domination, while opening to the Indian intelligentsia the floodgates of scientific and industrial civilisation and the democratic and ethical institutions of the West, killed much of the rural wisdom of the Indian people and mutually antagonised all the more Indian and Muslim minds through their old tactics of *divide et impera* policy that there were Hindu-Muslim clashes in India prior to the coming of the British cannot be denied but the fact that these were now fomented and harped upon to gain political hold on India of a third party and then leave the country mutilated through the help of vested interests of anti-national sections of Muslims is the blot of the British period—a blot to be wiped out through sane ideals of modern secular democracy based on the Fundamental Rights of Man and patriotic love.

The balance sheet of the last millennium of India's political slavery may be summed up as follows:

(1) The specific and unique cultural heritage of India, in its broad essentials, has been preserved to this day in such a way that the modern representative men like Ram Mohun Roy, Ramakrishna, Vivekananda, Sri Aurobindo, Tilak, Gandhi, Rabindranath, C.R. Das and Netaji Subhas Chandra can trace their spiritual genealogy back to the Upanishadic seers, to the Epic Period and to the remotest known history of India. This continuity of the cultural heritage of India in itself is a great achievement of which we may well feel proud, an achievement on the parallel lines of the transformed survival of the ancient Hellenic, Roman, Jewish and Chinese civilisations to our own days. This proves that the ancient spirit of India is pulsating with life to this day, that the tap-root is still there and that it is but a matter of national self-discovery for India to rise again from her present state of degeneration, frustration-complex and division we see all around today.

(2) The economic and social backbone of the country is broken. A major operation would now be needed to put it in order. Centuries of political slavery brought about economic and social bondage and that has created degeneration, not only among those who have accepted and fondled the religion of their political conquerors, but also among those who stuck to the old school and held on to it uncritically, unjudiciously, unintelligently. Thus, the problem of all problems for our national resurrection, for the uphill work of nation-building after political emancipation, boils down to the much-needed

economic-social transformation, which is the root-problem, crying for immediate solution throughout the country.

(3) The centuries-old walls of isolation are broken and India is again brought back to the international front which she held from the earliest dawn of her civilisation, long before the Greek soldiers and Roman traders touched her shores.

(4) Collective conscience and joint-enterprise and nationwide outlook have all fallen off before the moloch of caste and creed, communalism and provincialism, separatism and accentuated parochialism, sectional and party interests against the wider and broader interests of the country, nation, people. We have lost the power of imagination, of a nation-wide outlook, courage and strength to look beyond our immediate surroundings, our own caste, sub-caste and outcaste systems and look straight to the Motherland as a whole and the infinite skies hanging overhead.

(5) Inferiority complex and the loss of national character among the illiterates, as also among the 'learned', do not let them hold their heads erect and face the white man from the West, the rich and the powerful from within the soil of India and solve their day-to-day socio-economic and spiritual problems with manly vigour and creative imagination. The cheer and charm of life which characterised the ancient Indo-Aryans are gone. For, centuries of unnatural living under foreign political masters, domestic social cruelties and economic anachronism have emasculated, devitalised, degraded the majority of our countrymen.

III. Indian National Congress

The representative prophets of modern India, Ram Mohuns and Vivekanandas, Gandhijis and Netajis, have visualised the real situation in the country. The religious renaissance and social reform movements, which characterised the latter half of the eighteenth century and the entire nineteenth century among the loyal and thoughtful children of the soil, found their flow into the mighty political organisation of India, the Indian National Congress. From the year 1885, the new-born Congress was not only the political mouthpiece of nationalist aspirations but it also became the socio-spiritual expression of India that was to be born during the national struggle and after attaining political independence. Idealists, enthusiasts, philosophers, writers, journalists, orators, reformers, the elite, the intelligentsia of the entire country slowly rallied around the Congress, which, under Mahatma Gandhi's leadership, broke the narrow bounds of the select thoughtful few and flowed into the villages and plains of India, regenerating the Congress as a mass movement. The Congress, as the organised expression of India's national aspirations, freedom and unity, had as its pillars not only eminent men and women of character, but it had also such potential power and idealism as to leaven the whole country along the best nationalist traditions and the best India could profitably learn from other civilisations of the world, notably from the great European nations and their culture.

No critical historian, no person of sane thinking, can gainsay the plain fact that the Congress was largely instrumental in bringing about political independence to India, in spite of its many 'Himalayan blunders' committed by the academic and debating Congress of Dadabhai Naoroji and W.C. Bonnerjee of the Curzon period, and the aggressive, united, challenging Congress under Gandhiji's leadership during the two decades stretching from 1920 to 1940. The Trade Unions, Communists, Socialists, Anarchists, the Forward Blockists and various other Leftist organisations—all recognised the Congress as their parent body, even when younger, impatient, aggressive and practical trends of political ideology and advanced economic thinking persuaded their followers to break away from the paternal roof of the Congress and set up their own separate camps. They have, however, had this much in common with the Congress that they recognised the country above the party, perhaps the only solitary exception being of those opportunists who, during the last World War, became marionettes in the hands of foreign imperialists, entrapped with the enticing bait of the slogan of 'people's war' and betrayed patriotic interests at the psychological moment, when, after the august movement, the nationalist leaders were held locked-up behind British prison bars. Barring this unfortunate episode, Leftist and extremist parties of India were at least as equally patriotic and nationalistic as their parent body, the Indian National Congress, in devotion to their Motherland, in setting patterns of service and sacrifice, in purity of intention and sincerity of purpose.

It is significant that the most interesting, romantic and crowning sagas of the entire national freedom struggle in India did not end either with Gandhiji, or with the orthodox wing of the Congress, but with the Leftist Netaji Subhas, whose political realism and experience became the biggest challenge to the weal, security-seeking moderatism and undiluted, unconditional and unregenerate political pacifism within the Congress circles. The romance of the INA is not merely an isolated, outside episode of the extremist, radical Forward Bloc vanguard of the Congress, but it represents the vital urge of India's soul, the spirit of Pratap Singh, Sivaji, Lakshmi Bai of Jhansi, reincarnated—as it were—with a deep sense of political realism that should fertilise and crown India's spiritual idealism. The INA shows the direction; it is the finger-post to the revolutionary course India should adopt to solve her economic-social problems and, above all, it is a clarion call and challenge to the youth of the country to rise to the occasion and continue to fulfil the unfinished task of spiritual idealism of Gandhiji, on the one hand, and the economic-socio-political realism of Bal Gangadhar Tilak, Bipin Chandra Pal, Aurobindo Ghose and Netaji Subhas Chandra Bose, on the other.

The Congress of the Surat Session, of the non-co-operation and Swaraj Days, of the Civil Resistance Movement, of the Dandi March and *Satyagraha*, of the Tripuri Session and the Congress of the august movement, continue to stand out as the trumpet call and triumphant landmarks of awakened India in her onward march to freedom. The great patriotic zeal, nationalistic, idealistic, ethical fervour and revolutionary heritage of these landmarks in Congress history can hardly be forgotten, even if the old, orthodox Congress may have today fallen off almost completely from

India's ancient ideals of sacrifice, service, risking and venturing into the Great Unknown. The Congress may grow decrepit for lack of youthful blood, may grow reactionary and old for lack of assimilation of progressive and new ideas; it may succumb to the temptation of easy power-politics and cheap careerist security to the detriment of the people as a whole but no new, youthful, progressive and enterprising party or group can break away from those broad, patriotic, nationalistic, spiritual and philosophic-ethical traditions of the Congress. It is clear that no new organised force along the patriotic and humanistic, democratic and rational lines can be of any benefit to the people save when it inherits the spirit that gave birth to the Congress, which is still the main life-giving stream of our nationalistic politics. Besides, the Congress has an all India organisational machinery which can still be set in motion for the purpose of nation building, if new, creative, enterprising forces of the youth are linked vitally with the old Congress of Surendranath and Tilak, of Gandhiji and Subhas.

Continuity of nationalist policy and co-operation with the Congress is therefore not a liability, but an asset even to the most advanced economic-political trends in the country. We might learn the lesson from the Conservative, Labour and Liberal parties and the minor Leftist offshoots of the Labour Party in England, which, with their differences in policy and programme, have, nevertheless, one common uniting link—their loyalty and devotion to England, to the progress, social security, economic welfare and cultural and moral advancement of the British people. Similarly in India, whatever be the variety of old or new political and other progressive organisations, all must have this common ideal to place the country, the nation, the people, above parties and groups and serve unitedly the basic, broad, inalienable rights and interests of the people.

IV. Independence and Partition

India, although politically free today, is placed in a situation where almost all around her are seen burning fires, and at home the volcano is smoking. The country is divided into Pakistan and India on the basis of communal separatism of the Muslim League.

Congress that was born of the booing stream of nationalistic idealism and anti-communalism, as the representative mouthpiece of millions professing Hinduism, Islam, Christianity, Parsism and other religious faiths of the sub-continent, had finally to yield to the absurd, stupid, suicidal two-nation theory of the Muslim League. On the other hand, the Indian nationals remained internally weak and could take few practical, effective and energetic steps to resist this calamity, destroy untouchability, remove caste barriers, social disabilities and malpractices. No effective mass drive was launched to improve the socio-economic lot of the common man for the emancipation and education of men and women of India, for working out social cohesion and equality among the inhabitants of the country, the prerequisites of a mighty nation. Even the great reform movements initiated by the Brahmo Samaj, Arya Samaj, Theosophical Society and the Ramkrishna Mission, with minor socio-religious reforms here and there, touched but the fringe of educated Indian society, with the result that the old cleavage between individual eminence, the stalwart character of a few, and the mass degradation and degeneration of the many continued as wide as ever before.

The Congress became the united front of the Indian people against foreign domination and could, without much difficulty, rally mass sympathy and pool the energies and resources of the nation because all were agreed on attaining the main target, viz., that the British should quit India. But the positive side, what next after the quitting of the British, was depicted but in few paper schemes and wishful thinking. It was this lack of concrete, realistic and constructive plan after seizure of power to embark upon the uphill nation-building task that made the Congress leadership flounder at the trying hour of decision. Failure of the Congress to unleash the energies and initiative of the people, its continued dependence only on the governmental machinery, as it was bequeathed by the British power to the Congress, and an almost entire lack of new creative, imaginative, efficient and revolutionary vigour would mainly account for the increasing frustration-complex and sense of economic agony and despair among not only the have-nots of the country, but also among all the upper classes, as also in the middle class society of India which forms the backbone of the nation.

Whereas the imperialist policy of partition elsewhere, such as in Ireland, Germany, Palestine and Korea made the people all the more conscious of their national unity and solidarity, but here in India, hardly after a couple of years of Independence, have taken it for granted that Pakistan, born of either limbs of Mother India, brutally amputated from the main body, has come to stay and we have begun to plan and act on such unnatural assumption. If the absurd proposition of dividing the indivisible geographic-historical unit like India could be made practical and taken without question as having come to stay, some of our leaders think that the transfer of population, the logical corollary of admitting the premises, of the two-nation theory and dividing the country on that basis, is impracticable. If such assumption and contention of some of our leaders is to be accepted, then the whole partition business and vivisection of Mother India should have been made impracticable too. Mr. M.A. Jinnah, the protagonist and pro-pounder of the two-nation theory, himself foresaw and suggested transfer of populations as the necessary corollary of accepting partition of the country according to the demands of the League, which resorted to 'Direct Action' or violent bloodshed, for achieving their objective. The pacifist Congress had to yield, for violence was then believed to be the worst evil to be shunned at all cost but there was to be no transfer of population. And yet, the force of events and the tactics of communal genocide policy of the Muslim League have compelled the Hindu minorities in West Pakistan to leave their hearths and homes, their everything, and seek shelter within the territories of the Indian Union. In East Pakistan the situation became worse where Hindus had either to fly for their lives and honour to West Bengal and other parts of the Indian Union, or suffer the worst type of helotage in the Islamic State. How many Draupadis are abducted, how many Sitas raped, and yet no more *Mahabharatas* may be created! What callousness, indolence, and indulgence of our weak manhood! The refugees at Sealdah Station cry to Heaven for Justice. The situation reached such a huge stage when India and Pakistan were vibrating with fears of mutual warfare, until the Nehru-Liaquat Ali Pact in Delhi enforced 'peace' at any cost, and the danger of war has been warded off, at least, for the time being.

The logical conclusion of the secular, nationalistic and humanistic stand of the mighty Congress should have never been to allow the partition of the country and its deplorable socio-economic consequences that now eat up what is still left of vitality, humanity, vigour and courage among our people. The balance-sheet sheet of three years of political independence could have been more on the credit side, if the same revolutionary, self sacrificing and rigidly realistic policy of the secular, nationalistic and humanistic Congress had been pursued. This impeachment of the Congress acquiescence stands, even when we consider the attenuating circumstance that the leaders of the Congress were too soon entrusted with tremendous responsibilities of running the country, of which they had so little previous experience, and had to fill up the topsy-turvy void left by the British. Yet, frankly, considering the past, past one thousand years of the history of India, even to hold on the reins of the Government of the mutilated Indian Union for three years without any serious breakdown is no mean achievement. But then, greater achievement is that Pakistan has already built up a new stable Government almost out of nothing, from mere dreams, and it has reached a stage when Pakistan and India are contending for bones with equal barking and counter-barking from either side. Pakistan has raised an army of aggression, as evidenced in Kashmir, which India would think twice before facing. This reflection is by no means a disparagement, but realistic perspective which we, the Indian people, can ill afford to neglect or deny.

V. Birth-Pangs of Economic Freedom

What has been troubling the conscience and minds of the most thoughtful and and loyal of Indian patriots is our lack of political realism in the affairs of our new-born State and Nation. While our foreign policy is somewhat confused, our domestic economy is still largely dominated by foreign investments. The means of production of national wealth is still in the hands of profiteering elements and not yet either state-owned or controlled.

Gandhian economics, specially as embodied in the Wardha Scheme, may go some way for improving our rural economy. But to solve the problems of economic development of the entire country in the modern world set-up we need a powerfully organised and centralised State mac hinery with total control over all the human and materia resources of the country. Here parliamentary democracy, which unfortunately, we are apt to believe, is our only alter-native, after learning politics from England, is ill-suited to Indian conditions. Our centuries of political bondage should be explained not for lack of democracy in India, but due to over-doses of individualism, whereby individual and group interests prevail to the detriment of the larger interests of the nation as a whole. At this juncture the challenging personality of Netaji Subhas assumes a new significance as he still continues to inspire the hearts and minds of young men and women of India. Netaji Subhas' political philosophy and ideals loom brighter today as the economic and socio-political trends in the country arouse younger generations to a sense of political realism, after they have suffered disillusionment with the practical consequences of a utopian pacifist philosophy. For, the common masses of the people, used to a cruel lot of social injustices in the work-a-day life in a war-torn world, cannot be expected to reach the heights of pacifist ethics. In concrete terms, the creation of Pakistan has been as much the result of the pacifist philosophy in politics as it was the result of economico-social disabilities to the lower castes and outcastes of Indian society, with vast masses of men and women reduced to a state of servitude, as mere beasts of burden, drawers of water and hewers of wood.

Perhaps, in the interest of national resurrection, the partition of the country, refugee problem, semi-starvation of the larger part of Indian population, the swelling population tide overtaxing the existing economic resources of the country, were necessary to get the needed shock for the people and the youth of India to wake up, to realise their actual position and learn the political wisdom of rendering unto Caesar what belongs to Caesar and unto God what belongs to God. No, Government and politics cannot be made practical by turning all swords into ploughs, nor by converting Government barracks and Government offices into Basic Education centres and spinning colleges. Religion is religion, politics is politics and there is no way for identifying the one with the other. History and experience is ample proof of this categorical assertion. The feasible proposition then is not in identifying the State and the Church, but in creating conditions under which the material and spiritual interests of mankind may be best served with the slightest clash possible between politics, which is meant for the economico-social welfare of the masses, and religion, which is meant for the mental and moral freedom of the individuals. The identification of religion and politics, Swaraj with Ramrajya, in the Gandhian concept of the Congress was unfortunate. This gave the anti-national Muslim League an opportunity to spread the false impression that the Congress was for Hindus alone. It also weakened all sense of political realism among the Congressmen. The one outstanding exception that made the clear cut distinction between politics and religion and rendered unto Caesar what belonged to Caesar and unto God what belonged to God, and taught his people accordingly both in life and deeds, was 'Netaji Subhas Chandra and his I.N.A. India cannot afford to forget Netaji's political realism and Gandhiji's sacrificial ethics except to the detriment of her people. Spades are spades and mental confusion, moral weakness and appeasement politics do not pay in the end.

The Socialists, though born of the womb of the National Congress, are today decidedly against it. Communists, outlawed and driven underground, are certainly growing stronger. India cannot afford to ignore that international Communism advances and triumphs in those countries where the economic problems, viz., hunger, nakedness, disease and starvation, are not faced courageously and dealt with effectively. Historically, it is an undeniable fact that there is something like spiritual communism in the teachings of great thinkers like Pythagoras, Plato, Augustine, Kropotkin, More, Aquinas and Tolstoy, and in the redemptive message of such prophets like Buddha, Jesus, Muhammed, Francis of Assissi and Kabir. But this is quite different from those

Communists who with hedonistic frenzy exploit victims of poverty to serve their own ends. Such shallow Communism has no place anywhere in India.

The position of the Congress is not all too happy in the provinces and states of the Indian Union. Rival Congress organisations spring up and the Congress is losing important election contests here and there. The prospects for the Congress during the next general election, based on adult franchise of an overwhelming majority of illiterate electorate, though not hopeless, is not as bright as its past leadership, sacrifice and ideology would entitle it to hope for. Men of sterling qualities and eminent character are today few in the Congress ranks and those few who really are metamorphosed through the powerful personality of Ghandhiji and Subhas are not organised enough to come to the fore, lead the common herd and conduct them to the promised land. For, iron turned into gold through the touch of the philosopher's stone becomes iron again when the philosopher and the stone are removed from the scene. More than paper schemes and constitution clauses, what is so vitally and urgently needed are deeds, practical revolutionary steps to infuse new blood into fading limbs, remove social disabilities with an iron hand wherever sweet reasonableness fails, and bring about the much-needed socio-economic changes, in which every child of India will find employment, not merely through what one calls "self-help", but through planned,. organised State-regulated channels of nation-building service and employment. Human values are trampled under feet and money reigns. Not bank balance, but capacity to work and produce should be the real asset of a free citizen. Mental and moral powers are being prostituted to the money-lords. Justice, human dignity, virginal chastity, honour of women-folk, all violated by the dazzling glam glamour of Mammon. Once man created money for exchange purposes of his material life. Today money masters, dominates, controls man, Money speaks money wages wars money buys and sell, justice, girls, boys, everything underneath the sun. But this tyranny of money over man must stop. We are out to finish it; and Free India's millions will be freed from the bondage of Mammon and its entourage. The population increase is the biggest menace to India's economic situation.

The dismal reality of the situation expresses itself in mere increase of flesh and blood without corresponding increase of the means of sustenance, which leads our people to being born and brought up in incredible, chronic poverty and dying in abject misery. An Indian's average 27 years life-span threatens to be still shorter. Planned improvement of our race and the development of mental, moral and physical qualities, without which citizens become more liabilities than assets to the State and the Nation, are essential.

It is when scenes of desolation are multiplying in the country, with ever-increasing problems and fewer solutions, that the most patriotic, progressive, realistic, self-sacrificing, enterprising young sons and daughters of Mother India have started thinking and working for the socio-economic and political regeneration of the country. It is significant that the Congress felt the pulse of the Indian youth and have thought it necessary to organise the youth of Free India for the purpose of serving national interests. We recall how the youth of the country, notably the the Student Section, once responded to the call of the Congress in our national struggle for political independence. At that time the role of Indian youth was merely negative, viz., to join the mother Congress in forcing the British to quit our shores. But the British withdrawal was the negative side, whereas the positive side of nation-building is the urgent problem of today, when not mere slogans and agitations, civil disobedience and negative fights, but solid, positive, constructive thought and action become the urgent need of the hour for the youth of the country to contribute their share in building up the Nation.

VI. Youth Congress

It is gratifying to note that the Working Committee of the Congress at last felt the need of effectively organising the Youth Movement in the country for which a sub-committee has been set up with prominent and leading Congressmen, such as, Shri Jagjivan Ram, Shri Sankarrao Deo, Shri S.K. Patil, Prof. N.G. Ranga and Shri Gokul Bhai Bhatt as members. The sub-committee has concluded its work and appointed a Central Board for the organisation to be called the "Indian Youth Congress". The preamble to the constitution of the Indian Youth Congress reads:

"Whereas there is urgent need to organise the youth of our country to train them in the duties and rights of citizenship and to enable them to develop a positive and constructive approach to the ideal of a secular democratic state to the lofty principles taught by Mahatma Gandhi and to the establishment through peaceful means of a classless and democratic society, free from distinctions based on birth, caste, religion or class, now therefore an organisation to be known as the Indian Youth Congress is hereby formed."

The idea is clear the ideal is lofty and it is in the fitness of time that the Working Committee of the Congress felt the need of organising the youth of the country for constructive nation-building purposes.

Among the objects of the Indian Youth Congress are mentioned:

(1) To promote opportunities for the development of character, discipline, efficiency, knowledge and the spirit of service among its members,

(2) To organise study circles, classes, debates, study camps and research centres in order to give under-standing of the culture, history, social, economic, political and spiritual problems of our country;

(3) To impart training in the conduct of public work in close association with the Indian National Congress and organisations formed by, associated with, or recognised by the Congress,

(4) To promote opportunities for the youth to organise sport, physical culture clubs, and other cultural activities,

(5) To assist the Indian National Congress to combat communalism and social and caste orthodoxy and to carry on constructive and social work;

(6) To organise work-squads and touring parties, to tour the rural and urban areas of the country and to en-courage the youth to co-operate with farm and factory labour.

These objectives of the Indian Youth Congress are laudable and well worth achieving. It is significant that co-operation between the Youth Congress, the Indian National Congress, Ram Mohun Roy sounded the trumpet call of an enlightened, humanism and theistic faith, striking at the very roots of ignorant/ superstitions, caste, sub-caste and other anti-social inhumanities of the dark days of the country's history,—right in the soil of Bengal province of Mother India, where were heard the songs of poet Rabindranath, the singer of perpetual Youth and Beauty, where was born Swami Vivekananda, the prophet of youthful uthful divinised Humanity, the warrior-leader Subhas Chandra Bose, Bankimchandra, the patriot-singer of Vande-Mataram, the pioneer martyrs like Khudiram, Kanailal, Dal Bahadur Giri and Surya Sen;—where the powerful neo-Vedantic gospel of Sri Ramakrishna was first voiced, received and interpreted, right in this ght in this Bengal, today partitioned and called the "Problem Province" of the Indian Union, is born the first nucleus of the new Indian National Youth Movement, born of the loving heart and thinking mind of that Congress that once attracted the finest brains and the noblest characters into its fold. It is meet that Bengal should now show that it is capable of understanding, facing and solving the provincial and all-India national problems by rightly organising her youth as part and parcel of the wider all India Youth Movement, which will be the heir to the Congress when, following the laws of Nature, it grows decrepit and leaves its legacy to younger generations.

We are fully convinced that ideas instilled into young limbs are greater power than atomic weapons and bomber planes. Is not the human brains that released atomic energy mightier than the bombs that atomised Hiroshima and Nagasaki? Idea is the greatest power the world has ever known, for it is through ideas and ideals that the progressive wheels of history move. Accordingly we attach the greatest importance to the formation, organisation and discipline of the Indian youth on nationalist and patriotic foundations. Our country today is fading because there is no clear thinking, no practical planning, no enthusiasm, no energy, no sacrifice, no realism to translate ideas into actions in practical fields of social, economic, cultural and political life. The lack of high ideals is evinced from the fact that there is so little appreciation of human values, sense of social justice, equality, unity and brotherhood among the various sections of India's life today. In Europe and America, in spite of their materialism, capitalistic imperialism, there is more of human touch and sense of social justice than in India today. False patriotism should not make us blind to our own ills and calamities and deter us from taking those hard steps with which alone problems could be realistically faced and satisfactorily solved.

We believe in giving ideas and ideals to the youth. Even the bread-and-butter problem is not solved without having ideas in our minds—healthy, constructive, clear and creative ideology in our hearts. The classical instance of this is drawn from the great book of the last century, *Das Kapital* of Karl Marx, which is the one great book, one great idea that has revolutionised the economic-social life in various parts of the world. As in the sphere of political economy of modern times, no greater book has been written than *The Capital* of Karl Marx, so no greater revolutionary idealist and humanist has influenced so deeply and widely the socio-political life of modern times as Lenin. But India has her own soul. It will be up to the people of this country to study our own conditions and learn the lessons of history for solving our own problems. Of the various socio-political ideologies afloat in the air we should take and assimilate only those that will make the people of India vigorous, fully-employed, healthy, educated, prosperous, muted and invincible on the face of the earth.

Mahatma Gandhi, Netaji Subhas Chandra Bose and Pandit Jawaharlal Nehru have taught us the broad trends of an economic system which, to all sane-thinking children of India, must appear convincing. Mahatma Gandhi's life itself was a living commentary to socialist ethics which, if the majority of Indians had taken to heart, many of the problems of India's poverty, beggary and misery could have been solved outright without any violent revolution besmearing the face of India. Netaji Subhas Chandra's political philosophy is too well known and it is up to the youth of the country to understand his mission and message, the meaning of his life, struggles and martyrdom, and carry on the unfinished work of those great sons and daughters of Mother India for ushering in social justice and economic liberation to the working classes, including the intellectuals, educationists, artists, professional men in all walks of life. Pandit Nehru's ideology was such that he was once acclaimed as an 'international Socialist' by the progressive forces inside and outside India.

The world today is divided between two main ideologies of collectivism and socialism headed by the Soviet Union and monopoly capitalism headed by the United States. These two military giants divide up the loyalties of other countries of the world, even countries like England, France, Germany and Japan and other once-mighty powers, but today reduced to second-rate satellites. It is a misnomer to call socialism an economic collectivism where democracy is imperiled. But real democracy is not inconsistent with totalitarianism in countries where the great majority of citizens are illiterate, have-nots, victims of manifold social tyrannies and economic injustices and consequent nation-wide frustration complexes. That is why there was none to shed tears when Chiang Kai-Shek's Government was overthrown and Socialistic regime was solidly established in Peoples' China. It is the anachronistic economico-social factors, coupled with the increase of hungry stomachs and unemployed hands, that call for violent revolution, as the history of various revolutions from the days of ancient Romans to the days of the French, Russian, and Chinese Revolutions testify. But if Neroes continue to play harpsichord when Rome is burning, the just nemesis will overtake them, and in the struggle the have-nots will have nothing to lose save their bonds of helotage.

While the most outstanding personalities in the history of modern India have left no doubt as to the nature of economy that should lay the foundation-stone of the new classless and casteless Indian society, it is meet that the new Indian Nationalist Youth Movement start on its work with an appeal to different political parties and factions in the country, specially to the leftist groups, including the most radical and revolutionary organisations, to place the country above parties and factions and maintain the broad nationalistic, idealistic and patriotic patrimony which Congress, at its best, in the past has bequeathed to us. It is in spirit of co-operation with all progressive humanistic forces within the country that the Indian National Youth Movement (I.N.Y.M.) embarks upon its work, possibly with the blessings of the Congress, the Mother Church of Indian nationalistic idealism in the political life of the country in the past, and without her if necessary.

VIII. Three-fold Fields of Activity

The entire field of activity which the I.N.Y.M. proposes to concentrate upon is threefold, viz., the brain-side, training-side and the field-activity side. Westress much upon clear ideas and character-building ideals which are our best patrimony of not only India, but of the best in every culture underneath the sun. We believe in the power of ideas to enthuse the fading limbs, to instil new blood into a moribund society, to mobilize and utilise the available economic and human resources of the country to the great purpose of nation-building. It is far better to act and serve out of conviction than out of coercion. Although for social progress often coercion and legislative enforcement would be needed in countries where there is little of enlightened public opinion,-where the just nemesis of poverty and disease continue to grind the people, it is far better to create such healthy mental environment where men and women would act as free citizens, conscious of their duty towards their own self-culture, sacred duties to their family, society and State at large than to be goaded and moulded by a central authority dictating to and enforcing upon the citizens from the top. To think is power, idea is power, ideal is power. To will is power.

(1) The first, then, in our field of activity will be a centre from where clear, powerful, constructive, nation-building, patriotic and humanistic literature will come out regularly in Hindustani, the national language, and in all the principal vernacular languages of India, and also in English, which will continue to be our foreign link at home and overseas for outside contacts and exchange of notes.

(A) The I.N.Y.M. will have a Publishing House of its own, with press and premises of its own, owned and managed by a Committee on behalf of the Movement, which is meant to be the pioneer movement of its kind in Independent India to face problems courageously and solve them effectively, as are as it is humanly possible, through the youth forces, mobilised and canalised for nation-building purposes. Such a publishing house of the I.N.Y.M. may be called, something like, "The Young Patriot Publishing House", which will have its own rules and statutes, best calculated for the promotion of the patriotic, nationalistic and freedom ideals which it upholds.

(B) A weekly journal will be the mouthpiece of the Movement. It will be published in English, Hindi, Bengali, "Tamil and other vernaculars of India, with an All-India National Advisory Council, consisting of representative men and women helping to organise the youth forces in the country in various States. The Central Office of the Editorial Board will be located in Calcutta. Week by week our country will hear the policy and programme, the ideas and ideals, the practical work of the I.N.Y.M., reports and other news items of interest to all citizens, specially to the youth forces of the country. The weekly journal in English may be called The Young Patriot.

The main weekly features of the Young Patriot will be Lest We Forget quotations, regular editorials on current affairs, articles, short story, poetry, Stage and Screen, Youth Section, Discussion Forum, Question Box, Correspondence, Book Reviews and Gleanings. It therefore covers a wide and varied range of thought and news items. It will furnish an open forum for enterprising young men and women of this country to state their case and ideas clearly, freely and fearlessly before an open reading public all over India and abroad. It will give opportunities of expression of their personality to fresh young minds and also bring to light the hidden services and sacrifices of the youth, living and working in hitherto neglected and unknown spheres of life.

The flow of powerful ideas, we believe, will stem the tide of provincialism, communalism, separatism, self-interested intriguing party politics, and will become the powerful antidote against desert-sand-dry atheism, soulless materialism that denies spiritual values and ethical forces in human society, that discredits and disbelieves in Supreme Reality, the God of the heroes and heroines, of thinkers, sages and saints of all times. The journal and the publishing house will spread ideas of power that will show the youth of the country a plan and way of life, not merely in words and theories, in sheer exhortations and hollow propaganda, but as expression of actual lives, exemplified in the lives of those working and sacrificing in and through the Movement. For, we believe that only personal character, an ideal way of honest, integrated and purposeful life, with irresistible power and unending creativity born of purity and practice, can bear conviction to the general public. So few are real men today amidst this swelling flood of population in such a great historical country like India!

(2) The second field of activity will be a training centre for the workers of the Youth Movement, who will be chosen from among the best boys and girls, men and women with character, mentally and morally equipped, with capacity for independent initiative, courage, creativity and self-reliance. The trainees will come in batches in sufficient numbers as the training centre can conveniently accommodate them. As there is the training centre for the cadets of the army, airmen and sailors of the Armed Forces of a State, so we believe that there should be a regular training system for youth, who form the main bulwark of the nation, in whatever capacity they may later serve the interests of the country.

The vicious circle of the Government taking up the job and not fulfilling it, of private individuals or groups planning to do it, but not proceed beyond planning for lack of funds, must be broken at some end. Hence it is suggested that the Indian National Youth Movement, a private and independent organisation for public and inter-dependent national and humanitarian service, should undertake the establishment of a Training Institute and Youth Training Centres with the closest co-operation with the Government and the Congress and such other nationalistic and patriotic, political, social and cultural organisations at home and abroad, as may seem fit and proper for the Youth to associate with in furtherance of the aims and ideals of the Movement.

It may be profitably recalled that such Youth Centres were organised and financed by the young Governments of Italy, Germany and Japan in pre-war years and they proved to be the strongest bulwark of nation-building task. But in India somebody must show the way and the continuous vicious circle from the Government to the people and vice versa should be broken at some end. The people expect that the Government would do everything for them, as in most totalitarian and economically advanced countries. But the Government, tied down to so many bonds of past legacies, confronted with an anachronistic social and economic system in the country, can help the people little, unless they help themselves. But the people, worried all the twenty-four hours of the day with the sole thought of how to keep their body and soul to together and and maintain mainta their family, have neither the imaginat imagination, creativity, experience, nor guidance towards self-help, the beginning creativity, creative adventure, in individual and collective life.

Hence it is that centres for the training of Youth Organisers should first be started through non-official and private initiative of the I.N.Y.M., and then seek the backing, sympathy and support of the Government. Because in India today there is too much talk of planning and too little achievement, in the socio-economic fields of national life, it must be borne in mind that a grain of practice and achievement weighs more than tons of lectures and paper schemes. Some concrete result must be shown as the fruit of the Movement month by month, week by week, nay, day by day. What that concrete achievement will be must depend upon the clear scheme and practical working out of the various depart-mental items connected with the Movement. Hence the importance of the training of workers.

For historical and sentimental reasons we suggest that the first and central training centre and institute for our youth workers be called the "Netaji Subhas Youth Training Institute". The most appropriate place for such a training centre will be chosen in Calcutta to meet the requirements of the training purposes. We believe that among all the leaders of the Congress, Netaji Subhas

Chandra has a special appeal and message for the youth of India. This appeal is not for the youth of Bengal alone, but it is India-wide, like the songs and poems of Rabindranath, the Poet of Universal Humanity.

(3) The Youth Movement in its actual field work will assume the form of a country-wide network of Youth Camps. In towns and villages of every province and every state of the Indian Union, in every district and sub-division thereof, there will spring up youth camps. Now that the village Panchayat system and the Congress organisational machinery are still there, it will be of immense advantage for the I.N.Y.M. to make use of them as their spring-board to reach out to its national objectives.

These Youth Camps will be a country-wide network of an armys of boys and girls, young men and women, who will concentrate on the work of rural reconstruction, social disabilities removal, adult education, farming and husbandry, athletic clubs and physical culture, spread of healthy social, economic and cultural ideas among the rural population, and such other items which will have to be worked out in their minutest details in the statutes of the Youth Camps. Study circles, discussion forums, sports, recreational and rest centres, centres, village sanitation and social hygiene and, above all, village handicraft and self-sufficient domestic, rural and social economy will form the chief items of work in such Youth Camps.

National Youth Voluteers Organisation in every state, district and village will be another aspect of field activity of the I.N.Y.M. Today we see only gloomy faces, dejected and despondent boys and girls, grinded down by the devil of poverty and misery throughout the length and breadth of our Motherland. Lack of social hygiene and sense of personal responsibility have left no outlets for the people in the villages save in procreation. Where creative channels of man-making are lacking, the vital energy energy seeks outlets in procreation of sub-humans. What other God than bread and butter shall we give to those walking skeletons, shrivelled-bellies of India? To improve the quality of our citizens and to make them really men and women, truly citizens of free India, out of the huge waste of unproductive, unimaginative, uncreative mass of human flesh and blood, is by no means an easy task. The powerful voice of the great social reformers, consuming apostles of social emancipation, men like Ram Mohun, Keshub Chunder Sen, Justice Renade, Dayananda Saraswati, Srinivasa Iyyangar, Kamakshi Natarajan and others continue to ring in our ears, calling us all to remove the social cancers with our own hands with a sense of urgency. Entire rural India still needs the light of India's foremost social reformers. To reduce the population through consciousness of parental responsibilities among married couples in the villages and towns of India and through raising their standard of living is a great task. Our family system, social system, economico-political system need radical reforms, which, if not done in done in proper time, it may be too late to raise the country. A stitch in time saves nine, says the proverb. The process of degeneration has gone far too deep and we need cool brains, muscles of iron and nerves of cast steel to free the country economically and socially.

IX. Objectives and Organisation

The objectives of the I.N.Y.M. could be roughly stated as follows:

(1) Formation of men and women with character, developed will-power and intellectual clarity, with their hands, brains and heart trained for the purpose of advancing self-culture and promote the objective of national resurrection and socio-economic self-sufficiency of the Indian people.

(2) Formation of country-wide network of Youth Camps for the education and training of youths for duties and responsibilities of citizenship, for the spread of the most progressive social and political ideas, for vindicating human values and spiritual concepts that will raise human beings from mere animal life, that will give courage, courage, po power and ideals to fight for social justice, brotherhood and equality, for national unity and solidarity.

(3) To co-operate with the best of nationalistic, patriotic and idealistic traditions of the Congress and with other

socially advanced and economically sound groups, organisations and parties in this country and abroad.

(4) Preparing and publishing tracts, booklets and literature of dignified patriotic tone which serve as practical basis for the removal of social obstacles, such as, caste and creed distinctions among Indians, all traces of provincialism and communalism, and all those remnants of medieval feudal economy or capitalistic exploitation which retard the progress of the country and thus place her on a sure and sound economic footing.

(5) Defence of the basic Indian culture, the spirit of her civilisation and cultural exchange of the best of Indian heritage with the cultural and spiritual heritage of other nations of the world. As the I.N.Y.M. will fight heart and soul against the caste system, superstitions and degrading social customs in the un-enlightened quarters of Indian society, so it will fight against trends of exotic and separatist character of considerable sections of people living in India, primarily as religious groups and not as the children of the same soil of the common Motherland.

(6) Help to promote international understanding and co-operation based on the Fundamental Rights of Man and the Rights of Free Nations. We believe that ultimately a World Government must come; that is the necessary corollary of the world-culture and world-citizenship of the modern world. It may take still more wars to achieve that; but a new World Order is bound to come.

Objectives of such a national youth organisation may be numerically multiplied, but the main, central and essential idea is that we seek to organise a band of workers in every province and state of India, beginning from Bengal, who will continue the work analogous to that of the "Servants of India Society", founded by G.K. Gokhale, who will be the servants of Free India, nurtured on the most advanced socio-political ideology. The long and short of the purpose of such a nationalistic youth organisation is nothing but the fulfilment of the great ideals which the greatest and most outstanding of our national leaders and prophets and bards of Modern India have bequeathed to our people.

Though practical details of the organisation still needs to be worked out, the broadest outlines of the organisation may be briefly touched touched upon in this Manifesto for the information of the public, and public, and of those who are specially, and more directly concerned or are connected with our work. In fact, further developments of the I.N.Y.M. will be nothing nothing but a practical life-blood-commentary on the central ideals, as outlined in the Manifesto.

There will be a strict well-disciplined organisational machinery to control the entire Movement. The self-imposed organisational rigour and discipline will become really sweet to those who, through conscious understanding of the nature and mission of the Movement, freely and voluntarily become part and parcel of it. For the purpose of completing the general picture and perspective of the organisational machinery, a few clauses pertaining to membership, organisation and fields of activity are included in this Manifesto:

1. Membership. There will be two main age groups of active membership of the Indian National Youth Movement, viz., Junior and Senior. Although physical age is not always the necessary infallible criterion to decide upon youthfulness or old age, for purposes of organisational and structural efficiency some broad canons are necessary.

The membership may be divided into (a) Active and (b) Honorary. The active members will be subdivided into (i) Junior and (ii) Senior units according to age groups. Junior members shall be between the ages of 7 and 18, further sub-divided into Junior (a), (b) and (c) groups, comprising of the ages between 16 and up to 18; 12 to 16; and 7 to 12. Senior members, between the ages of 18 to 45, are sub-divided into (a), (b) and (c) according to age limits between 35 and 45; 25 and 35 and 18 and 25.

Honorary members are those who, though not actually and actively participating in the work of the Movement, are, nevertheless, associated with the organisation and help it through their advice, guidance, sympathy and support.

Members are required to take and live by the spirit and letter of the following pledge.

I (Name)..........enrol myself as a member of the Indian National Youth Movement with a view to contributing my best services and sacrifices to the economic, social, cultural, educational and political progress of Mother India. Whatever avocation of life I may pursue, under whatever circumstances I may be placed, I will have as the supreme purpose of my life the service of my fellow men and the upholding of the principles of social and economic justice, national solidarity and human brotherhood not in India and Asian countries alone, but throughout the world. I believe, the service of visible man is the best form of service to the invisible God.

There is no limit to recruiting members to the Movement, The annual subscription, if any, must be nominal, say, not more than a rupee per head per annum. Whether the Movement receives help from Government or any other private sources or not, the policy should be to make it self-supporting, with the ambitious scheme of increasing its material and human resources to be utilised for the expansion and consolidation of the work of building up India through her own young sons and daughters, cemented into one disciplined national army.

It must be noted that only men of eminent character, young men and women who, through serious thought and inner discipline, have acquired power to serve and sacrifice, should be selected as office-bearers for holding any responsible post in the organisation. Power comes from self-knowledge, self-controlled self-realisation, which must be considered the best and highest passport to enter the sancta sanctorum of God's work in the Movement. To those who would consecrate their whole time and energy, mind and soul, to the service of Truth and Humanity, is recommended Brahmacharyya, or complete sublimation of sex urge into creative channels of Love, Thought, Art and Service.

2. Organisation. The Movement, for its effective functioning, must have its organisational machinery well set up with strict cordons all around and tight screws inside. Discipline and organisation are traditionally so poor in India, and the result is

that individual freedom is preserved to the detriment of collective security and general good of the nation. Today the world trends are towards collective security and fulfillment of individual growth and capacity, not as an entity in itself, but as part and parcel of a larger whole, Society and State. This concept of totalitarian hold of Society and State over individuals predominate not only in Fascist and Nazi ideologies and Socialistic and Communistic States as well, but also in the most advanced and realistic sections of democratic institutions, including the constitutional and parliamentarian types, in the Anglo-Saxon world, not in times of war-emergency alone, but in peace time also Organisation, more organisation, strict organisation, is what is needed in India. If the Movement itself is not strictly disciplined it will become a poor show without having any exemplary and moral force behind it to convince or compel the members and adherents to be conscious of their duty and perform it to the best of their ability. Personalities, men and women with character, do not fall on earth by chance, casually, but they are the creatures of an environment, social and political, and of strict discipline and regimentation imposed upon them during the early stages of their formation, and through self-imposed discipline when they have grown up to maturity. Hence ancient Sparta, the modern State of Israel and the German youth, the Fascist G.I.L. and the Russian and Chinese youth organisations should be patterns of organisational efficiency and discipline which we can ill afford to ignore, tone down or neglect. Everything depends upon organisation, which must be fully centralised and totalitarianised and made strictly disciplined with muscles of iron, nerves of steel, strong minds and stout hearts.

From the central office will be controlled all the provincial and district centres with their affiliated village units. The Congress organisational structure could be profitably studied. The organisation of the I.N.Y.M. and the Congress can profitably work hand in hand for the socio-economic redemption of the country.

3. Fields of activity. Social work of national regeneration, training for citizenship and enlightened leadership, conducting study circles and discussion forums, lecture tours and inter-provincial trips, tours and exchange of workers, teachers,

organisers and members of the Movement, physical culture and field work in the form of Youth Camps, as already described, will be the main items of activity. Fine arts, specially choral music, street-marches and parades, painting and sculpture and such other pieces of art that are likely to enhance the breadth of vision and infuse enthusiastic optimism of life, must be encouraged. Literature, poetry, classicism and romanticism also are congenial fields for the youth movement of India to enter into and develop.

To achieve these ends, the I.N.Y.M. proposes to make the full use of the most potent means of propaganda like films, cinema, wireless, television, press and platform, which, unfortunately in India, are not often used for man-making and nation-building purposes. They are oftener used for frivolous merriment to the detriment of the character of the Indian youth.

The rules and regulations that will build up, strengthen and expand the movement are to be framed from time to time to meet existing needs, knowing full well that organisation, being part and parcel of human life, must be organic, living and adjustable to fulfil the purposes for which it came into being. Living organisations survive through vital adjustment and transformation.

X. Our Stand and Our Faith

Our stand is clear and we seek no recognition or outside canonisation of our humble efforts to fulfil the duties connected with citizenship of free India at this critical juncture. The work the I.N.Y.M. undertakes is not for the selfish interest of this individual or that, but it is the selfless sacrifice of each for the good of all, for it has its eyes fixed upon rapid socio-economic changes which will create such conditions under which alone the population flood could be arrested, the quality of the citizens of India be improved and the majority of the citizens, at least, will become strong assets and not mere burdens to the society as, unfortunately, it is in India today.

Our stand is clear, our objectives are clear, our means are also equally clear. We are believers of human and spiritual values. We believe that man is not merely his body and physical being, but he is primarily and essentially his mind, soul and spirit. But at the same time we are strongly convinced that physical, material and economic well-being is the condition sine qua non, the first and indispensable step, for the spiritual and ethical unfoldment of man, according to the Sanskrit proverb "Shariramadyam Kheladharma Sadhanamt Here we accept the financial and economic basis of all civilised life to be fundamental. Historically the dialectics of economic materialism is unassailable. But at the same time, on a higher plane, not Marx, but Hegel, not economists and industrialists, but sages, seers, philosophers and prophets have the final word in life. We accept, respect and assimilate the best of teachings of such spiritual teachers also. But, here again, the problem of food, clothing and shelter, education and health are the five pillars, as it were, on which the higher stages of civilised life with social refinement and intellectual and spiritual achievements are to be based. Change the economic basis of a given society, then the whole superstructure, such as religion, art, literature, all are changed. The immutable, permanent and eternal human values underlying all changes is the perennial philosophy, the Sanatana Dharma, the Manava Dharma, the Religion of Humanity, which we accept, support and uphold, as the un-derlying unifying core of all religions and philosophic systems, including Hinduism, Islam, Christianity and Buddhism.

The Indian National Youth Movement is independent in the sense that it is a new born child of Mother India to meet certain needs, both permanent and transient, in post-independent period of Indian history. It is no primarily a political party, though politics is not precluded from the spheres of its activity. Its strength lies mainly in being born of the f the permanent and vital idealism of the Nationalist Movement, of which the organised and the most powerful and representative and historical expression was the Congress. As a child of that idealism the I.N.Y.M. looks to the old Mother, the Congress, for its inspiration, guidance and help.

Though a small germ, at present, active in Bengal, a seed sown in the "problem province," its arms already stretch out to the entire country. It cannot be otherwise. The Corsican Napoleon, Prussian Bismark, the Austrian Hitler, though started with localised field activity, had to embrace the entire State and bequeath the fruits of their ideology as a permanent legacy to the people of their country. They may be militarily defeated, but the spirit of their movements is invincible, eternally there in modern France and Germany. While we have eyes fixed on the whole globe to learn the best social, educational and economico-political institutions, we do not hide our special leanings and sympathies towards the young and creative, energetic and comparatively more industrious and enterprising nations such as Germany, Japan, Italy, Soviet Union, modern China, Young Israel and those other countries, where the youth of the country achieved wonders in transforming medievalism into modern up-to-date society through challenging and enterprising ideology.

We believe in God and Humanity. Our first duty being to the land of our birth and love, we believe to serve the country to the best of our ability, along the lines of Truth, which is God, is the best way to serve the rest of mankind. Our youth will regain their past idealistic heritage whereby they will regain faith in eternal verities of human spirit. The life that is given to us is a sacred trust from God, whose economic justice we will struggle to bring down on earth, and make this vale of tears and hell of misery transformed into a veritable abode of peace and joy, a terrestrial paradise come true for all. This is not mere rhetoric, not merely sweet utopian dreams of More, Companella, Mazzini, Morris and Emerson. We know we have all the materials necessary in our country to achieve that end. All that is needed is calm thinking, cold planning and enough canalised energy and needed idealistic enthusiasm of the youth to carry them out. Our country's position is not at all happy today and children of the soil, soil, conscious of their duty, cannot sleep quietly by night, for the fires are burning all around and there is neither enough water nor enough hands to quench the devastating forest-fires of poverty and misery in the country due to lack of ideals and creative vision, a healthy enterprising Humanity.

The youth of the country will come forward to give their best, sacrifice their all, their dear and near ones, if necessary, so that they may continue to live for their God who is Perfect Humanity, for Humanity which is the highest God, God made flesh and blood-God who is first Motherland-and then this wide Human Family.

We understand the significance of human pilgrimage on earth. We believe that the only supre supreme purpose of human life is nothing but self-culture and service of society, where social injustice and economic iniquities are to be fought against and human and spiritual values to be vindicated, each one contributing his or her share to the best in the advancement of Humanity, for the progress and peace with honour for all citizens in the country. We are not undiluted pacifists, for we believe that injustice, dishonour, social iniquities are greater evils than police action or military operations on a battlefront. Kurukshetra is the Dharmakshetra. The law of struggle for existence is universal and only the fittest and strongest survive the ordeal that is human life.

We bow our heads before God, the Universal Spirit, the Cosmic Over-Soul, the Source of all Light, Life and Love, of all Progress and Peace for all. Brotherhood of man and Fatherhood of God is our accepted faith. We bow our heads to the Fundamental Rights of Man in all countries, under all skies, in all climes. We bow our heads before Mother India from whom we have received our best and to whom we pledge our loyalty and service and sacrifice. We bow before the valiant heroes and heroines of all nations, specially those who have given us and bequeathed the highest ideals of human freedom and economico-social justice. We bow our heads to the innumerable martyrs of freedom struggle in all countries, specially in India, and to those future soldiers who will fall fighting to bring socio-economic justice, not in an ideal paper constitution, but in actual everyday life.

The Youth of India is on its march. Their die is cast. "Do or die" is their motto, for, they know, to die like heroes and heroines in the battle-field is far better than to survive as vanquished slaves. Freedom, freedom, freedom is their watchword, Freedom, Brotherhood, Socio-economic Equity, International Understanding and World Peace.

'*सत्यमेव जयते*—Truth alone Wins-is Free India's motto. Yes, Truth, thy kingdom come! *असतो मा सद्गमय, तमसो मा ज्योतिर्गमय, मृत्योर्मा*

अमृतं गमय'—Lead us from untruth to Truth, from darkness to Light from death to Immorality!

Victims of economic injustice and social slavery unite! Youth, Youth of India, Youth of Asia, Youth of the world, unite! For union is strength; union is invincibility; union is Freedom.

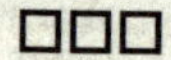

PHILOSOPHY AND ACTION OF THE R.S.S. FOR THE HIND SWARAJ

By: Anthony Elenjimittam; Published by the Laxmi Publication, 43, Tamarind Lane, Fort, Bombay 1, Pp. 241; Price Rs. 4/8.

As a sympathetic attempt to understand the ideology and working of the R.S.S. this book is welcome despite its shortcomings, arising mainly from the natural incompleteness of an outsider's insight into the Sangh. Though it is unfortunate that Shri Jamnadas Mehta's foreword as also the author's opening chapters should lend an anti-Nehru, anti-Congress tinge to the book, yet the author's endeavour to view and assess the mission of the Sangh from the cultural i.e. the supra-political, plane is in the right direction, as it is from that high position alone that the essential and timeless positivity of the Sangh's ideology can be grasped and appreciated.

Anthony

The quintessence of the Sangh's stand-point is that Hindu is not a narrowly religious but a catholically territorial-cum-cultural concept and the author of this book is to be congratulated upon being one of those very few out-siders who have grasped it, though he has expressed his understanding a bit clumsily.

The somewhat unmarshalled use by the author of his wide philosophical and religious studies has given the thesis a discursive appearance, while the endless array of quotations, in which Shri Guruji's naturally predominate, make it still more lose in presentation.

Yet the book can be recommended as the best yet written to advocate and uphold the R.S.S. and its ideology.

The book, priced a bit high, is nicely printed, except for the copious misprints in the Sanskrit quotations.

Review of this book that appeared in 'Organiser' in 1951

PHILOSOPHY AND ACTION OF RSS FOR THE HIND SWARAJ

By: Anthony Elenjimittam; Published by the Laxmi Publication, 43, Tamarind Lane, Fort, Bombay 1, Pp. 241; Price Rs. 4/8.

Anthony Elenjimittam

As a sympathetic attempt to understand the ideology and working of the RSS this book is welcome despite its shortcomings, arising mainly from the natural incompleteness of an out-sider's insight into the Sangh. Though it is unfortunate that Shri Jamnadas Mehta's foreword as also the author's opening chapters should lend an anti-Nehru, anti-Congress tinge to the book, yet the author's endeavour to view and assess the mission of the Sangh from the cultural i.e. the supra-political, plane is in the right direction, as it is from that high position alone that the essential and timeless positivity of the Sangh's ideology can be grasped and appreciated.

The quintessence of the Sangh's stand-point is that Hindu is not a narrowly religious but a catholically territorial-cum-cultural concept and the author of this book is to be congratulated upon being one of those very few out-siders who have grasped it, though he has expressed his understanding a bit clumsily.

The somewhat unmarshalled use by the author of his wide philosophical and religious studies has given the thesis a discursive appearance, while the endless array of quotations, in which Shri Guruji's naturally predominate, make it still more lose in presentation.

Yet the book can be recommended as the best yet written to advocate and uphold the RSS and its ideology.

The book, priced a bit high, is nicely printed, except for the copious misprints in the Sanskrit quotations.

Review of this book that appeared in 'Organiser' in 1951

About the Author

Father Anthony Elenjimittam (1915-2011) was an Indian Catholic priest, philosopher, and prolific writer dedicated to fostering interfaith dialogue and spiritual understanding. Born in 1915 in Kerala, India, he was ordained as a Catholic priest in the Dominican order and pursued higher education in philosophy and theology.

A staunch Indian nationalist, Elenjimittam was also a committed advocate for interreligious harmony. Throughout his life, he was a student of Advaita Vedanta, and his works often emphasised the commonalities between Eastern and Western spiritual traditions, seeking to bridge the gaps between different faiths.

As an author, Father Elenjimittam wrote more than fifty books on topics related to spirituality, philosophy, and interfaith dialogue. His writings reflect a deep commitment to exploring the universal truths present in various religious traditions.

Father Anthony Elenjimittam passed away in 2011, leaving behind a legacy of efforts toward spiritual unity and mutual respect among diverse religious communities. His life's work continues to inspire those engaged in interfaith initiatives and the pursuit of global harmony.

Works in English

- *The Hero of Hindustan (On Subhas Chandra Bose), Orient Book Company, Calcutta, 1946.*
- *The Poet of Hindustan, Foreword by Dr. S. Radhakrisnan, Orient Book Company, Calcutta, 1947.*

- *Hindustan Hamara—Our India, Orient Book Company, Calcutta, 1948.*
- *Philosophy and Action of RSS, for the Hind Swaraj, Luxmi Publications, Bombay, 1951.*
- *Saint for the Young Men of Today, St. Paul Publications, Allahabad.*
- *National Songs and International Hymns, Aquinas Publications, Bombay.*
- *St. Francis of Assisi, the Bhakti Yogin, Aquinas Publications, Bombay.*
- *The Voice of Silence, Aquinas Publications, Bombay.*
- *Monasticism, Christian and Hindu-Buddhist, Aquinas Publications, Bombay.*
- *The Dhammapada, Aquinas Publications, Bombay.*
- *Buddha's Teachings, Aquinas Publications, Bombay.*
- *Saint for the Young Women of Today, St. Paul Publications, Allahabad.*
- *The Philosophy of Yoga Patanjali, Aquinas Publications, Bombay.*
- *Cosmic Ecumenism, Autobiography of an Indian Dominican Monk, Aquinas Publications, Bombay.*
- *Tao Te King of Lao Tse, Aquinas Publications, Bombay.*
- *The Upanishads, Aquinas Publications, Bombay, 1977.*
- *Vedantic Gnosis for Blessedness, Aquinas Publications, Bombay.*
- *Mahatma Gandhi and St. Francis of Assisi, Aquinas Publications, Bombay.*
- *The Psalms of a Solitary Sailor, Aquinas Publications, Bombay, 1980.*
- *Interreligious Understanding, Aquinas Publications, Mumbai, 1982.*
- *The Bhagavad Gita, Aquinas Publications, Bombay, 1982.*
- *Thoughts for Daily Meditation, Aquinas Publications, Bombay, 1983.*

- *Meditation for Self-Realisation, Aquinas Publications, Bombay, 1990.*
- *Dharmadvaitham parts 1 and 2, K.V. Krishnamoorthy, Bombay, 1992.*
- *Dharmadvaitham part 3, K.V. Krishnamoorthy, Bombay, 1993.*
- *Mind Training for Self-realisation, Sat Cit Ananda Edizioni, Assisi, 2010.*

Works in Italian Language

- *The Bhagavad Gita, Mursia, Milan, 1987.*
- *Meditation for the Realisation of the Self, Mursia, Milan, 1990.*
- *The Quintessence of Religions, Verdechiaro Edizioni, Modena, 2000.*
- *From Politicised Religions to Self-Realising Religions, Verdechiaro Edizioni, Modena, 2002.*
- *The Yoga Philosophy of Patanjali, Sat Cit Ananda Editions, Assisi, 2005.*
- *Upanishad—Isa, Katha, Mundaka, Mandukya, Sat Cit Ananda Edizioni, Assisi, 2007.*
- *Dialogue with the Eternal, Sat Cit Ananda Edizioni, Assisi, 2010.*
- *Mind Control for Self-realisation, Sat Cit Ananda Edizioni, Assisi, 2010.*
- *Vedantic Gnosis, Sat Cit Ananda Editions, Assisi 2010.*
- *Sublimation of Sex, Sat Cit Ananda Editions, Assisi 2010.*
- *Yoga Vashista Sara, Sat Cit Ananda Edizioni, Assisi 2010.*
- *The Gospel of Purity, Sat Cit Ananda Editions, Assisi 2010.*
- *Mahatma Gandhi, Sat Cit Ananda Editions, Assisi 2010.*
- *Spiritual Perfection, Sat Cit Ananda Editions, Assisi 2010.*
- *Vedanta for All, Sat Cit Ananda Editions, Assisi 2010.*
- *Cosmic Ecumenism, Sat Cit Ananda Editions, Assisi 2010.*
- *Thoughts for Daily Meditation, Sat Cit Ananda Edizioni, Assisi 2010.*
- *Psalms of a Lonely Sailor, Sat Cit Ananda Edizioni, Assisi 2010.*

- *Saints for Today's Youth, Sat Cit Ananda Edizioni, Assisi 2010.*
- *The Saints for the Young Women of Today, Sat Cit Ananda Edizioni, Assisi 2010.*
- *The Religion of Religions, Sat Cit Ananda Editions, Assisi 2010.*
- *Liberating Wisdom, Sat Cit Ananda Editions, Assisi 2010.*
- *Bhagavad Gita: Divine Poem and Esoteric Philosophy of India, Sat Cit Ananda Edizioni, Assisi 2010.*
- *Psychology of Self-Realisation, Sat Cit Ananda Editions, Assisi, 2011.*